D1375791

BOURNEMOUTH LIBRARY

610352706U

MAGICIANS' TRICKS

MAGICIANS' TRICKS

Henry Hatton
and
Adrian Plate

BOURNEMOUTH
2003
LIBRARIES

Dover Publications, Inc.
Mineola, New York

Bibliographical Note

This Dover edition, first published in 2002, is an unabridged reprint of *Magicians' Tricks: How They Are Done,* originally published by The Century Co., New York, 1910.

Library of Congress Cataloging-in-Publication Data

Hatton, Henry.
    Magicians' tricks / Henry Hatton and Adrian Plate.
       p. cm.
    Originally published: New York : Century Co., 1910.
    ISBN 0-486-42516-9 (pbk.)
      1. Magic tricks. I. Plate, Adrian. II. Title.

GV1547 .H3 2002
793.8—dc21

2002034824

Manufactured in the United States of America
Dover Publications, Inc., 31 East 2nd Street, Mineola, N.Y. 11501

TO OUR BROTHER CONJURERS,
PROFESSIONALS AND AMATEURS
IN THE HOPE THAT
IT MAY AFFORD SOME ENTERTAINMENT
AND A LITTLE INSTRUCTION,
THIS BOOK IS FRATERNALLY DEDICATED
BY THE EDITORS

CONTENTS

I WITH CARDS

vii

V SOME AFTER-DINNER TRICKS

VI . MISCELLANEOUS TRICKS

ACKNOWLEDGMENT

The Editors beg leave to acknowledge their indebtedness to Messrs Trewey, Germain, Fischer, Blind, Conradi, Caroly, Goldston, Okito, Ducrot, Elliott, De Lion, Fuigle and others of their brother conjurers who have generously contributed explanations of tricks to "The Magicians' Tricks."

FOREWORD

THERE is a distinct fascination about conjuring not easy to understand. In the many years that we, the writers of these papers, have practised the art, we have known many men, and some women, who took it up for pleasure or money, or both, and we have never known one to lose interest in it. Shakspere, that master "mind-reader," must have understood this ceaseless hankering, for he makes Rosalind say: "I have, since I was three years old, conversed with a magician most profound in his art," which undoubtedly means that she had taken lessons in conjuring all those years. We preface our instructions "with these few remarks" as a warning, so that we may not be blamed should our readers find themselves possessed of this undying love for "conjuration and mighty magic."

That "the hand is quicker than the eye," is one of those accepted sayings invented by someone who knew nothing of conjuring—or, as is more likely, by some cunning conjurer who aimed still further to hoodwink a gullible public. The fact is, that the best conjurer seldom makes a rapid motion, for that attracts attention, even though it be not understood. The true artist in this line is deliberate in every movement, and it is mainly by his actions that he leads his audience to look not where they ought, but in an entirely different direction. Mr. David Devant, who for a number of consecutive years has entertained London with his ingenious tricks, has said: ''The conjurer must be an actor. By the expression of his face, by his gestures, by the tone of his voice, in short, by his acting, he must produce his effects.'' He is certainly right, but as it is not our purpose to furnish an essay on conjuring as a fine art, let us turn on the lights, ring up the curtain, and let the magician make his bow.

MAGICIANS'
TRICKS

MAGICIANS' TRICKS

INTRODUCTION

Before beginning any explanations we shall have to trespass for a few minutes on the patience of our readers while we describe certain articles that are almost necessities for the successful production of many tricks. The first are:

THE CONJURER'S CLOTHES.

The coat is generally provided with four special pockets, in addition to the several pockets found in every well-made garment of its kind. Of these special pockets two are in the breast, one on each side, and two inside the coat tails, also one on each side. The breast pockets are inside the coat and nearly under the arms. They open perpendicularly and are spacious enough to hold a rabbit, a pigeon, or other large object. The tail pockets are about seven inches in width and six in depth, and the opening slants slightly, being higher at the back than at the front. They are placed so that the performer's knuckles touch the opening when his arm hangs at his side. They are professionally known as *profondes,* and into them is dropped anything of a reasonable size that the performer wishes to be rid of. Some performers have a tempered wire stitched around the opening to make it more accessible.

3

The trousers, at each side of the back just above the thigh, have a small pocket, called a *pochette*, of a size to hold a billiard ball.

On each side of the vest, inside, there is often a large pocket with a perpendicular opening, to hold large objects that the performer may wish to produce during his performance. It is also well to have a broad elastic band sewed to the lower inside edge of the vest. This makes the vest fit tightly around the waist, and prevents concealed articles dropping out prematurely.

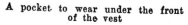

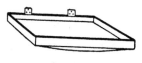

A pocket to wear under the front of the vest   A servante

Some performers wear under the front of the vest a pocket of which the mouth comes just to the opening of a dress vest, and the lower part passes under the waist band of the trousers. It is made of an aluminum plate, about seven inches in width and five in depth, bent to conform to the shape of the performer's body and tapering down to a rounded point. From side to side of the upper part is riveted a narrow strip of hard brass, convex in form, and the whole is covered with white canton flannel, the smooth side on the outside, to form a pocket, as shown in the accompanying illustration. Into this may be dropped any small article to be got rid of, as, for example, a ball that has been palmed, etc.

This pocket may be slipped in place or removed in a moment, which is a great advantage.

As most amateurs will not wish to have their clothes cut up for the sake of the pockets we have described, they will find that detachable pockets made of some black stuff and fastened in place by black safety pins will prove entirely satisfactory.

THE SERVANTE.

At the back of the table of the professional conjurer, just a few inches below the top, is a padded shelf or shallow box, technically known as a *servante*, and intended to hold or catch whatever is laid or dropped on it. Where a performance is at a club or a private house a portable *servante* that may be attached to any table or to the back of a chair is frequently used. An oblong frame, about five by four inches, made of strips of narrow, hard brass, having a small upright brass plate about an inch from each end, is one of the best. The plates are blackened and in each is driven three small holes, into which are thrust thumb tacks to fasten the frame in position. The frame is covered with soft black cloth, which should sag a trifle in the center of the frame, so as to hold whatever may be dropped on it. See illustration on the opposite page.

THE WAND.

This is a round stick about thirteen inches long and five-eighths of an inch in diameter. It is best made of polished hard rubber or of ebony, and at each end has an ivory or a silver-plated tip or ferule, about two inches long. While it is generally looked upon as an ornament or, perhaps, an emblem of power, the performer will find it highly useful.

Some few other things that are commonly used in conjuring, when not described or explained in the trick in which they are used, will be found at the end of the book.

WITH CARDS

Before the would-be conjurer may hope to mystify an audience successfully with a pack of cards he must master certain sleight of hand moves that are a part of every card trick that requires skill. These moves can be attained only by constant practice. There are a number of these sleights, but in this book only such as are necessary successfully to perform the particular tricks herein described will be explained.

Of late years a number of so-called "card kings" have appeared whose sole ability consists in making what is known as "the back-hand palm," a bit of card jugglery which is utterly useless in those beautiful and bewildering card illusions that may be shown with an audience on every side of the performer. Besides being useless this particular move has so frequently been exposed, intentionally or carelessly, that it is now very generally understood by the average theater goer.

The Pass:

One of the foremost artifices resorted to in card conjuring is that known as the "pass," "shift," or *sauter la coupe,* as it is called in French. By this sleight a card which has been placed in the middle of the pack is transferred to either the top or the bottom without any one perceiving it. The position of two or more cards may be changed as readily as that of one card.

In order to do this the lower part of the pack on which a chosen card is placed must take the place of the upper part, which, in turn, goes to the bottom; in other words the positions of the two halves or portions are reversed.

When a card that has been selected is to be replaced in the pack, the performer opens the pack, as shown in Fig. 1. The card is received on the lower portion of the

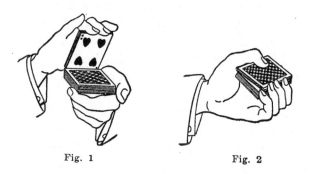

Fig. 1   Fig. 2

pack, which is then closed. In closing it, however, the tip of the little finger of the left hand is inserted between the two portions. The pack is now lying in the left hand in the position shown in Fig. 2, that is, with the thumb on the top of the pack and the fingers on the opposite side, the little finger dividing the pack in two.

Placing his right hand over his left, the performer grasps the lower portion of the pack between the thumb at the bottom and the second finger at the top, as in Fig. 3. The top packet which is now held by the fingers of the left hand, the little finger below and the other fingers on top, is drawn away by opening out the fingers, and when it is clear of the lower packet the fingers are closed again, bringing it thereby to the bottom. So that the two packets may clear each other in passing, the right side of the lower packet must be raised a little, as shown in Figs. 4 and 5. The part marked A in Fig. 4

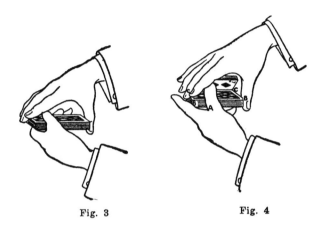

Fig. 3   Fig. 4

presses steadily against the root of the left thumb. At BB it is held between the ball of the thumb and the second finger of the right hand. While in this position if the lower part of the left thumb exerts a pressure at A, the side CC will be raised, the thumb and second finger of the right hand at BB acting as pivots. The movements of the two packets must be simultaneous, and be made noiselessly. The right hand acts as a screen to hide the manipulations and should be held motionless. The pack is held at an angle of about forty-five degrees.

The manipulations should be practised before a mirror and slowly until the exact moves are reached, but until then speed ought not be sought.

Instead of opening the pack bookwise to receive the selected card, it may be spread out like a fan between

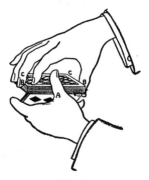

Fig. 5

the hands, and the little finger inserted when closing it.

When it is desired to bring the selected card to the bottom of the pack instead of the top, the little finger of the left hand must be placed *under* the card.

The ''pass'' may be made with one hand, but as it is almost impossible to make it invisibly it is of little practical use, and need not be considered here.

There is still another method, an excellent one, whereby the position of a card is changed and it is brought from the middle of the pack to the top or the bottom or from the top to the bottom and *vice versa*. This is known as

The Clip:

The proper way of doing this is not so generally understood as the ''pass'' proper. The pack is held the same as for the ''pass,'' and as soon as the selected card is replaced on the lower part of the pack the left thumb pushes the card a little toward the right, as shown in Fig. 6. At the same moment the pack is closed. The result is that the selected card protrudes about half an

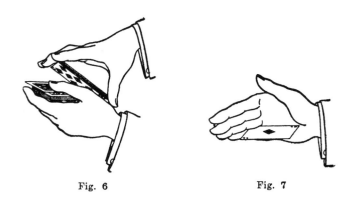

Fig. 6   Fig. 7

inch to the right. This can not be seen by the audience as the card is covered entirely by the right hand. The upper right hand corner of the card is now grasped between the base of the third and little fingers, the card is drawn entirely away from the pack and placed on the top or the bottom. By the same move the top card is brought to the bottom or the bottom one to the top.

The card is not palmed, but is grasped between the fingers, as described, and as shown in Fig. 7. The position of the hand is perfectly natural.

The "Diagonal" or "Dovetail" Pass:

While used for the same purpose as the two-handed "pass," the manipulation of this "pass" is altogether different. By its means not only one card, but several cards in different parts of the pack may be brought together to be kept on the top of the pack.

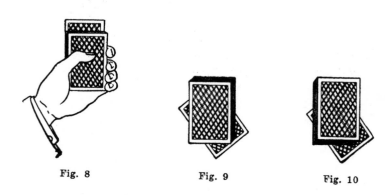

Fig. 8   Fig. 9   Fig. 10

Let us suppose that several cards are selected by the audience. Holding the pack, as shown in Fig. 8, the performer presents it in turn to each one who has drawn a card, with a request that the selected card be placed in any part of it. He sees to it, however, that no card is pushed home entirely, but that about three-quarters of an inch of each protrudes from the pack. For this purpose the left thumb, which is on top of the pack, presses the cards together slightly.

The performer now places his right hand on top of the cards as if to push them flush with the others. What he really does, however, is to twist them to the left, by help of the thumb, first and little fingers, so that they are in the position shown in Fig. 9. The first finger then presses them downward as far as the left thumb, which is across the top of the pack, will allow. The cards are now in the position shown in Fig. 10.

Then the second, third, and little fingers of the left hand press against the side of the protruding part of

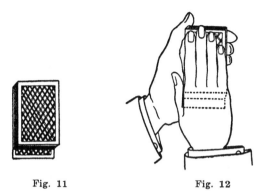

Fig. 11   Fig. 12

the cards and straighten them flush with the rest of the pack, as shown in Fig. 11.

These movements must be blended into one and take up only a fraction of a second.

The right hand is now removed from the pack for a moment, ostensibly to show that the cards are well home in the pack, care being taken to conceal the protruding parts at the bottom. Then the right hand rests on the back of the pack, and the protruding cards are clipped at the left lower corner between the thumb and forefinger of that hand, as shown in Fig. 12. The left hand is moved forward a little from the right which move separates from the rest of the pack the selected cards that are held between the thumb and forefinger and they are now placed on top of the pack. A slight upward motion of both hands will completely conceal any suspicious movement.

If the trick requires that the cards should be at the bottom of the pack they may be brought there by the two-handed "pass."

The Card Palm:

By means of this sleight the performer is enabled to steal a card or cards from the pack without fear of detection and without even touching the pack with the right hand.

The pack is held in the left hand with the cards that are to be palmed lying on top. The thumb and third finger keep these cards in place and the little finger is under them. As the right hand approaches the left and is about three or four inches from it, the little finger pushes the cards up toward the right hand, the thumb and third finger relax their pressure, and the cards spring or shoot into the palm of the right hand, where they are retained by partly closing the hand. At the very moment the cards are palmed the left hand moves away slowly. This move which is known as "the spring palm" is absolutely imperceptible.

Should the performer wish to hand the pack to one of the audience with the right hand, in which the card is palmed, he places the left hand little finger under the card or cards that are to be palmed. The right hand grasps the pack between the thumb and the second finger, as if to make the "pass." The cards that are to be palmed are pushed by the left hand little finger into the right palm. Then the wrist of the left hand is turned outward, while the right hand grasping the pack at the left hand upper corner between the thumb and first finger hands it to the one who waits for it, as in Figs. 13 and 14.

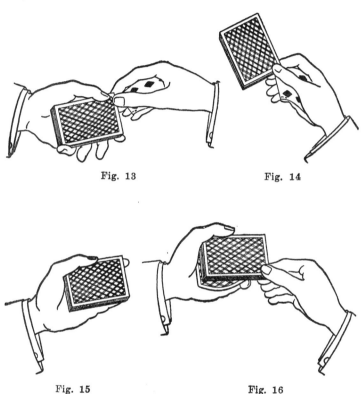

Fig. 13   Fig. 14

Fig. 15   Fig. 16

The Bottom Palm:

In this method of palming a card the pack lies lengthwise in the left hand, the lower end in the fork of the thumb, the upper end against the first joints of the second and third fingers, and the tip of the left thumb resting on the face of the cards as shown in Fig. 15.

As the right hand approaches to take the pack the fingers of the left hand press slightly against the bottom of the pack, and then partly close, as in Fig. 16.

The result is that the bottom card of the pack is separated from the rest of the pack and is retained in the (left) palm by the bent fingers, while the right hand removes the pack.

The Change:

By this sleight one card is imperceptibly changed for another under the very eyes of the audience. There are several ways of making this exchange, but the following are about the best and apply to the proper performance of tricks hereafter described.

The Top Change:

When the top card is to be changed the pack is held in the left hand, the thumb resting across the back and the fingers at the bottom. The card that is to be changed for the top card of the pack is held between the tips of the right hand thumb and the forefinger, the thumb on top of the card and the forefinger below it.

The hands are brought together for just a moment, and the left thumb pushes the top card of the pack an inch or so to the right. At the same time the card held in the right hand is laid on the top of the pack and slid back by the left thumb. At that moment the first and middle fingers of the right hand clip and carry off the original top card of the pack, as shown in Fig. 17. Care must be taken to bring the forefinger, which, with the thumb is on top of the card, to the bottom, thus replacing the second finger, so that the card will be between the thumb and forefinger. The slight noise which is unavoidable, must be reduced to a minimum, and as soon as the change is made the left hand is drawn away, but not too quickly, while the right hand is held motionless. The body must not be turned sideways to the left at the critical moment, nor should the hands be brought together suddenly and then separated in a jerky

Fig. 17

fashion, as if something were snatched away. The necessary moves ought to be made in a natural, careless way in the course of the remarks that accompany the trick. While it may seem that these moves will be apparent to every one, they are, in fact, almost imperceptible.

The Bottom Change:

In this change the card to be changed is left at the bottom of the pack instead of at the top. It is somewhat easier of execution than the top change, and has the advantage of being almost noiseless and the still greater advantage that instead of one card, two or more cards may be exchanged equally well.

The pack is held in the left hand, as in the top change. The card to be changed is in the right hand between

the thumb and first finger. On its way to meet the left
hand, however, the fingers are shifted. The first finger,
which is below the card, is brought to the top to join
the thumb, and, consequently, the card is held between
the first and middle fingers. In this position the thumb
and first finger can grasp the top card of the pack, while
the card to be exchanged is brought to the bottom of
the pack where the second, third, and little fingers of

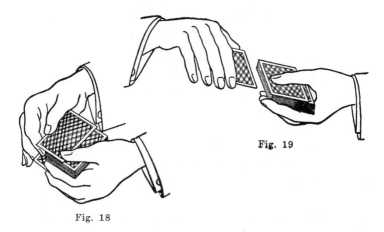

Fig. 19

Fig. 18

the left hand are extended to receive it. At the same
moment the first finger of that hand, which is between
the pack and the card which is substituted for the one
that is to be exchanged, is brought to the bottom, as
shown in the illustration, Fig. 18.

A New Top Change:
The pack is held in the left hand, as in the other
changes. The card to be changed is held lengthwise
in the right hand between the forefinger and the thumb,

the forefinger at the upper end and the thumb at the lower, as in Fig. 19.

As the hands come together to make the change the left thumb slides the top card of the pack about an inch to the right. The right hand lays the card it holds on top of the pack, where it is held by the left thumb, and at the same time carries off the top card of the pack between the first and second fingers and the thumb, preserving the same position as that of the first card. The card is laid on the table or handed to one of the audience. This change is noiseless and very little known.

The Single Change:

This is made without the help of the pack. It is useful when a selected card has been replaced in the pack and passed to the top, where it is still to remain though the pack is shuffled. The performer takes the two top cards, holding them so that they appear as one, and lays the pack on the table.

The cards, slightly bent inward so as to keep them together, are held up between the forefinger and the thumb, as shown in Fig. 20, and the audience are asked if they recognize the selected card. As they see only the card that was the second on the top and now conceals the selected card behind it, they are not slow to declare that the performer has made a mistake. Naturally he is somewhat crestfallen, but at once sets about remedying the mistake. Taking the card, face down, between the forefinger and thumb of his left hand, he gives it a fillip with the first finger of the right hand, and when the face of the card is shown again it proves to be the chosen card.

When the performer transfers the cards to his left hand, the thumb of that hand rests on the top card, while the fingers are on the bottom one. Then the

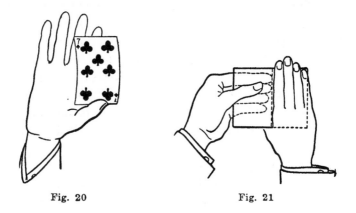

Fig. 20   Fig. 21

thumb draws the top, the chosen, card into the left hand, while the fingers push the bottom card into the right hand, where it is palmed. See Fig. 21.

As the right hand is advanced to strike the card the fingers naturally contract or partly close, thus concealing the palmed card.

False Shuffles:

Without a knowledge of the false shuffle the conjurer would be obliged to omit most of the best card tricks from his program. By its aid he can, apparently, mix up the cards of the pack in a most hopeless manner and yet not disturb their arrangement in the least. By another variation of this shuffle he may leave undisturbed in their original position two or more cards while appearing to shuffle them thoroughly.

To Leave a Prearranged Pack Undisturbed While Seeming to Shuffle It Thoroughly:

The pack is held lengthwise in the right hand between the thumb at one end and the second and third fingers at the other, the forefinger bent over the upper side. The left hand, palm upward, is under the pack. The right hand drops a few cards from the top of the pack into the left hand, which places them at the bottom of the pack, where they are held by the right thumb, assisted by the second and third fingers, as shown in illustration, Fig. 22. Again the right hand drops some cards from

Fig. 22

the top into the left hand. Then the right hand appears to drop more cards in front of those in the left, but merely goes through the motion without dropping any. Then a few are really dropped but *behind* those in the left hand, and this is continued, pretending to drop them in front and really dropping them behind until all the cards in the right hand are used with the exception of the first parcel which is dropped in front (the top) of the pack.

The pack is now in the order it was before the shuffle.

To heighten the deception the cards in the left hand should be kept moving backward and forward. When cards are *apparently* dropped in *front* of the cards in the left hand, the left thumb pushes the cards already in the hand toward the fingers, and when cards are *really* dropped *behind* those in the left hand the fingers tilt them back toward the thumb. This tilting motion is continued until all the cards in the right hand are disposed of.

Another Method of Shuffling a Pack Without Changing Its Order:

The pack is held in the left hand, the thumb on the top, the fingers at the bottom. The left thumb pushes a few cards into the right hand. Then the rest of the pack is placed in batches of five or six cards alternately

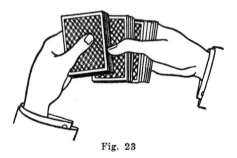

Fig. 23

above and below the cards in the right hand, but in the following way: The cards that go above are taken from the bottom of the pack, whilst those that go below are from the top. While there will be no difficulty in pushing the *top cards of the pack below the packet in the right hand* it will not be found so easy to *push the cards from the bottom of the pack above those* in the right hand. The difficulty may be overcome, however, by placing the right hand thumb against the right side of the pack while the left fingers push the bottom cards on top of the right hand packet. In this way the right thumb will act as a check, as shown in illustration, Fig. 23.

It only remains now for the performer to run his eye over the pack in order to find the card that was originally at the bottom, and making the pass at that point bring the pack back to the order in which it was first arranged.

To Shuffle the Pack so as Not to Disturb the Position of the Top or the Bottom Card or of Both Cards:

In order that the bottom card of the pack may be in the same position after the shuffle as it was before, the pack is held in the right hand as is usual when shuffling. Then the left hand squeezes it between the thumb and fingers, the thumb on top and the fingers below. Now if the rest of the cards are lifted out from between the top and the bottom cards by the thumb and second finger of the right hand, as if to shuffle the pack, it will be found that the top and the bottom cards will be clipped together by the left hand, and the pack may be shuffled over these two cards, leaving the bottom card in its original position.

The same procedure will keep the top card in its place, but two shuffles will be necessary, for after the first shuffle the top card will be next to the bottom card of the pack. By repeating the same shuffle the top card will be brought to the bottom of the pack, and then by shuffling it may be brought to the top.

As will be seen, this shuffle keeps both top and bottom cards in place.

To Force a Card:

By this very necessary artifice a performer induces one of his audience to select a particular card which is to be used in the course of a trick.

Like all tricks it requires some practice, but above all it needs much audacity. The card to be forced is, at the beginning, either at the top or bottom of the pack. By means of the "pass" it is brought to about the middle of the pack, the tip of the little finger of the left hand being held on top of it. As the pack is offered to the person who is to draw, the cards are

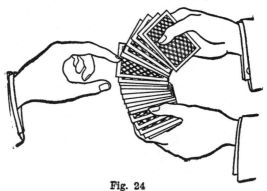

Fig. 24

pushed one by one with the left thumb into the right hand apparently to afford the selection of any desired card. Just at the very moment that the card is to be taken the forced card must be almost at the finger tips of the one who is to draw, and be exposed, if possible, a trifle more than the other cards. (See Fig. 24). The unsuspecting victim will almost invariably draw that card.

If, by any chance, another card be drawn than the one the performer desired, he must not be disconcerted, but must try to force his card on some one else. With the first card drawn some minor trick may be performed, as, for instance, when the card is returned to the pack the performer passes it to the bottom and learns what it is. Then addressing the one who drew it, he says: "It would not be fair to use that card for the trick, as I chanced to catch sight of it." Then he names the card and proceeds with his trick. This ruse generally averts all suspicion.

The Second Deal:

The object of this sleight, as its name implies, is to deal the second card of the pack, while, apparently, dealing the top card, which remains unchanged in its position after the deal.

The cards are held loosely in the left hand with the thumb on top of the pack, in the position usually adopted in dealing.

The left thumb pushes to the right the two top cards, so that they will be between the thumb and middle finger, the thumb on top of the first card and the tip of the middle finger under the second card. As the hands come together, the thumb and forefinger of the right hand grasp the two top cards, the thumb pushing the top card back to its original position on top of the pack, in which movement it is assisted by the left thumb. The right forefinger by a closing downward movement draws away the second card, which is now held between that finger and the thumb free from the pack. At the same moment the left hand moves back a little to the left.

The different movements must melt into one another, so to speak, and with a little practice, the most keen-eyed observer will be deceived.

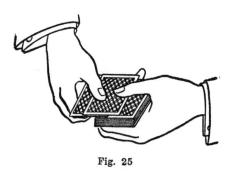

Fig. 25

It will greatly facilitate the proper working of this sleight, especially when it is to be repeated several times in immediate succession, if the little finger of the left hand is held as a rest or stop against the lower part of the pack. This will keep the cards safely together. See the illustration, Fig. 25.

The False Count:

This is a very deceptive sleight. By it the conjurer leads his audience to suppose that he has many more cards in his hands than he really has. For example, let us suppose that the performer holds only six cards, while from the nature of his trick the audience believe he has eight.

He holds the pack in his left hand, backs up, and the front cards pointing in a slanting direction toward the stage. The first card is pushed by the thumb of the left hand into the right hand, the thumb of that hand drawing it away, and the hand itself moving away a trifle toward the right. Then the hands come together again and the next card is pushed off in the same way,

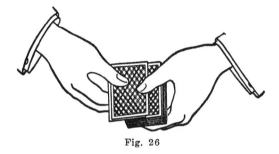

Fig. 26

falling on number one. Now the third card ought to follow, but at the very moment that the right hand is about to draw it away it is quickly drawn back by the left thumb on top of the cards in the left hand. The hands separate again, as in the case of the first two cards, as shown in Fig. 26.

Bear in mind that the performer counts "one, two, three," etc., whether or not a card leaves the left hand. So, when he counts "three" this time, he has only two cards in his right hand. Then he continues "four," really counting a card into his hand; "five" (drawing back the card), "six, seven, eight." Apparently he has eight cards in his right hand, while in fact he has only six.

As there is always a sound when a card is drawn

away, the performer is careful to imitate it when a false count is made by sliding his right thumb downward along the card just at the moment the left thumb draws it back.

If these instructions are carefully followed and the count is made deliberately the most astute observer will be deceived.

The "Ruffle":

To heighten the effect of a trick, as, for example, when a card is to disappear from the pack or to mark the passage of a card from one place to another, a crackling sound with the cards is sometimes introduced. It is made by holding the pack in the left hand, with the thumb at one side along the edge, the forefinger doubled under the pack and the other fingers on top at the opposite side, as shown in the illustration, Fig. 27. Now with the thumb the cards near the upper left hand corner are bent toward the inside of the hand. The bent forefinger which is under the pack, presses against the cards in the opposite direction. When the thumb lets the cards escape again the rebound of the cards to their normal position will produce a peculiarly sharp, explosive sound.

To Spring the Cards From One Hand to the Other:

Hold the pack in the right hand, the thumb at one end, the first, second and third fingers at the other. Now by pressing the ends of the pack so that the thumb and fingers are brought toward one another (see Fig. 28), the cards will be bent and be inclined to spring from the hand. By continuing the pressure the cards will slide out from under the finger tips. The open left hand which must be held some inches below the right, must catch the cards as they fly downward and be *brought up to the right hand,* squaring up the pack.

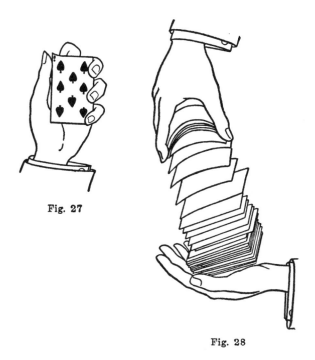

Fig. 27

Fig. 28

By practice the distance may be increased and the springing be made in a horizontal and also in an upward direction. Care must be taken not to follow the cards with the right hand to the left, as that will scatter them.

The Slide:

By this useful little sleight the card next following the one at the bottom of the pack is substituted for the bottom card.

The pack is held face down in the left hand, the thumb on one side, the fingers on the other. As the right hand approaches the pack, ostensibly to draw away the bottom card, the third finger of the left hand slides that card back about an inch toward the wrist. (See Fig. 29.) The thumb of the right hand is then

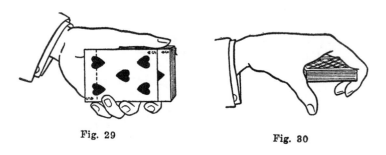

Fig. 29   Fig. 30

placed against the pack and the forefinger under the now partly cleared card that is next to the one at the bottom. This card the forefinger draws out and with the help of the thumb it is removed from the pack. The audience imagine it is the bottom card, which they saw but a moment before. As soon as the card is removed, the forefinger of the left hand presses the front end of the pack and pushes it back to square it with the bottom card.

When practicing this sleight it is well to moisten slightly the tips of the third finger of the left hand and the forefinger of the right hand.

In the illustration the hand holds the pack so that the cards may be seen. This is done in order to give the reader a better idea of the position of the cards; in doing the trick, however, the pack is held with the faces downward, as in Fig. 30.

The Forcing Die:

This is a most useful adjunct to the conjurer who wishes to force number *two* or *three* by the throw of a die.

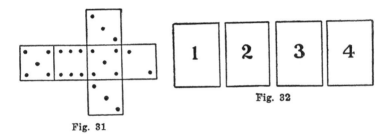

Fig. 31

Fig. 32

From the diagram it is seen that the "one" and the "four" spots are missing from the die, and are replaced by an extra "five" and "three." The spots are arranged as follows: The two "three" spots are on opposite sides, as are also the two "fives," while the "six" and the "two" are opposite, as shown in Fig. 31. When the performer places four heaps of cards on the table, and wishes to force one, he takes care that this heap is either the second or the third in the row.

Let us suppose that number *three* is to be forced. He announces that the spots on the die will indicate which heap is to be selected or used, and as there happens to be only four heaps, it will be necessary to count backward, should *five* or *six* be thrown. The heaps are in the order shown in Fig. 32. If two is thrown, the performer begins to count from the right, which will make the third card, number *two;* if *three,* he counts from the left, when the third heap will be number *three.* If *five* he counts from the left and one number back; if *six,* he begins to count at the right and then two numbers backward, which will cause him to end with *three.*

It is evident that no matter what number may be thrown on a die made in the way described, the counting may always be done so that it will stop at *three,* the desired heap. Should it be necessary to force the *second* heap, the counting must be in an opposite direction.

The Prearranged Pack:

Difficult as most card tricks are there are certain others that may almost be said to do themselves, and yet are by no means to be despised.

There is little, if any, sleight of hand called into play, the essentials being a clear head, a good memory, a prearranged pack of cards, and some practice. The cards are not mechanical affairs, but an ordinary pack, *discarding the "joker,"* arranged in a certain order. The better to remember this order, resort is had to a sentence made up of words having almost the same sound as the numbers they represent. The preparation of this sentence may be left to the ingenuity of the performer, or the following may be used.

4	9	king	ace	10	6	jack
Four	benign	kings	won	a tender	sick	knave

5	3	8	queen	2	7	
fifty-three	hated	queens	to	save.		

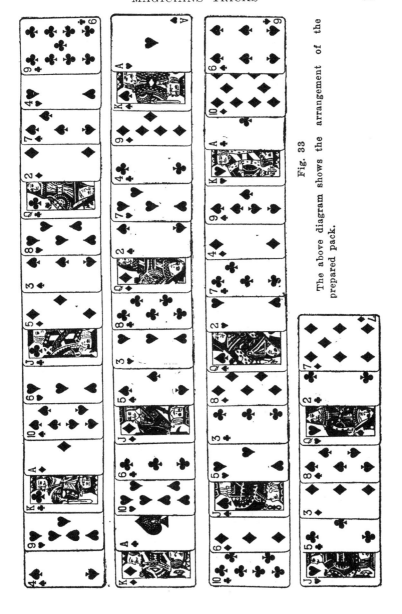

Fig. 33

The above diagram shows the arrangement of the prepared pack.

This is not very brilliant verse, nor is it clearer than some of Lewis Carroll's lines, and yet it answers its purpose admirably.

So much for the numbers, or spot values, of the cards. As it would not do to have all of one suit together, they also are arranged, say, as follows: spades, hearts, clubs, and diamonds, and the more easily to remember this sequence, we bear in mind that the four consonants of the words "SHow CoDe," here printed in capitals, represent the order of the suits.

To prepare the pack, we begin by laying the four of spades, face upward, on the table. On top of this place the nine of hearts, next the king of clubs, and then the ace of diamonds. We proceed in this way with the rest of the pack, always following the values as suggested by the formula and the suits as laid down in the "SHow CoDe." The accompanying diagram may help the inexperienced in arranging the pack. When the cards are all laid out it will be found that *every fourth card is of the same suit, every second card the other suit of the same color,* and *every thirteenth card is of the same spot value* and of *the next suit in the order of suits.*

When these instructions on the arrangement of the pack are thoroughly mastered, it is surprising what an expert performer at cards the merest tyro may become.

This pack may be *cut* (not shuffled) as often as desired without disturbing its order in the least, and when cut four or five times in quick succession it will appear as if the cards are thoroughly mixed. To still further mislead the audience, the performer may resort to the *false shuffle.*

Now for the wonders that may be worked with this pack.

The performer requests some man or boy to empty the breast-pocket of his coat. Then placing the pack behind his own back, he asks the one who is assisting to draw one card and, without looking at it, to put it into the empty pocket. As soon as this is done the performer inserts the little finger of his left hand at the place in the pack from which the card was taken, and, without disarranging the order of the cards in any way, cuts the pack at that place, putting the upper part under the lower, in fact, making the *pass*. Bringing the pack in front of him, and getting sight of the bottom card, he recalls the memorized formula and will know almost immediately which card was drawn, for it must be *the one that comes just after the bottom card of the pack*. For example: should the nine of diamonds be drawn, and the pack be cut as directed, the bottom card will be the four of clubs. "Clubs," the performer says to himself "are followed by diamonds and four by nine." Turning to the one who has the card in his pocket, the performer says: "There are two colors in a pack, red and black. Which do you choose?" Should the answer be *red*, the performer says: "Red, be it." If, on the contrary, the answer be *black*, the performer simply says: "You take the black? Very well; then I shall use the red." This system of *forcing*, by *always interpreting the answer to suit the purpose of the performer*, is followed throughout the trick, and is rarely detected by the unsuspecting audience, as a long experience proves. The next question of the performer is: "There are two red cards, diamonds and hearts. Which do you choose?" A slight emphasis on *diamonds* will generally cause that suit to be mentioned, but should the answer be *hearts,* then the performer, following his forcing method, says: "You choose hearts? Very well; then I have *diamonds.*" Continuing, the next question is: "Let us divide the thirteen cards of that suit into two, say, the ace, king, queen, jack, ten, nine, and eight in one part, and the deuce, trey, four, five, six, and seven in another. Now which do you choose?" And no matter which is mentioned, the first pack is used for the trick. Again and again the pack is divided until at last but two remain, and of the two the *nine* is chosen by the performer, who says: "There is now only one card remaining, the *nine of diamonds.* Take it from your pocket, please." Which is done.

Another mystifying trick is that of calling for the cards that some one has selected at random.

Having gone through the pretense of shuffling the cards, the performer offers the pack, without letting it leave his hands, to one of the audience with the request that it be cut. This done, he takes the upper portion in his right hand, and holding the lower part in his left he extends it to the one who made the cut with the remark, "As it would be impossible for me to know what these cards are, will you be good enough to take as many as you wish, without letting me see them?

"I would suggest," he continues, "with a view to saving time, that you select only seven or eight, but that is not material. Take as many as you please." As soon as the cards are drawn, which must be in a lump from the top, not from different parts of the pack, the left hand pack is placed on the other and the performer gets sight of the bottom card. "Now, sir," he says, "how many cards have you?" and as he knows the card that follows the bottom card, he begins to ask for them in their routine until all are handed to him. It is not even necessary for him to ask how many cards are drawn, for by slightly raising the inner corner of the top card with the left thumb and getting a glimpse of its index he knows the number almost immediately. There is little danger that this will be noted by the audience, for their attention will be fixed on the one who has drawn the cards.

When, by continued practice, the performer has become proficient in the handling of this prearranged pack, he may give further evidence of his skill by telling the name of the card that will be found at any number in the pack; and for this the bottom card is the key, and to begin the first thing is to find the suit. This is learned by dividing the number called for by four. If there be no remainder the suit is the same as that of the card at the bottom of the pack. If the remainder be one, it is the next suit in the arranged order; if the remainder be two, it is the second suit in the order, or the other suit of the color of the bottom card, and if the remainder be three it is the third suit in the order. When the suit is known, which takes a moment only to learn, the performer mentally divides the number called for by thirteen, which is the number of cards in each suit. That is easily done when one reflects that thirteen goes into twenty-six, thirty-nine, and fifty-two (the number of cards in a pack) without a remainder. In dividing the number called for by thirteen, should there be no remainder the spot value of the card is the same as the bottom card, though this rarely happens. When there is a remainder, count over mentally in the prearranged order (four, nine, king, etc.), beginning with the top card of the pack, and when as many cards are counted as equal the number of the remainder, the last card will have the same spot value as the card that is called for. To illustrate this, let us suppose that the bottom card of the pack is the seven of hearts, and the thirtieth card is called for. Dividing thirty by four we find a remainder of two, by which we know that the card is a diamond. Dividing thirty by thirteen, the remainder is *four*. In the order of the formula, after the bottom card, which is a seven, comes the four, the nine, the king, and, finally, the ace, so it follows that the thirtieth card from the top is an ace, and consequently the asked for card is the ace of diamonds. To prove this, try it with a prearranged pack.

It is always a great mistake to repeat a trick that has impressed an audience; of course, the professional is not called on to do this, but the amateur will frequently find himself urged to "do it again." As to refuse might seem ungracious, the young magician ought, whenever possible, to have another similar trick to present that is effected by entirely different means.

With the trick just described it frequently happens that the performer has no sooner told that the thirtieth card (in this case) is the *ace of diamonds* than some one will call out another number. "It is as easy to tell one number as another," says the performer, "and it would be merely a repetition of what I have just done. Let me show you the same trick in a different form. If some one will call the name of a card I will tell him what number it will be found in the pack. Now, who speaks? You, sir? The deuce of clubs? Certainly; that is the twenty-fifth card, as we shall see." He counts off the cards, laying them face down on the table, and when he reaches the twenty-fifth card, he turns it face upward, and, sure enough, it is the wished for card.

To gain this knowledge the performer, to begin, must know the location number of the first card which corresponds in the number of spots to that of the card called for. Glancing at the bottom card, he counts mentally, beginning with the top card of the pack, until he reaches the card he is in search of. The number that this card holds in the pack, which must be less than thirteen, he divides by four. Should it be of the suit called for he need go no further, but simply announces that number as the one at which the card called for is located. But should the proper suit be the next in order, he adds thirteen to reach the proper number; if the suit be the second in order, he adds twenty-six, and if third in order he adds thirty-nine.

On the first reading this may not be perfectly clear, but to make it so, let the reader take an arranged pack, and suppose the *deuce of clubs,* already quoted, to be the card named, and the *seven of hearts to be at the bottom of the pack.* Begin to count with the top card, which will be the four of clubs; then the nine of diamonds, the kings of spades, the ace of hearts, the ten of clubs, the six of diamonds, the jack of spades, five of hearts, three of clubs, eight of diamonds, queen of spades, *two of hearts*—which is the twelfth card, but as the required suit, clubs, is next in order to hearts, thirteen must be added, and counting off the cards the twenty-fifth will prove to be the desired card.

Just here, let us say, that when doing a trick, whether of cards or anything else, the performer should never look at his hands, unless he wishes to direct attention to them. How then may we "glance at the bottom card of the pack," as directed in doing the foregoing trick? In this way: holding the pack across the palm of the left hand so that it may be raised just a trifle by pressing the thumb against the edges of the cards, the performer raises his hand almost on a level with his eyes, and extends his arm naturally and carelessly toward his audience, making, at the same time, some trifling remark, as, for instance, "Pretty tricks, these card-tricks, aren't they?" At this moment he sees the bottom card. Other methods will suggest themselves as one grows more proficient.

One more trick that may be done with the prepared pack, which is very easy: that is, professing to deal oneself all the trumps in a whist hand. It is simplicity itself. Have the pack cut for trumps in the usual way, and then deal out four hands on a table, the faces of the cards down. Let the fourth hand be the dealer's. When all the cards are dealt, turn up the dealer's hand, and it must, necessarily, be all trumps, since every fourth card is of the same suit. But do not, on any account, show the other hands, as they might reveal the whole secret of the trick.

The Color Change:

By means of this sleight the bottom card of the pack, which the audience have seen only a moment before, is made to disappear or rather to be replaced by a card of a different color and suit.

Method 1. When this method is followed only the left hand is used.

The pack is held in the left hand, faces toward the audience. The top card is reversed, that is, it is turned back to back with the other cards. To the audience it will appear as if the pack were lying face upward in the left hand. It is held with the face of this one card

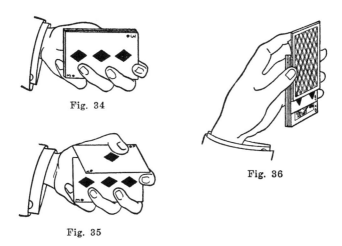

Fig. 34

Fig. 35

Fig. 36

toward the audience and the fingers of the left hand arranged as follows: The forefinger is at the left bottom corner; the second and third fingers are along the bottom edge, and the little finger is behind the pack near the right bottom corner. The thumb is behind the pack with its ball against the hindmost card, as shown in Fig. 34. The pressure of the four fingers maintains the pack in a standing position. Now if the thumb presses gently against the hindmost card (really the first card of the pack), slides it up and over the other cards, the top of the pack serving as a pivot, and then presses it down (see Fig. 35), it will come over and cover the face of the reversed card. The fingers help it into position, and if the entire movement be accompanied by an up and down motion of the hand, the operation will be imperceptible. Should the performer choose, he may repeat this change until every card that faces him has been exhausted, but it is not wise to do this more than four or five times.

Method 2. The pack is divided in two, and the cards are held so that one packet covers the other about half way. The faces of both packets are toward the audience, with the exception of the front card of the upper packet which is reversed, as in Fig. 36. To the audience it will appear as if the cards of the packets face in opposite directions. The cards are held in the left hand as in the illustration. The pack is now covered with the right hand and with the first finger of the left hand the back card of the upper packet is pushed down. This card will now cover the card of the lower packet that was in sight, and it will appear as if the face of the card had changed in some mysterious way. Even if the audience imagine that a card from the upper packet was brought down they will soon abandon that idea since they suppose the cards of the upper packet face the other way, and pushing one down would bring it with its back to them.

Method 3. In this the pack is held in the left hand, the faces toward the audience, the fingers on the top, the thumb on the bottom, and the little finger at the back, as in Fig. 37. The right hand, perfectly straight, is brought in front of the pack, the tips of the fingers of the left hand resting on it, as in Fig. 38. The pack,

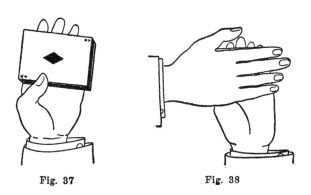

Fig. 37   Fig. 38

which is held between the forefinger and thumb of the left hand, is now turned round. The little finger which presses against the back card prevents that card from turning also, and it is kept in position and pressed forward into the palm of the right hand. The second and third fingers of the left hand, which are on top of this card, keep it down so that its upper edge does not show above the right hand. (See Fig. 39.) In the illustration the card is shown to make this explanation clearer, but it must always be kept so that the audience can not see it, being pushed down by the second and third fingers into the palm of the right hand.

The pack in the left hand has the thumb on top and the three fingers below, while the little finger presses the card against the palm of the right hand. The right hand is just below the pack. (See Fig. 40.)

When the right hand is now brought upward with a sliding motion over the pack it leaves the card which is in its palm on the pace of the pack.

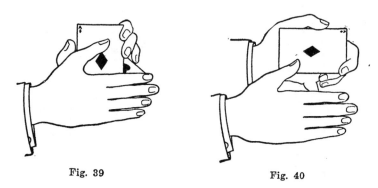

Fig. 39   Fig. 40

Method 4. While very simple, there is no better method of making the color change than the following: The performer holds the pack horizontally in his left hand, the thumb at the upper side, the fingers at the lower. The cards face toward the audience, as shown in Fig.

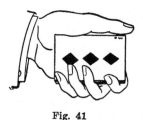

Fig. 41

41. Holding the pack in this way, the palm of the right hand is turned outward so that every one may see it is empty. Then, as if to show that no cards are concealed

in the left hand, the performer passes the pack to the right hand, taking it, the faces toward his palm, with the thumb at the lower corner of the end near the wrist, the forefinger at the lower corner of the opposite end. When the left hand has been shown to be empty the performer passes the pack back again to that hand, which seizes the cards with the thumb at their upper sides and the fingers at the lower, in the position they were held at first. At the same moment, or may be just a fraction of a second before, the tips of the second and third fingers of the left hand push the back card of the pack down and into the right palm. The right hand is now brought over the face of the pack, and the palmed card is left there.

Care must be taken that the fingers of the right hand are kept close together, so that when the card is palmed it will not show itself above the first finger. Instead of palming the card in the orthodox way, the "clip," described on page 10, may be used. The moment the pack is to be replaced in the left hand the hindmost card, as in the first instance, is pushed downward, but this time between the root of the third and little fingers of the right hand which clutch it at the lower right hand corner. The pack in the left hand is held as at the start. The right hand, which must be held perfectly straight, is removed a little way from the pack. It then covers the pack and with a sliding motion leaves the card it holds at the front of the pack.

Method 5. In this method the pack is held almost horizontally in the left hand, the thumb on the upper side, the second, third, and little fingers on the lower; the forefinger is at the back of the pack. The per-

former shows his right hand to be empty, and with it
covers the front card of the pack. As he does this, his
left forefinger slightly frees the upper edge of the back
card, by picking at it, and then pushes the card backward into the fork of the thumb and forefinger of the
right hand, where it is secured by clipping it, care
being taken that the card does not show above the first
finger. The hand, which is held perfectly straight, de-
posits the card over the face of the first card as it
passes over. The color change is made.

This color change may also be made when a thin
elastic band is placed crosswise around the pack, thereby
precluding the idea that the card is taken from the back
of the pack and placed on the front or taken away from
the front. On three or more cards a black line is drawn
on the face lengthwise and another crosswise with ink,
while on the back of the cards only a line lengthwise is
made (See illustrations, Figs. 42 and 43).

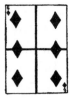

Fig. 42

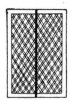

Fig. 43

When the bonafide color change has been made two
or three times, the prepared cards are secretly added to
the back of the pack. A thin elastic band worn black
by use and large enough to go crosswise around the
pack is placed first, lengthwise around the pack without
including the prepared cards. To do this so that it will

not be noticed, the pack should stand on its long edge in the left hand, with the face toward the audience, the little finger dividing the prepared cards from the pack. The band is now stretched and placed crosswise around both the pack and the prepared cards. The pack may now be thrown in the air and shown back and front as the inked line on the back will be taken for an elastic. The color change in the last method may be made as the elastic will in nowise prevent cards being pushed downwards with the left forefinger and being placed in the front of the pack with the right. All the prepared cards may be changed from back to front of pack.

To Make a Card Disappear from a Glass:

For this trick the performer will require:

1. A tumbler that is wide enough at the top to admit a card, but is a little taller than a card. It should taper towards the bottom, and, by preference, be ornamented, as shown in Fig. 44.

Fig. 44

Fig. 45

2. A piece of transparent celluloid, cut to the exact size of a card.

3. A playing card that is bent double. A court card

is the best for the purpose, as the crease is not readily seen when the card is not folded.   (See Fig. 45.)

4. A handkerchief, which may be borrowed from the person who is to assist in the trick.

The tumbler stands on the table, also a pack of cards with the creased card, not bent, on top and beneath it the piece of celluloid.

Some one is asked to assist and he is allowed to examine the glass, which he is told to hold up with his right hand.

The performer picks up the creased card with his right hand and with it the celluloid, which is kept concealed behind it.   The assistant is asked to call out the name of the card.   The performer holds the card with his thumb at the bottom and his second finger at the top, bending it out a little the better to keep the celluloid in place.   Then with his left hand he throws the borrowed handkerchief over it and asks the assistant to place the tumbler under it.   As soon as the card is covered, the performer takes hold of it through the handkerchief with his left hand, while the right hand, which is still under the handkerchief, bends the card in two and palms it.   As it is only half size now it may be palmed without being detected.   The left hand holds on to the celluloid shape and its outlines under the handkerchief give the impression that the card is still there.   The assistant is now requested to take hold of the card (the celluloid) from outside the handkerchief.   "You are sure you have it?" asks the performer.   "Of course I am," is the answer, and every one will endorse what he says, since the outlines of the supposed card may be seen plainly.   He is told to push the card into the tumbler, which is still covered. The performer gets rid of the palmed card by dropping it into a convenient pocket, and informs the assistant that the card will leave the tumbler in a moment, without his knowing it.

Pulling up his sleeves, the performer puts his left hand under the handkerchief and grasps the glass near the bottom, telling the assistant to let go of it. At the same moment catching hold of a corner of the handkerchief and crying "Go," the performer jerks away the covering and shows the tumbler empty. It may be turned around, for there is no danger that the fake will drop out. The tapering sides of the glass hold the celluloid firmly, which, besides, is curled slightly inside the lower part of the glass. The design traced on the tumbler helps in the deception and effectually conceals the celluloid.

The card may be produced from the performer's pocket or in any way that may suggest itself..

The Transformation of the Jack of Clubs:

Three of the Jack of clubs are distributed as follows in the pack: One is laid on the top, a second is placed the third from the top, and the third next to the bottom. The performer makes the "pass" so as to bring the top Jack to the middle of the pack, and forces it on one of the audience, who is asked to look at it, so as to know it again, and then put it back in the same place in the pack. Again the pass is made and the card is brought back to its original position. The performer now ruffles the pack with his left hand and, showing the bottom card to the one who drew the card, asks whether that is the card he selected. As the bottom card is, let us say, the seven of spades, the answer, necessarily, must be "No." "That's a bad beginning," says the performer, "and as that particular card is the most fractious one in the pack, always pushing itself in where it is not wanted, I'll get it out of the way and lay it on the table." Lowering the pack, face downward, he slips back the seven of spades with the third finger of the left hand, which is at the bottom of the pack, and with the second finger and thumb of the right hand takes instead the card that follows, a Jack of clubs, and places it, face down, on the table. Then putting his little finger between the two top cards and the rest of the pack he passes those two cards to the bottom. There will be now one Jack of clubs on top of the pack and another next to the bottom, while at the bottom is some indifferent card, say, the nine of diamonds.

"As I was so unfortunate with the first card," continues the performer, "I hope to do better this time. I think you will find, sir, that the card now at the bottom is the one you selected."

He shows the card and is again told he is wrong. "Dear me," he exclaims, "I don't know that I can do better than put it alongside of the other on the table." He proceeds as with the seven of spades and lays the second Jack of clubs on the table. "As many good things go in threes," he says, "let me try once more. As I have had no luck at the bottom of the pack, suppose I try the top for a change." He now, apparently, shows the top card, but, really, shows the two top cards as one, the second being, we will suppose, the ten of hearts. Keeping the two cards well together, his thumb at the top and first finger beneath, he slides them to the right. protruding about an inch. The thumb of the left hand keeps them in position. Now the thumb and first finger of the right hand turn up the two cards just a trifle, so as to bring in sight the ten of hearts, as shown in Fig. 46. The moment he is

Fig. 46

told that it is not the selected card the performer presses the cards down to their normal position, and with the right thumb slides the Jack of clubs free of the ten of hearts, holding it between the thumb and first finger. At the same time the left thumb draws the ten of hearts back on the pack. With a little care this change is imperceptible.

The Jack of clubs is now placed on the table, face downward, with the others.

The seven of spades and the nine of diamonds are now brought from the bottom of the pack to the top, and they will be in the following order: First, the top card, which is the seven of spades; second, the nine of diamonds; and third and last, the ten of hearts.

The three Jack of clubs are on the table, faces down.

"So far," says the performer, "my endeavors have come to naught." Then turning to one of the audience, he says, "Perhaps this gentleman may be more successful. Will you, sir, be good enough to select one of those cards that are on the table?" The performer picks up the one that is pointed out, and shows it to be the Jack of clubs. As he is putting it back on the table he exchanges it, by the bottom change for the top card, the seven of spades. Then a second card is selected and that proves to be a Jack of clubs. "That's very remarkable," he says, "the Jack of clubs has evidently come to life." While saying this he makes the exchange again, this time for the nine of diamonds, which he throws carelessly alongside the other card, face down. He then turns over the third card. "Jack of clubs again! Why, it seems to be nothing else," he says, and exchanging it this time by the top change for the ten of hearts, lays that on the table. As there can not be more than one Jack of clubs in the pack, the performer declares there must be a mistake somewhere, and asks some one to turn the cards over, and they prove to be the cards that were first shown, which were declared to be wrong. In the meanwhile the performer gets rid of the two bottom Jacks, and throws down the pack so that it may be examined.

The Prediction:

A pack of cards is handed out to be shuffled. When it is returned the performer learns what the top card is by simply bending the left hand bottom corner, so that he may see the index. Laying the pack on the table, face down, he asks some one to divide it in two.

He informs his audience that by looking at a card in one packet he is enabled to tell which card is on top of the other packet.

In proof of this he lifts a few cards from the packet which was the lower part of the pack, and looking at one card he names the top card of the other packet. As he knows that card, this is an easy matter. Looking at the cards of the lower packet is merely a ruse to learn what card is on top, for while the audience imagine he is looking at one of the cards when he opens the packet he is really shifting the top card so that he may see its index, as shown in Fig. 47. When the

Fig. 47

performer has named the top card of the upper packet and it is found to be correct, he deliberately places the former lower packet on top. Then he shuffles the pack without disturbing the top card, and proceeds as at first. In this way he may continue indefinitely, without fear of discovery.

He is careful to give his audience the impression that

when he lifts at hazard the cards from the lower packet, as already shown, that the particular card he sees enables him to tell the top card of the upper pack. To strengthen this impression, when he looks at the card of the lower pack he says: "Ah! the five of diamonds—" or whatever it happens to be—"naturally, the top card of the other packet must be the Jack of Clubs, just as naturally as day follows night." It is wonderful how this little subterfuge tends to mislead even intelligent people; most of them will imagine that the trick is the result of some mathematical formula worked out by the performer. Not for a moment must any one be led to suspect that the performer's sole object in handling the lower packet is to get sight of its top card.

To Discover a Card Drawn from the Pack:

Method 1. A card is drawn, and when it has been replaced in the pack, the one who drew it is asked to square up the cards. When the card is put back the performer watches to see in what part of the pack it goes. He puts the pack behind his back. He knows about where the card is, that is, whether it is near the top, the bottom, or the middle of the pack. Let us suppose it is near the top, and the performer thinks there are nine or ten cards above it. (Let us say, just here, that an expert handler of cards can tell almost the exact number, at a glance.) Holding the pack behind his back he takes three cards from the top, and showing them asks if the drawn card is among them. Of course it is not. He throws the three cards on the table, and then with three more cards taken from the top he goes through the same procedure. To take three more cards from the top would be extremely hazardous, as the selected card might be among them and there would be no way to know it. Instead of pursuing the same course he takes one card only from the top and two from the bottom. Should the selected card be one of these three, he knows at once that it is the card he took from the top. Should the selected card be placed near the bottom the same procedure is followed, but instead of showing cards taken from the top of the pack, he begins to show from the bottom. If the selected card has been placed in the middle of the pack, the performer brings a number of cards from top to bottom so that the selected card will be nearer the top, and proceeds as at first.

There is another way of doing this trick. Some one is asked to draw seven or eight cards and to think of one. These cards are replaced on top of the pack, which is then shuffled without disturbing the drawn cards. Then the pack is placed behind the performer's back, and he takes four cards from the bottom and one from the top and throws them on the table faces upward. He asks if the card that was thought of is among them. If it proves to be, he knows it must be the one he took from the top of the pack. Should the selected card not be among them, he repeats the proceeding just described until he reaches the card thought of.

Method 2. The cards are shuffled and one is drawn. Taking the pack in his left hand the performer holds it at the bottom in an upright position between the thumb and first finger. The thumb is stretched across the back of the pack and the first finger across the front. The cards face toward the audience. With the second finger of the right hand the performer opens the pack about the middle, by drawing the upper part toward himself, as shown in the illustration, Fig. 48.

Fig. 48

This gives him an opportunity to see the bottom card of the upper part. The drawn card is placed in the opening thus formed. Then the cards are cut or shuffled, and it is simple enough to locate the card as it will be below the card that was at the bottom of the upper part. The cutting or shuffling of the pack will seldom, if ever, separate the two cards.

Method 3. A card is selected from a previously shuffled pack. The pack is in the left hand and about half of it is lifted off with the right hand, which holds the pack between the thumb and second finger. The selected card is laid on top of the lower packet and the upper packet is placed above it with a little sliding motion toward the body. At the same time the thumb of the right hand slides the top card of the lower packet, which is the selected card, a little out toward the wrist, where the performer may easily turn it upward with the thumb and catching a glimpse of the index, learn what the card is.

Method 4. When the card has been drawn, the pack is bent almost end to end, as in Fig. 49. When the card is replaced and the pack is shuffled, all the cards will be curved slightly except one which is, of course, the one that was drawn. Sometimes the pack is curved lengthwise, as in Fig. 50. In that case when the se-

Fig. 49   Fig. 50

lected card is replaced and the cards are shuffled they may be sprung from hand to hand without disturbing the bridge and the selected card may be found in a moment.

Method 5. If done with care it is almost impossible to detect this trick. A faint line is drawn with ink or a pencil across the edges of the pack at B, as shown in the illustration, Fig. 51. To exhibit the trick the pack is first thoroughly shuffled, and then one of the audience is asked to draw a card. While he is looking at it, the performer turns the pack, so that the line which was near the bottom of the pack is now near the top. When the drawn card is replaced, the performer need only look for the little mark that is on the edge to know the card. Shuffling the pack does not interfere with the accomplishment of the trick, provided of course, that the position of the cards are not changed. More than one card may be drawn when necessary. Of course, the mere telling of what card has been drawn does not amount to much as a trick, unless in combination with something else.

A Flying Card:

A card is selected from an unprepared pack which has been thoroughly shuffled. When the card is returned the pack is again shuffled. The performer holds the pack in his right hand, and asks the name of the selected card. The answer is no sooner given when the card jumps out of the pack, and high in the air.

Before the knack of this trick is acquired, there will be no little practice spent on it. When the selected

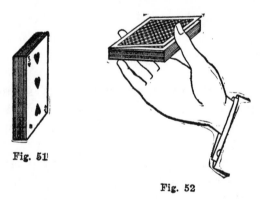

Fig. 51

Fig. 52

card is returned to the pack, it is brought to the top by the "pass," and left there, even though the cards are once more shuffled. Then the performer places the

pack, face down, on the right hand, the thumb on one
side, the first and second fingers on the other. The selected card (which is on top) rests on the side where
the fingers are, and its opposite edge, where the thumb

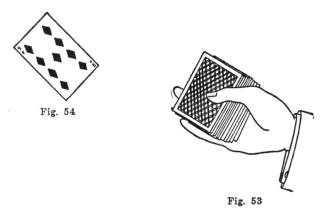

Fig. 54

Fig. 53

is, is raised about a quarter of an inch, and held loosely
by the thumb, as shown in Fig. 52. The muscles of
the hand which must be kept tense, suddenly press the
pack into the position shown in Fig. 53; the thumb
slips between the top card and the others, while the
first and second fingers glide along the bottom of the
pack. Almost at the same moment the top card will
spring out of the hand and go flying in the air, as
shown in Fig. 54. In its descent it will be found
possible to catch the card on the top of the pack, but
that means more practice and plenty of it.

A Greek Cross:

A number of cards is dealt out in four or more (not
less than four) heaps, faces upward. Each heap con-

tains four cards, and, for effect, they are arranged in
the form of a Greek cross, as shown in Fig. 55. The
performer turns his back to the table and requests some
one to think of one of the cards. When this is done,
the performer faces the table once more, and asks in
which heap the card is lying. When he learns this he
again turns his back to the table, and tells the one who

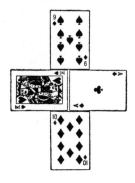

Fig. 55

thought of the card to mix up the cards indiscriminately. Then the performer rearranges them in cruci-
form heaps, and once more asks in which heap the card
appears. Then he picks out the card at once.

It is a very simple trick. The performer uses a prearranged pack (page 32) and when the heap containing
the thought-of card is pointed out, he has only to
glance at the top card of the cross to know the other
three cards. As he turns his back immediately no one
will imagine that he can memorize all four cards in
the heap. When he arranges the heaps a second time,
he is careful to have each card of the designated heap

in a different heap, that is, one only in a heap. As soon as the heap is pointed out the second time it is a simple matter to pick out the one card that was in the original heap.

A Selected Card Appears at Any Desired Number from the Top of the Pack:

A card that has been drawn by one of the audience and replaced in the pack is brought by means of "the pass" next to the top card of the pack. The performer asks at what number, counting from the top, the audience would like the selected card to appear. Let us suppose that number *eight* is decided on. Holding the pack in his left hand the performer shows that it is neither the bottom nor the top card. Taking the top card off the pack and holding it between the thumb and fingers of the right hand, face down, he counts "one." The second card (the selected one) follows immediately as "two," but instead of putting it on *top* of "one," which he holds in his right hand, he puts it *under*, his hands moving together slightly and quickly up and down, prevent the audience from seeing just whether the card goes on the top or the bottom of "one," and as the third card and all the other cards that follow go on top of "one," any suspicion that may be aroused is set at rest. When the eighth card is reached the performer throws it, face down, on the table. When the one who drew the card turns this up, he at once declares it is not the card he selected. While the attention of the audience is fixed on the card, the performer brings his hands together for a moment. The cards in the left hand lie flat, while the others are held

lengthways above them between the thumb and the first
and second fingers at the ends, so that the pack assumes,
somewhat, the position of a half-opened book, as shown
in the illustration, Fig. 56. With the fingers of his

Fig. 56

left hand the performer slips the bottom card of the
packet held by his right hand (the selected card) on
top of the cards in the left hand. By pressing lightly
on this card while the right hand keeps the rest of the
pile in the one position, the selected card will appear
face upward on the left hand heap. The performer
immediately places the cards in his right hand on top
of it, face down, of course. It is the work of a moment
only, and the audience ought not to notice it. Picking
up the card that is lying on this table, the performer
places it on the pack, which he hands to the person who
selected the card, telling him that though in spite of the
evidence of his senses, his card is not the eighth from the
top, it will by the magic power of the performer be
brought there. Taking the pack in his hands and ruf-
fling it, he hands it back to the man with the request that
he count off eight cards. The request is complied with,

and much to the astonishment of the gentleman he will find, when he reaches the desired number, the selected card staring him in the face.

A Card Apparently Placed at the Bottom of the Pack, Appears at the Top:

The performer takes two cards from the pack, and holding them tightly together they appear like one. (See "The Single Change," page 19.) Holding them up, he calls attention to the bottom card, calling it by name. He then places the two cards in the middle of the pack, which is in the left hand, allowing them to protrude about an inch. The two cards are held between the thumb and first finger of the right hand. These fingers draw the top card of the two slightly forward, while, at the same time, the forefinger of the left hand, which is under the pack, pushes the bottom card, which is the known card, back into the pack. By keeping the cards slightly tilted downward at the front and the left thumb extended alongside of the pack, the card will slide between the thumb and second finger of the left hand, without showing itself. Now the cards below the protruding card, which the audience suppose to be the card that was shown to them, are placed on top of the pack, the protruding card being thus brought to the bottom. In this position, the pack is placed on the bottom of an upturned goblet. Then the bottom card is pushed slowly home. "Where is the card now?" asks the performer. Of course every one declares it is at the bottom, but much to the surprise of all it is found to be not at the bottom, but at the top.

A Question of Sympathy:

When the pack has been shuffled and returned to the performer, one of the audience draws a card and replaces it in the pack. The pack is again shuffled and the person who drew the card is asked to *think* of another card. When he has done this he is further requested to draw a card from the bottom of the pack, which the performer holds in his left hand, and to lay it, face upward on the table. This he continues to do until he draws the card he thought. "Now, my dear sir," says the performer, "by some mysterious and inexplicable bond of sympathy the next card you draw will be the one you first selected." And so it proves to be. The explanation is simple: The card that was drawn was at once passed to the bottom of the pack, where it was left undisturbed when the pack was shuffled.

When the one who drew it is about to take the cards one by one from the bottom of the pack in his search for the card he thought of, the performer draws back the bottom card toward his wrist, in the manner already explained in the description of "The Slide," on page 30. The result is that *the card next to the bottom one* is drawn each time by the one who is searching for the thought-of card until the time is reached when the bottom card is wanted. Then the performer moves it into place.

The Card in the Pocketbook:

A card is freely selected from a thoroughly shuffled pack and marked. It is shuffled back into the pack around which is placed a rubber band. The pack is then returned to the person who drew the card, with the request that he hold it. The performer now takes from his breast pocket a large letter case or pocketbook, which is securely tied with a string. He cuts the string and takes out a sealed envelope from the book. Tearing off one end of the envelope he asks the one who drew the card to put his fingers into it and take out the contents. When the request is complied with the marked card is brought out. On examining the pack it is found that the card has left it.

The successful performance of this trick depends, in part, on the skilful palming of the bottom card of the pack, a sleight which is described on page 15. The peculiar arrangement of the pocketbook and the envelope are also essential features of the trick. Any letter case or pocketbook may be used, provided it is the proper length, which is about four by six inches. In it is placed a sealed envelope, which has one end neatly slit with a sharp knife, at the part AA, shown in Fig. 57. Into this open end is inserted two strips

Fig. 57

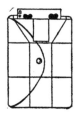

Fig. 58

of rather stiff paper, each an inch and a half wide and four inches long; two inches of each going inside and the other two inches remaining outside. The outside ends are slightly curled outwardly or, better still, each is folded over the side of the book. The book is then securely, but not too tightly, tied around, twice each way, with a string. This cord must be separated at the open end far enough to admit of the card being slipped into the envelope. (See Fig. 58.) The pocket-book is kept in the right breast pocket of the coat.

When the drawn card is to be replaced in the pack,

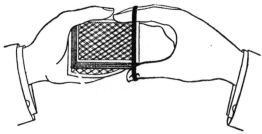

Fig. 59

the performer has it put about the middle and making the "pass" brings it to the bottom. This move he follows with a false shuffle, which leaves the card undisturbed. Taking the pack in his left hand, the thumb on top and the fingers below, the performer takes from his vest pocket with his right hand a rubber band, and stretching it over his thumb and the first two fingers, slips it over the pack. At the same moment the fingers of the left hand close up and palm the bottom card, as shown in Fig. 59. The palming of the card and the affixing of the rubber band being made simultaneously, conceal the stealing of the card. The performer now takes the pack in his right hand, while his left hand goes into the breast pocket, and slipping the card between the strips of paper, pushes it down into the envelope. The strips of paper are then pulled out and left in the pocket, and the cord is properly adjusted. The pocketbook is now brought out; the pack is handed to the person who drew the card and he is told to find the card, but fails in his quest. The performer then removes the string from the pocketbook, tears off the open end of the envelope, and requests the one who drew the card to take it out of the envelope and identify it.

The Disappearing Queen:

A pack of cards is shuffled and afterwards all the spot cards are taken out and laid on the bottom of an inverted glass or tumbler, which is then covered with a handkerchief.

Picking up the court cards, the performer shows the bottom card to one of the audience, whom he asks to take the card and place it in an envelope, which the performer hands to him.

Then the bottom card is shown to a second person, who, in turn, is asked to take it from the pack and place it in another envelope, as in the first case. And so the performer continues, showing the bottom card, and having it placed in an envelope, until all the court cards are disposed of.

Returning to his table, the performer requests them to call out simultaneously, when he shall say, *three*, the name of the card placed in the envelope. "Now, then," he says, "one, two, *three*," and with one voice there is a cry, "The Queen of Hearts." "What, every one the Queen of Hearts? Impossible!" says the performer. "Why think for a moment. There's only one Queen of Hearts in the pack, and here it is," he says, and taking the handkerchief off the cards that are on the tumbler, he picks up the top card, and shows that it is the Queen of Hearts. The audience are now asked to open their envelopes, and, to their surprise, each one finds an entirely different court card.

For this trick are needed a pack of cards, a tumbler, a handkerchief, a pack of envelopes, and a half Queen of Hearts of another pack, as shown in the illustration, Fig. 60.

Fig. 60

Fig. 61

When the cards have been shuffled and the spot cards are removed, including the Queen of Hearts, which the performer places on top of the others, he runs the cards over before the audience, so that they may see all are spot cards, taking care not to let the Queen of Hearts be seen. The packet of spot cards he lays on top of the tumbler, and covers it with a handkerchief. Picking up the court cards, the performer secretly places the half-Queen at the bottom of the pack. Taking the pack in his right hand, he covers the lower part of it, the forefinger covering the lower edge of the half-card, as shown in Fig. 61. Then going to one of the audience, he asks him to remember the bottom card, and then to remove it and place it face down in an envelope. At this, the critical moment of the trick, the performer lowers the pack and places it, face downward, in his left hand, the thumb near the top edge, the fingers beneath. With his right hand he grasps the pack, his thumb at the end toward the body, the fingers at the opposite end. Without changing the position of the left hand, which grasps the half-card, the right hand moves the pack forward a trifle. The result will be that the top edge of the half-Queen will be about the middle of the bottom card and be covered by the left forefinger. When the right hand is withdrawn the man who is assisting will take the bottom card, which he believes to be the Queen of Hearts, and place it in the envelope. Again the performer places his right hand on the pack, while the left hand moves the half-card to the front once more. The same procedure is repeated until all the stock of court cards is exhausted. With the last card care must be taken to press the half-card well against it and to palm the half-card neatly.

The persons who assist in this trick should sit well apart, and the cards should be held close to their faces, so that they may not be seen by those who draw them or by others. Of course each one imagines he has the Queen of Hearts in his envelope, and there is no little surprise when that card is found on top of the inverted tumbler, and a different one in the envelope.

The Changing Card:

A card is selected by one of the audience and when replaced is put in the middle of the pack. Placing the little finger of his left hand under this card the performer makes the "pass," and brings it to the bottom of the pack, which is then shuffled, but the selected card is kept at the bottom. The pack, backs upward, is held in the left hand, which is kept flat, the thumb at one side, the fingers at the other. Then, with the thumb and second finger of the right hand the pack, with the exception of the bottom card, is shoved forward slightly so that this card protrudes about an inch at the lower end as shown in Fig. 62. The front of the

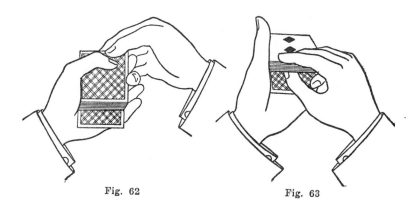

Fig. 62   Fig. 63

pack is lifted a trifle, the better to conceal this. The selected card is then ordered to pass to the top of the pack, and the performer, taking off the top card, shows it and asks whether that is the one that was drawn. The answer, of course, is "No." "Then," he continues, "it may, possibly, have traveled to the bottom," and he shows the bottom card. In showing it he takes hold of the end of the pack with the right hand and turns it over completely, as shown in Fig. 63, so that the faces of the cards are upward. The pack remains in the left hand. When he shows the visible card, which is supposed to be the one that was originally at the bottom, that, also, is declared not to be the selected card. It will be apparent to our readers, who by this time must have fairly good ideas of how some tricks are done, that the real bottom card which protruded from the lower end of the pack, was not turned over with the other cards, and is now back to back with the rest of the pack. The performer turns the pack to its original position,

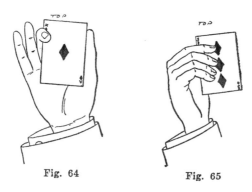

Fig. 64   Fig. 65

being careful, however, to keep it upright as the selected card which is now on top, face upward, must be concealed. Picking up the top card again he asks the person who drew the card whether he is certain that the card shown is not his. Of course the answer will again be that it is not. Instead of one card, however, the performer picked up two, holding them as one, as described on page 20. Laying down the pack, he takes the two cards for a moment between the thumb and forefinger of the left hand at the upper left hand corner so as to allow his right hand to shift its position by taking the cards between the thumb and second finger, as shown in Fig. 64.

Now, when it is asserted that the card shown is not the selected one, he says he knows no other way out of the difficulty except by changing the card. "What was your card, sir?" he asks, and being told, he bids the card to change. His command is obeyed instantly, the card between his fingers being now the one that was drawn. This change is brought about in this way: While the two cards are held by their edges the tip of the forefinger presses against the center of the hinder card. By bringing the thumb and second finger together the cards are curved outwardly at the center and at last the second finger releases its hold and the thumb and forefinger clip the cards between them. This will cause the cards to make a semi-revolution, bringing the card that was at the rear to face the audience, as shown in Fig 65. The left hand takes the cards away from the right to square them up in case they should not cover each other perfectly.

A Wonderful Change:

A court card is prepared by punching in the middle a hole about the size of a large pin head. This card is placed on top of the pack. A card is taken from the pack at random by one of the audience, who marks it. In the meanwhile, the performer brings the prepared card to the middle of the pack, by means of the "pass," and it is on top of this that he has the drawn card laid, when it is returned to the pack. Then he makes the "pass" again, and brings both cards to the top. These he palms and hands out the pack to be shuffled. When the pack is returned to the performer he ruffles the pack, and announces that by his power he has brought the drawn card to the top. In the meantime he has laid the palmed cards on the top. Picking up the two top cards he holds them close together, bending them slightly by the pressure of thumb and fingers, so that they look like one. "Here is the card that was drawn," he says. This will be denied, of course, by the one who selected it. As the front card is a court card the hole will not be visible. Lying on the performer's table is a fine needle threaded with about two feet of sewing silk on one end of which is a knot. This knot, however, must be of a size that will pass through the hole in the court card. Running the needle through the hole, the performer draws the thread till the knot rests against the selected card. Taking a handkerchief he passes the needle through it and then spreads it over the pack, which is scattered somewhat over the table. It is clear that if the thread is pulled up, the handkerchief will be raised, bringing with it the selected card attached to the thread and leaving the court card on the pack, to the surprise of the audience. Still keeping card, handkerchief, and thread together the performer carries them to the one who drew the card, for identification by the mark.

With a String—a Reminiscence:

It was about the year 1845 that one of the editors of this book learned his first conjuring trick. At that time Alexander Heimburger, a foreign conjurer, came

to New York. Under his stage name of Herr Alexander he appeared at the Minerva Rooms, a cozy hall
that stood on Broadway between Walker and Canal
streets. His manager was a personal friend of this
writer's family and the writer, then a little boy, had
not only the run of the house, but became intimate with
Alexander. One afternoon while the conjurer was arranging something for the evening's performance the
boy came into the hall and, boylike, began to ask questions, and then the conjurer, in turn, asked some. One
of these was, "Which of my tricks do you like best?"
"The one where the card comes up out of the pack,"
was the answer. "Good. And how is it done?"
"With a string." "Ah, that is the boy's answer. It's
always with a string. But how; but how?" "Don't
know, but it's with a string." And with a string, that
faithful ally of the conjurer, that potent motive power
of so many tricks, it proved to be. Then and there the
conjurer, who had taken a liking to the boy, explained
the trick. The secret is known to many now, and as
Alexander Heimburger, dexterous conjurer and genial
gentleman, has passed away, the little boy, now an old
man, will explain the trick for those who do not know
it, and moreover will tell many other ways of doing
it that have been invented since that day, years and
years ago.

The Obedient Cards:

In its original form the trick presupposes a certain
amount of skill in handling cards, for the reason that
the performer *forces* certain cards on the audience.
There is, however, an easier way, by use of what is

known as a *"forcing pack."* This is a pack made up of, say, only four different cards, as, for example, the King or the Jack of clubs, trey of hearts, the eight of spades, and the deuce of diamonds, each being repeated ten or twelve times. All of one kind are kept together, and when one lot is placed on another, the Queens at the bottom, it makes a respectable looking pack.

With such a pack, a decanter nearly full of water, a metal case with a cork at the bottom (known as an *houlette*), to hold easily, say, forty cards without binding the edges in any way, and a fine, strong, black silk thread, the performer is almost ready to begin his trick.

Fig. 66
The Houlette.

We say *almost* ready, for there is still one more matter, a most important one, to be attended to. This is the *threading* of the cards. For this, besides the forced cards, six other indifferent ones, which we will call *a, b, c, d, e,* and *f,* are used. The first card, *a,* should be, preferably, the King or Jack of clubs. In this a slit about a quarter of an inch in length is cut in the center of the lower edge, and in the slit is inserted one end of the thread, on which there is a large knot to prevent the thread from pulling through. From the bottom the thread is carried up back of the card, and *b, c, d, e,* and *f* are placed back of *a*. Over the tops of these five cards, as near the center as possible, the thread is laid. Taking, say, the trey of hearts, the performer presses it down between *b* and *c*, the thread going with it; then the eight of spades is pressed down between *c* and *d* and the deuce of diamonds between *d* and *e*, the thread being carried down in each case. When this is done the bottom of each of the forced cards rests on the thread, and, as will be readily understood, a gentle pull will cause these cards to come up from the pack, one after another, the trey of hearts the third, and the King of clubs, the card with the knot in it, the last.

The cards thus arranged are laid face down on the performer's table, the loose end of the thread being passed through a small staple or a screw-eye (which is entirely closed, so that the thread may not slip through) at the back of the table, and thence off to a concealed assistant who is to pull it when the time comes. In front of these cards lying on one side is the *houlette*. Everything being ready, the performer may begin his trick. Taking his forcing pack he goes to a lady whom he requests to draw a card. Remember, there are only four different cards—the ten top cards are all deuce of diamonds; the second lot of ten cards are all eight of spades; the third lot, all the trey of hearts, and the bottom lot the King of clubs. As the lady is about to draw a card the performer runs off the top cards and she naturally takes an eight of spades. As he goes to another lady he passes the top cards to the bottom of the pack, and running over the deuce of diamonds forces one of those, and so on with the trey of hearts and the King of clubs. In order to know when the last card of one kind is reached some performers have the card marked, say, by clipping off a small piece of the lower right-hand corner. When the four cards are drawn and returned to the pack, the performer steps to his table, ostensibly to get the *houlette* and the decanter, so they may be examined by the audience. As he reaches the table he places the pack of cards upon the threaded cards which are lying behind the *houlette*, taking care to keep the thread free. When the decanter and *houlette* are examined the performer places them on the table, the *houlette* being fixed in the decanter. Then the cards are taken up, placed in their case, and the trick proper begins.

Addressing the lady who drew the deuce of diamonds, he asks the name of her card and requests her to bid it rise. The concealed assistant, holding in his left hand the thread, gently taps it with the side of his right hand; the card obeys at once, and when it is almost entirely out of the pack the performer lifts it out, and takes it to the one who drew it. The second card, the eight of spades, is treated in the same way, and then comes the trey of hearts, and finally, the King of clubs. When this card is ordered to come up it does not obey.

"That's very strange," says the performer. "Are you sure, Madam, that you drew the King?"

"Very sure," answers the lady.

"Please repeat your demand, Madam."

Again she orders the King to come up, but all to no purpose.

The performer shows that he is perplexed. Suddenly his face lights up.

"Ah, I see," he says. "Probably we ought to be

more ceremonious in addressing a King.   Let us try it.''

Turning to the cards, and bowing politely, he says:
''Will Your Majesty graciously condescend to honor us
with your presence?''

Scarcely is the request made when the card rises from
the pack and jumps out.

By adding a duplicate of any one of the cards and
threading it so that it will rise just before the card it
represents and with its back toward the audience, the
performer may create the impression that the card
turns over in the pack.

Where it is not practicable to have an assistant to pull
the thread, the performer can gain the same effects by
fastening the loose end of the thread to the back of the
table.   In this case he will have to hold the decanter
in one hand (See Fig. 67), and by carefully moving it

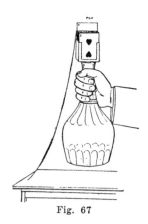

Fig. 67

forward the least bit he can cause the cards to come up
without exciting any suspicion.

A few years ago, a clever conjurer who, like young

Lochinvar, came "out of the West," claimed to have puzzled an old and accomplished performer with another version of the trick. He did not *force* his cards, but he had an entire pack prepared as follows: On the back of each card near the top and at the center was glued a bit of cardboard about half an inch square. It was glued only at the top of one edge and formed a sort of flap. This pack was held by an assistant at the back of the stage. When the performer began his trick he requested the audience to call out the names of the cards with which he should do the trick. The assistant, who heard the names, immediately selected those cards and arranging them in the order called for, quietly laid them on a table on the stage, from which the performer picked them up and placed them at the back of his pack.

Stretched across the stage at about six feet or more above the floor was a fine black silk thread. One end was fastened to a hook in the scenery frame, the other end passed through a screw-eye in the scenery frame on the opposite side of the stage. On this loose end were fastened two or three cards to act as counter-weights.

Standing under the thread and about a step back of it and holding the pack in his left hand, the performer raised his right hand above his head as if to show there was no thread used and in doing so pressed down the thread and passed it under the loose part of the cardboard on the last card. He held on to the other cards tightly. Then with his open right hand about two feet above the pack, he called the card by name and bade it ascend. Loosing his grip of the pack, the prepared card, propelled by the weights on the thread, sprung at once into the outstretched hand. In this way all the chosen cards were made to ascend. (See Fig. 68.)

A second American performer having seen the trick thought out another way of doing it,—and a better way, because it may be done anywhere, as well as on the stage. Here is his method. (See Fig. 69):

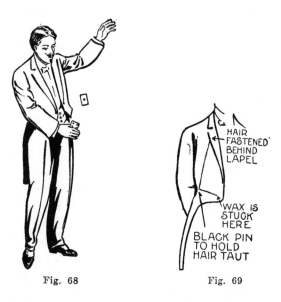

Fig. 68   Fig. 69

The performer procured a long brown hair, from a woman's head, and tied one end of it firmly to a black-headed pin. On the other end he stuck a bit of wax. So that the hair might not pull out of the wax he cut a piece of thin cardboard about one eighth of an inch square. Through this a slit was made about two thirds of the way across. A knot was made in the loose end of the hair which was slipped into the slit and pulled through till the knot caught fast; the hair was then wound through the slit and around the card two or three times which finally was trimmed as small as possible and imbedded in the wax of which only a tiny piece is needed. When the performer was to do the trick he secretly fastened the black pin under the lapel of his coat on the right side, brought the hair down to his hip at which point in his coat he had stuck a second blackheaded pin, passed the hair round the head of the pin and stuck the waxed end on the bottom button of the coat. With the hair fixed in this manner there is little danger of it getting in the way, and the performer might wear it all the evening.

For this form of the trick any cards may be taken, they need not be *forced*. We should advise not more than three be used. As the performer gets them back he has them placed in the center of the pack, and one on top of the other, without it being noticed. To do this easily, he merely slips the little finger of the left hand, in which the pack is held, in the place he opens the pack. When all are gathered he deliberately cuts the pack, and so brings the selected cards to the top. The performer's next move is to pull out the pin at his hip, which will allow the hair to swing loose; remove the waxed end from his coat button, which he may do with his thumbnail, and stick it on the point of his thumb. As he takes the pack from the left hand to stand it upright in that hand he presses the wax on the back of the top card near the top and the center. Then holding the pack upright in his left hand, the right is waved to and fro, under and over, around and about, to show that the cards are not connected with anything, and while making these motions he gets his thumb under the hair.   Then by raising the right hand slightly and lowering the left, the back card will shoot up into the right hand which goes down to meet it.   The second and third cards are treated in the same way.

Sometimes a mechanical pack is used to make the cards rise.   In this form a number of cards are glued solidly together and afterward are cut away, with the exception of the first and last cards, so as to leave nothing but a framework and make a box into which the necessary mechanism is introduced.   This consists of a watch movement somewhat similar to that in a musical

Fig. 70
The Mechanical Pack.

box.   This movement sets in motion two small toothed wheels of steel or rubber, which protrude through slots cut through the front card, about an inch and a quarter apart and about half an inch from the top, as shown in Fig. 70.   A tiny projecting pin at the top of this box, sets the movement going or stops it.   It is not worth while to go into detail about the mechanism of this box-pack for it is not always reliable.   It is an old arrangement, though claimed by a modern conjurer, but has never been popular.

Recently another mechanical pack has been made that dispenses with the aid of an assistant.   This consists of a tiny spindle around the center of which is wound a fine silk thread, one end fastened to the spindle, the other to the back of the table on which the goblet rests and holds the cards. At each end of the spindle is a small wheel covered with a little rubber band. The mechanism is simple and seems to be practicable. The spindle rests in a metal frame that fits over the edge of the goblet. With this, as with the other mechanical device, the cards are not forced.

Besides these, a glass tumbler is made, as shown in Fig. 71. In one part of this a narrow slot is cut, run-

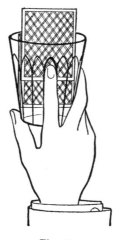

Fig. 71

ning from the bottom of the glass to within an inch of the top. Through this slot the performer, holding the glass in his right hand, sticks his forefinger, and pushes up, one by one, the cards that were drawn by the audience. The cards are not forced, but as they are replaced in the pack are brought to the back by the "pass."

There are other ways of doing this popular trick, all more or less ingenious, but we shall omit mention of them and describe a method that has stood the test of years in the hands of one of our editors, who has exhibited it without failure under most trying circumstances, with the audience on every side of him. The main requisite is a piece of the finest sewing silk, that known as 000, about eighteen inches long. At one end is a bit of conjurer's wax (see Appendix), and at the other is a piece of blackened match. The latter is run through the lowest buttonhole of the performer's vest; the wax is stuck inside of the opening of his shirt front. These three articles with a large goblet, a many-colored Japanese folding fan, and his wand under his right arm, constitute all the "properties." Three cards are freely drawn by the audience, and as they are replaced in the pack are brought to the back by means of the "pass" and false shuffle. If so inclined, the performer may palm these and allow the pack to be shuffled by the audience, replacing the cards at the back before proceeding with his trick. Now mark the exact routine of the movements: Going to his table, the performer places the pack in the goblet with his left hand. At the same time he removes the wax from his shirt front with his right hand and secures it with his thumbnail. "Ah!" he says, "I have neglected to show you this glass. Please examine it and satisfy yourselves that it is not prepared in any way." As he says this he takes out the pack with his right hand and sticks the wax on the back card, near the top edge. The left hand picks up the goblet and when it has been examined replaces it on the table. Then the left hand takes the pack from the right and puts it reversed into the goblet, thus bringing the wax to the lower end of the card. "Pray," says the performer, addressing the person who drew the last card, as the wax is attached to that, "what is the name of your card?" When he is told this he makes a few mesmeric passes over the goblet, and picking up the fan with the right hand opens it and slowly fans the right side of the goblet. As he does this his body bends naturally, pulling the thread taut, and the card slowly rises from the pack. Laying down the fan, he takes the card from the goblet with his left hand; at almost the same moment the right hand takes hold of the card at the bottom, as if to show it better and in doing so removes the wax with the thumbnail and sticks it on his wand, which, as will be remembered is under his right arm. At the same time the left hand puts the card back in the pack. Then the cards are taken from the goblet and sprung from hand to hand, to satisfy the audience that they are not connected with any contrivance to make them rise. The cards are held up with the left hand, while the right rests naturally on the wand, secures the wax with the thumbnail and sticks it on the back card. The left shows the glass and the trick proceeds, following the same routine as described for the first card. When the last card has risen from the glass the wax is replaced on the shirt front. The varicolored fan screens very effectually the presence of the thread from those of the audience who may be at the side. It will be found to be an advantage if the goblet is placed on a slight elevation, say, on a box or some books.   Some performers stick the wax on the top button of the vest, but the thread is apt to curl and tangle.

The Rising Cards in a Case:

Several cards are drawn from the pack by the audience.   They are returned, the pack is shuffled, and placed in an ordinary paper or pasteboard case, such as cards now usually come in.   This the performer then holds up, and as the cards are called for, they rise, one at a time.

Fig. 72

72a

72b

The case, which is the ordinary affair, has a slit cut in its face, lengthwise, as shown in Fig. 72.   This is imperceptible, for it is merely a slit made with a sharp knife, not a slot.   At the lower end of it is a tiny hole. At Figs. 72a and 72b is shown a little concave disc of metal; on the convex side of this is soldered a needle point, so that it somewhat resembles a small drawing pin.   The concave side is filled with adhesive wax, and the whole disc is painted a flesh color.   This is stuck on the tip of the forefinger.

When the drawn cards are replaced in the pack, they are brought to the top, by means of the "pass" and the pack is placed in the case with the top cards next to that part of the case in which is the slit. The flap of the case is turned back or upward, so that it will be out of the way.

Holding the case with the thumb on one side, the forefinger at the back and the other fingers at the other side, the cards are raised, as called for, by the pin point which enters the slit, the little hole at the end making the entrance easy.

The Rising Cards, as Exhibited by Buatier de Kolta:

Four cards are prepared as shown in Fig. 73. A is a double card, that is, two cards pasted together, back

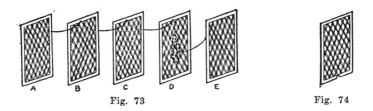

Fig. 73   Fig. 74

to face, so as to secure a piece of fine black silk thread between them. The loose end of this thread comes out at the back of the back card A through a tiny hole punched in the exact center of this card at about an eighth of an inch from the upper edge. A similar hole is punched through B, C, and D. At the bottom of each of three other cards is cut a little notch, as shown in Fig. 74. These cards are placed between A and B, B and C, and C and D, one between each pair, the notched part resting on the thread, which is slackened so as to come under the cards. These are the rising cards, and cards corresponding to them in suits and spots are forced on the audience. When the cards are in place the remaining part of the thread ought still to be about a yard long. This part is curled up on the back of D, and the free end is fastened securely to the card E by pasting over it a piece of court plaster. When everything is prepared, the cards are gathered together and secured by passing a light rubber band over them.

When about to exhibit the trick the packet of prepared cards is placed in the performer's pocket or under the front of his vest. Then duplicates of the rising cards are forced on the audience, and when replaced, the pack is given out to be shuffled. In the meanwhile the performer palms the prepared packet, which he places on top of the pack when it is returned to him. Then he announces that in order to keep all secure he will place a rubber band round the pack. He goes through the motions of taking one out of his vest pocket, but really takes out nothing, but slips the band that holds the prepared packet around the whole pack.

As the little holes and notches in the cards perfectly conceal the thread, the performer may safely hand the pack to some one—preferably a lady—to hold for a moment, while he goes to his table for a goblet.

When the goblet has been examined the person who holds the cards is requested to drop them into the glass, which the performer then stands on his table. Then he asks the name of the first card that was drawn, and announces that he will try to blow it out of the pack.

He removes the rubber band from the cards and taking out the last card in the pack, which is E, he rolls it into a tube. This he puts to his mouth and blowing in the direction of the goblet, while he draws back the thread a little bit, the first named card slowly rises from the pack. In like manner the other two cards rise. As each card comes out the thread naturally increases in length, so the performer must imperceptibly draw further back.

After the pack is shuffled, it will be well for the performer to note whether one of the selected cards is at the bottom, and should it be, he must, for very obvious reasons, slip it out of the way.

One More Version of the Rising Cards:

The performer shows a Japanese fan, of the kind shaped like the bamboo fan, but covered with variegated paper, and a skeleton case for holding a pack of cards, with a loop of cord at its rear top corners. Cards are freely selected and returned to the pack; this is placed in the card case, and that is hung on the face of the fan, the loop resting on two little slots or nicks in the top of the fan. The performer holds the fan in his hand, and, at command, the chosen cards rise from the pack and return again.

The card case is without preparation, the mechanism of the trick lying in the fan, (Fig. 75) which is double and fastened around the edges. The handle is hollow. Between the two surfaces of the fan is a sort of lazy-tongs riveted at A, Fig. 76, to the fan, and pivoted to the top of this is a watch spring, working between two little staples or bands, BB, Fig. 76, made fast to the fan. Attached to the lower long arm of the lazytongs is a short piece of cord that runs over a tiny pulley, and is fastened to a spring rod working in the hollow handle of the fan. A small stud, attached to this rod, projects through a slot in the handle. A slight movement of the stud raises or lowers the watch spring by opening or closing

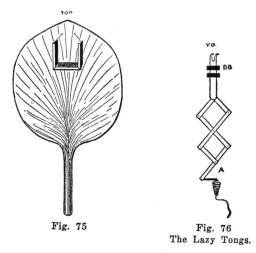

Fig. 75　　　　　　　Fig. 76
The Lazy Tongs.

the lazytongs. The end of the watch spring which inclines forward has two sharp points that go through openings in the fan, and pressing against the back card in the pack, pushes it up or down at the will of the performer. The selected cards are, of course, all at the back of the pack. The lazytongs will move up about four inches to every quarter of an inch movement of the stud.

The Seven Heap:

The four sevens are sorted out of a pack and placed in a heap on the table. Then seven indifferent cards are placed in a second heap alongside the first, and some one is asked to come forward and assist the performer.

Looking the man earnestly in the eyes for a moment, the conjurer writes on a slip of paper: "You will select the seven heap." This is folded and handed to the assistant with the request that he put it in his pocket. He is then asked to select one of the heaps of cards. When this is done he is requested to read what is written on the paper. When he has done so, he is told to turn over the heap. No matter which heap is selected the prediction is verified. Should it be the heap with the four sevens, the conjurer turns over the other heap with the remark, "You see these are all different cards." On the other hand should the heap of seven cards be selected, the performer merely counts them out one by one, without showing the faces of the other heap, merely spreading the cards apart to prove that there are only four cards there.

The Sympathetic Kings and Queens:

The performer hands out an ordinary pack of cards with the request that some one will pick out the kings and queens and lay them, faces upward. When this is done the performer arranges them in four pairs, a king and queen in each. These pairs are now arranged one over another in one packet, which is laid, faces down this time, on the table. Several persons are asked to cut the cards (not to shuffle them, remember), so as, apparently, to disarrange their order. Declaring that his sense of touch is so delicate that without seeing the cards he can separate the kings from the queens, the performer puts the packet behind his back, and, almost immediately bringing his hands in front shows that in one hand he has the kings and in the other, the queens, which he throws on the table.

"Now," says this wonderful man, "by this same acute sense of touch I shall reunite the separated pairs."

Picking up the kings he places the queens on top of them, or *vice versa*. This packet he lays on the table, as in the first instance, faces downward, and again has them cut by different persons, until kings and queens seem to be hopelessly mixed. Once more putting his hands at his back, he produces the cards two at a time, laying each pair, faces downward on the table, and when, at his request, they are turned up, it is found that each king has the queen of his suit for a companion.

And now for the secret of this marvel: When, in the first part of the trick, he puts the cards behind his back, he takes in one hand the first, third, fifth, and seventh cards, counting from either the top or the bottom, and in the other the second, fourth, sixth, and eighth cards. When they are brought to the front all of one kind will be found in one hand, and all of the other in the other hand.

When the performer picks them up again for the second part of the trick he apparently takes them at random. In fact, however, he takes them in the old SHow CoDe order, the kings first and on top of them the queens. When, with their faces downward, he has them cut several times, and has put the packet behind him, he divides it in two equal parts. Then he takes the top or bottom card of each part and lays these two cards, faces down, on the table. This he repeats until four pairs are on the table, and when they are turned up they will be found in proper order, each king with a queen of his own suit.

Should the performer be proficient in making a false shuffle he may introduce it with good effect in the course of the trick.

Correcting a Mistake:

The pack is handed out to be shuffled and some one is asked to select a card and without looking at it to lay it on the table, face down, and place something on it. A second person is then asked to select three cards, at random, and without looking at them to place them also on the table.

Now the performer declares that by virtue of a certain hypnotic power he possesses, he has caused the two persons to select four cards of the same value. To prove the truth of this the three cards last chosen are turned over and are found to be of the same spot value, but when the first card is turned up, it proves to be, to the great humiliation of the performer, of an entirely different value. "Ah," cries the embarrassed conjurer, "I remember now, that the moon is in a different quarter from what I thought it to be. However, that can be remedied, and I shall yet do what I set out to do. Please turn the three cards down once more. I shall now simply wave my hands over the cards and mentally repeat the mystic formula. Be good enough to turn the cards face up again. I knew I could do it!" To the surprise of the audience, the cards are seen to be of the same value as that of the card first chosen.

Clever as this trick is, it is very simple. At the start the pack is arranged with an ace on top; immediately under it are three queens, and under these are the other three aces. To begin, the performer makes the "pass," so as to bring the top cards to about the middle of the pack, and forces the first ace. Again making the "pass" he brings the pack again to its original arrangement. The ace is laid on the table and covered with something. On his way to the second person the conjurer palms at least six cards from the top of the pack. The second person now draws three cards, without looking at them, and places them on top of the pack. When the pack is returned to the performer he lays the palmed cards secretly on top of the pack. A third person is now requested to take the pack and lay the three top cards, supposed to be those that were selected, faces downward, in a row on the table. Carelessly taking the pack in his left hand the performer picks up with his right one of the three cards, turns it over, and shows that it is a queen. Then he asks some one to turn over a second card, and that also proves to be a queen. While the attention of the audience is drawn to the second queen, the performer, by means of "the bottom change" exchanges the queen that is in his hand for one of the aces, which he lays on the table. Some one is now asked to turn over the third card, and that being a queen, the performer remarks that so far he has been successful. Picking up the two queens in an off-hand way, he says, "We have had the Queens of spades, hearts, and clubs. All we need is the Queen of diamonds. Will some one turn over the covered card and see if it is she?" While attention is directed to that card, Mr. Conjurer exchanges the two queens, that are still in his hand, for the two aces that are on top of the pack, and throws them, faces down, on the table. The trick is done and needs no further explanation.

Thought Anticipated:

When properly presented by one who is an adept at palming, this trick is wonderfully effective.

Two euchre packs and two other cards that are not in a euchre pack, say a five and a six, are required for the trick. To make everything clear let us call the two packs A and B. The two odd cards are placed on pack B. The packs lie on the table: A to the left, B to the right.

Picking up pack A and going to one of the audience, the performer without giving the pack to him asks him to *think* of a card. When he has done so, the performer looks him in the eyes, and then spreading out the pack looks it over and finally selects a card, which he lays on the table, without showing what it is.

The same procedure is gone through with a second person, and a second card is laid on the table.

Laying the pack on a goblet and deliberately taking the two cards, still without showing them, the performer lays them on top of the pack.

Picking up pack B, he requests the first man to take from it the card he thought of, but before handing him the pack Mr. Conjurer palms the two odd cards that are on the top. When the card has been taken from the pack the man is told to keep it for the time being.

The same routine is followed with the second man.

The reader will now understand why two odd cards are placed on top of the pack, for if two cards belonging to the pack be palmed it is possible that one or even both might be the ones thought of and would be missed from the pack. The two odd cards are also necessary for the concluding effects.

The pack is now offered to a third person, with the request that he take a number of cards and count them secretly. Placing the rest of the pack on the palm of his left hand and at the same time having the two selected cards laid on top of it, the performer asks the man who is assisting to place the cards he counted on top of those. Taking the pack in his right hand the performer lays the two palmed cards on top. Addressing the third assistant he asks how many cards he placed on the two selected. Let us suppose the answer to be fourteen. Very deliberately sixteen top cards are counted on the table. To the audience it will appear as if the two selected cards are on top of the pile, and so they would be, had not the performer added the two odd cards. In reality the selected cards are on top of the others of the pack. While putting aside this packet the performer palms these two top cards and taking pack A off the goblet leaves them on top of it.

Addressing the two who selected the cards the performer remarks that it would be a simple matter to read their minds and that the two cards which at the start he placed on top of this pack must be the ones they thought of. That there may be no question of this they are asked to name their cards, first, and then turn up the two cards. To their surprise they will find them to be their cards.

Putting the two cards aside and picking up the sixteen cards, which he adds to the rest of pack B, the performer announces that he will command the chosen cards to leave pack B and pass to pack A. Both packs are now examined, when it will be found that the cards have passed from one pack to the other, as ordered.

In order to avoid the possibility of the two persons thinking of the same card, which would spoil the trick, it would be well to have them tell each other the names of their cards.

The Spots on a Freely Selected Card Will Indicate the Number of Cards Secretly Removed from the Pack:

At the bottom of the·pack are eight cards arranged as follows: a deuce, trey, four, five, six, seven, eight, and nine, of varying suits. The undermost card must be the deuce, on top of this follow the trey, four, and so on to the nine. By slightly turning up the left hand bottom corner of the nine spot, these arranged cards may be easily found when the rest of the pack is on top of them. These arrangements must be made before attempting to show the trick.

To begin, the performer lays the pack on the table and requests some one to remove "a good portion" and from this to take away as many cards *between* one and ten, as he sees fit; that is, excluding one and ten. These cards are to be placed on top of the pack. The assistant puts aside the rest of the portion removed, so that the performer can not possibly know how many cards were placed on top of the pack. As soon as the assistant at the beginning removes "the good portion," the performer picks up the pack, and by the "pass" brings the eight arranged cards from the bottom to the top, the turned up corner of the nine helping him in this. When any number of cards between one and ten is placed on top of the pack the tenth card from the top will indicate by its spots the number. For example: If five cards are placed on top, first counting off these five, the sixth card will be a nine, the seventh, an eight, the eighth, a seven, the ninth, a six, and the tenth, a five.

The effect of the trick may be improved by allowing the one who assists to select a number between one and ten. As soon as the cards are placed on top of the pack the performer passes three cards to the bottom, in which case the seventh card from the top will now tell by its spots how many cards were placed on top. It is a psychological fact that eight out of ten men asked to select a number between one and ten will choose "seven." In that case hand the pack to the assistant and tell him to look at the seventh card. If, by any chance "five" should be called for, two more cards must be slipped to the bottom, and so on for other numbers.

The Ace of Diamonds Changes to a Trey:

To begin the trick the performer has the ace of diamonds on top of the pack and the trey of the same suit at the bottom. Making the "pass" he brings the two cards together in the center of the pack, and forces the ace of diamonds on one of the audience. The trey is now the bottom card of the top section of the pack. When the pack is closed the performer separates the two packets by inserting between them the little finger of the left hand. When the ace is to be replaced he

opens the pack at the place of separation, so that it
will be directly under the trey. Putting his little finger
between the ace and the trey, he makes the "pass,"
bringing these cards to their original position on top
and at the bottom of the pack. "Now," says the performer, "I will despatch the ace on its travels, by send-
ing it from the middle of the pack to the bottom." He
ruffles the pack and shows the ace, apparently, at the
bottom. What he really does is to hold the pack at its
ends by both hands, the fingers covering the end spots
of the trey. Then he covers the face of the cards with
his left hand and presses the pack against his forehead. With his other hand he strikes the hand that
holds the pack. This, he says, is to drive the ace
through the pack. He removes the pack from his forehead and the ace is seen sticking there. This is effected
by having the forehead dampened before beginning the
trick.

Removing the ace from his forehead the performer
spins it through the air, and catching it as it falls
shows that it is really the ace of diamonds. "Now
watch it," he says, and once more sets it spinning
through the air. Every one can see that it is the ace.
This time as it comes down the performer does not
touch it, but allows it to reach the ground. "Will
some one," he asks, "be good enough to pick it up, and
tell us what card it is?" And to the surprise of all it
proves to be the trey.

The secret of this is that the performer changes the
ace for the trey, and when the latter is spun in the air,
by some principle of optics, which is not clearly under-

stood, it is impossible to distinguish the one card from the other, the end spots of the trey seeming to be drawn into the center spot.

The Four Aces:

The performer hands out the four aces with the request that some one will place them in different parts of the pack. He sees to it, however, that they are not pushed down all the way, but stand up at the top about three-quarters of an inch. In this position every one can see that they are not in one place, but are separated. Taking the pack in his left hand the performer apparently pushes the cards down with his right hand. What he really does is to push them through the pack by means of the "dovetail pass," explained on page 11, until they come out at the lower end. Then they are grasped between the thumb and forefinger of the right hand, pulled clear of the pack and placed on top of it. The pack is then shuffled without disturbing the position of the aces which, finally, are passed to the bottom.

The pack is now held in the performer's left hand, the faces down, with the first finger at the upper end and the thumb at the lower. The thumb of the right hand resting on the left hand side of the pack lifts about a quarter of it bookwise and with the fingers which are beneath the pack take away that quarter section and at the same moment slip away with it the bottom ace. Naturally that ace will be at the bottom of the heap when it is placed on the table. As the pack is held in a half slanting position this move can not be seen. This operation is repeated twice; the cards remaining in the left hand make the fourth heap.

It is placed on the table alongside the other heaps. When they are turned over an ace will be seen at the bottom of each heap.

Another Method.—In this method the aces instead of being found at the bottom of the heaps at the conclusion of the trick will be at the top.

The performer proceeds as in the preceding method, but brings only three aces to the bottom of the pack, leaving the fourth on the top. He now requests some one to take away about a quarter of the pack and lay it on the table. Then he goes to two others with a similar request, and while passing from one to the other, he brings each time an ace from the bottom to the top of a heap, by means of the "clip," explained on page 10. The fourth heap he lays down himself, after bringing the last ace to the top in the same way.

From Pocket to Pocket:

In this trick a number of cards which one of the audience has in his pocket are transferred invisibly to the pocket of a second person. As usually exhibited only the cards in one pocket are counted and the number to be transferred is restricted to three, four, or five. If the right number, say, four, is named, well and good, but should the selection fall on three or five the ruse is resorted to of taking one card visibly from one pocket and putting it in the other, under the pretext of "showing the others the way." As here described, these decided drawbacks are evaded.

Two of the audience are requested to assist the performer. One is placed at the left of the table, the other at the right. The performer stands between them, back of the table. A euchre pack, of thirty-two cards is counted and divided in two. When each part is counted each of the volunteer assistants takes a packet, places it in an envelope and puts it into the inside pocket of his coat. Then a number is selected by one of the assistants, and the trick proceeds as already described.

As far as the audience is aware only thirty-two cards are used, but in reality there are thirty-five. At the start the performer spreads out his pack fanwise, with the assertion that he has thirty-two cards. Before handing the pack to the gentleman on his left to be counted, the performer inserts the little finger of his left hand below the three top cards and palms them in his right hand. The better to conceal them he takes hold of one end of his wand, which is under his right arm, without removing it.

When the assistant has counted the pack aloud and announced that there are thirty-two cards, he is requested to square up the pack and, without counting, to divide it in two nearly equal packets.

The other assistant, the one on the right of the performer, is asked to select one packet and hand it to the first assistant to count. The other packet is laid in front of the performer.

The assistant is now asked to count slowly on the table the selected heap. While he is doing this, the performer spreads out the cards a little, so that when he drops the three palmed cards on them, it will not be noticeable.

When the count is finished and announced, as, for instance, fifteen, the performer pushes the cards that are scattered on the table toward the assistant, and in doing so drops the palmed cards on them. At the same time to attract the assistant's attention he remarks, "I should have preferred another number, but let it go as it is. Square up the cards, please."

These few words of misdirection naturally turn the assistant's eyes from the cards to the performer.

When the cards are squared up, the assistant is asked to place them in one of the previously examined envelopes and to put all into an inside pocket of the other assistant's coat.

Picking up the remaining packet, the performer says: "Fifteen of our thirty-two cards are in this gentleman's pocket. How many should be here? Seventeen? That is correct. But to make sure, let me count them." Slowly he counts them on the table, one on top of another, until he reaches the fifteenth card, which he lays a little to the right, so that it overlaps the other cards about half an inch, and on it the remaining two cards are placed.

With his left hand the performer picks up the seventeen cards, taking care to place his little finger under the fifteenth card. "Now let us see just how we stand. This gentleman"—turning to his right—"has fifteen cards in his pocket, which, with the seventeen we have here make thirty-two." The second pack he requests the assistant on his right to put into the second envelope and place them into the other assistant's pocket.

While turning to the assistant on his right the performer palms the three top cards in his right hand, using the spring palm, explained on page 14, after which he grasps his wand that is under his arm.

The trick is now almost done. Turning to his audience the performer says: "Of the thirty-two cards fifteen are in this gentleman's pocket, as you will please remember, and seventeen in the other gentleman's pocket. Bear in mind, too, that both packets have been carefully counted. Now I shall order any number of cards that you elect to pass invisibly from one pocket to another. That there may be no suspicion of collusion, let chance decide the number."

Putting his hand into his own pocket he brings out ten cards, numbered one to ten, in large figures. As he does this he leaves in the pocket the three cards that he holds palmed.

Holding the numbered cards with their faces towards the audience, he passes them from hand to hand, calling out the numbers. Then he gives them to the assistant on his left to be shuffled. When they are returned he again spreads them out, calling attention to the thorough manner in which they are mixed. While doing this he locates card numbered three and slips it to the top.

Turning to the assistant on the left he says: "I will begin at the top, and taking off these cards one at a time lay them face down on the table. When you call out *Stop,* I will take the card that happens to be the top one." The performer begins to deal the cards, but by means of the second deal he keeps number three always on top. When the command to stop is heard the performer hands the packet to the assistant and asks him to take the top card. "Let all see what it is. Number three! Then that number of cards I will pass from the envelope in your pocket to the envelope in this gentleman's pocket.''

Touching the gentleman's pocket· with the tip of his wand he commands a card to ''Go!'' This he repeats twice.

Turning to the assistant on his left, the performer says: ''You selected number three. You had seventeen in your pocket, but as three have gone you now have only fourteen. While you, sir, ''turning to the other assistant, ''if you will count your cards, will find that you have eighteen instead of fifteen.''

The cards are counted by the two assistants, the performer not laying a finger on them, and found to be exactly as was foretold.

While this form of the trick calls for some skill on the part of the performer it also calls forth much applause.

A Second Method.—In this form of the trick three mentally selected cards are passed from one packet to another.

The performer asks some one of the audience to assist him. This assistant he places at the right of the table, and hands him a pack of cards, with the request that he shuffle it.

When the cards are thoroughly mixed the pack is divided in two. Each packet is counted and the assistant is asked to put one into his pocket.

Picking up the other heap and taking five cards from it, the performer asks one of the audience to think of one card as he calls out the names of the five. Then taking five more he repeats this procedure with another of the audience and again with a third person by calling out the rest of the cards, so that the same card may not be thought of by more than one person. Finally, the entire packet is handed to the person who thought of the first card, and at the same time the performer commands the three cards that are thought of to leave the packet and join the cards which the assistant has in his pocket.

The man in the audience who holds the second packet of cards is requested to count it, and on complying he reports that there are three less than when first counted. The assistant at the table is asked to count his cards, and doing so finds three more than when he put them in his pocket.

To prove that the thought-of cards have really left the second packet, the persons who selected them are unable to find them in the packet.

When the assistant at the table examines his packet, the missing cards are found in it.

For this trick a pack is used that has been trimmed to taper, so that all the cards are narrower at one end than at the other. The pack is known to conjurers as a *biseauté* pack, a word which the French dictionary tells us means *beveled*. Such a pack may be bought from any dealer in conjuring goods.

A euchre pack is best for this trick. The cards are arranged in a certain order known to the performer, as, for example, the following:

TABLE A	TABLE B
King of Spades	King of Clubs
Ten of Hearts	Ten of Diamonds
Eight of Clubs	Eight of Spades

TABLE A, cont'd	TABLE B, cont'd
Nine of Diamonds	Nine of Hearts
Jack of Spades	Jack of Clubs
Ace of Hearts	Ace of Diamonds
Seven of Clubs	Seven of Spades
Queen of Diamonds	Queen of Hearts
King of Diamonds	King of Hearts
Ten of Spades	Ten of Clubs
Eight of Hearts	Eight of Diamonds
Nine of Clubs	Nine of Spades
Jack of Diamonds	Jack of Hearts
Ace of Spades	Ace of Clubs
Seven of Hearts	Seven of Diamonds
Queen of Clubs	Queen of Spades

To prepare for the trick the pack is divided in two equal packets; one containing the cards in Table A, the other, those in Table B. The packets are placed together with the narrow ends of the cards in opposite directions. No matter how often the pack is shuffled the two packets may be separated by holding the pack in the middle between the hands, the thumbs on one side and the fingers on the other, and drawing the cards apart.

When the assistant has shuffled the pack the performer divides it, as explained, and adds secretly to the packet which the assistant chooses and counts three cards which he holds palmed in his right hand, in the manner described in the first method of doing the trick. These cards must be entirely different from those in either packet, say, two "fives," of different suits, and one "six." In this way there is no danger that any duplicates may be found later.

The cards that are called out by the performer for the three people to select from are not those he has in his hands but are the names of some that are in the assistant's pocket.

While going toward the person who thought of the first card, in order to hand him the second packet, the performer quietly palms three cards, which he gets rid of as soon as may be, by dropping them in his pocket or disposing of them in any way that suits his convenience.

The trick then proceeds as already described.

The Vanishing Card:

In this trick a double-faced card and some clever manipulations are used.

A card is prepared with a nine of spades on one side and a Queen of hearts on the other. If preferred any other two cards may be substituted for these. The manner of preparing such a card will be found explained later on.*

When beginning the trick the prepared card is next to the top card of the pack, the spot side down. The top card is the real nine of spades. The performer palms these two cards and gives the pack to be shuffled, replacing the palmed cards on getting it back. These he lays a little to the right, but draws back the top card, so that the prepared one will protrude a trifle beyond the right side of the pack. In this position the right hand, which covers the pack, seizes it by means of "the clip" and transfers it to the bottom of the pack. The prepared nine of spades is now at the bottom and the real nine at the top. The latter is now forced on one of the audience. As the prepared card

* See the "Sense of Touch," page 121.

might be exposed if the regular method of forcing were used, the performer resorts to the "second deal." Asking one of the audience to say which card he will take, counting from the top, he forces the nine of spades by the second deal. The performer shows the card, holding it, face up, between the first and second fingers of the right hand. At the same time he turns the pack, which is in his left hand, face up, taking care that the prepared card is not exposed. He now announces that he will place nine cards on top of the nine of spades, making ten altogether. Bringing his hands together, the performer makes "the bottom change," substituting the prepared card for the real nine of spades. At the same time his left hand goes up, so as to be in a position to count off the cards. This makes "the change" easy, and as the audience still see the nine of spades (the prepared one) after "the change," they will not suspect that anything is out of the way. Counting the prepared nine of spades as one, the performer, apparently, counts nine more, always with the faces up, on top of it. Apparently, we say, for after he has counted five or six cards he makes a "false count," so that he will have nine cards only, instead of ten, in his right hand. Laying the cards, faces down, on the table he announces that he has ten cards, one of which is the nine of spades. He takes it from the bottom and spreading out the other cards places it in the center, "the better to show it." While again closing up the cards, the fingers of the right hand which are just under it, turn it over deftly, bringing the side on which the Queen of hearts is, in sight, and closes up the packet.

He now announces that he will cause the nine of

spades to leave the packet and go to the pack. He ruffles the cards, and then counting them deliberately on the table, faces up, it is found that there are only nine cards, the nine of spades being missing. He picks up the pack, on top of which is the real nine of spades, and again using the "second deal" brings it back to the number from the top, from which it was originally selected.

The Cards in the Envelopes:

A pack of cards is thoroughly shuffled by the audience. While this is being done the performer palms four cards of the same suit and number, as, for instance, four of the ace of diamonds, which he has had concealed either in a pocket or that have been lying on top of the pack, at the start. When the pack is returned to him he places these four cards on top of it. Going among his audience he "forces" these cards on four different persons who are seated some distance apart, so that they may not be able to compare notes. To each of these persons he hands an envelope with a request that he places his card in the envelope, seals it, and places it in an inside pocket. Going to his table, the performer lays the pack aside, and asks some one to come forward to assist him. Taking a second pack he requests his volunteer assistant to shuffle it. Spreading the pack out he calls attention to the fact that it is a regular pack and thoroughly shuffled. This gives him the opportunity to locate the ace of diamonds and slip it to the top. Then he spreads the cards in a row on the table, taking care that the ace of diamonds is about the middle of the row and that it projects a trifle beyond the line of the other cards. He requests the assistant to take a card. By pointing carelessly to the ace of diamonds it is almost certain that that card will be selected. Then the assistant is allowed to mix up the cards as they lie on the table and take a second card, without forcing a card this time. This is repeated twice more till he has four cards, one being the ace of diamonds. Addressing his audience the performer explains that four of the company have each drawn a card. That each card is in a sealed envelope and each envelope is stowed away in an inner pocket.

Under the circumstances it is impossible for any one, except those who drew the cards to know what they are. He further calls attention to the fact that the person who is assisting in the trick drew from a second pack four cards at random, at least it is supposed he did, but by some undefined influence he was forced to select the same cards as the gentlemen in the audience had taken. Then the cards that the assistant drew are shown to the four persons in the audience, and as each sees the ace of diamonds he admits that he sees his own card. Following this, the assistant is requested to collect the envelopes from the men in the audience, and a plate or tray is handed to him, so that the envelopes may be laid on it, and thus exclude any suspicion of a change. The assistant collects the envelopes and mixes them indiscriminately, and of the original holders each draws an envelope at random. "Again," says the performer, "this subtle influence is at work, and each one of you shall draw the envelope he held originally. The envelopes are opened by the holders of them and each admits that he finds his own card.

Instead of spreading out the cards for the assistant to select one, the ace of diamonds may be forced on him and he may take the others at random, but the better way is the one described.

A Missing Card Found:

Two cards, let us say, the three of hearts and the three of spades, are freely drawn by one of the audience, and afterward are returned to the middle of the pack. Placing his little finger between them, the performer makes "the pass," which brings one to the top, the other to the bottom of the pack. He then announces that though placed in the middle of the pack the cards have of their own volition, traveled to the bottom. "Here," he says, "is the three of hearts and following it, the three of spades." To make good his assertion he shows the three of hearts and removes it to show the next card. But to his dismay, an altogether different card is seen. He replaces the three of hearts, with the remark that he will send it in search of the missing card. While saying this, he places his right hand over the pack for a moment, stretches his left arm, ruffles the pack, and then shows the face of the cards once more. The three of hearts has gone, as the performer foretold. He rubs his hand over the face of the cards, and lo! there is the three of hearts and following it directly, is the three of spades.

When he first covers the pack for a moment, the fingers of his right hand are over the face of the pack and the thumb is at the back. With a gentle pressure and moving the hand downward toward the body the front and the back cards of the pack are removed and retained between the fingers and thumb. The fingers close over the thumb, which presses the cards out of sight against the palm. The hand is held against the stomach, a natural position and yet one that completely conceals the cards. The forefinger points to the pack and the attention of the audience is thereby directed to it. The cards are ruffled and when the face of the pack is shown again, the three of hearts is gone. Then with an upward sweep of the hands, the performer places the two cards on the front of the pack, removes the right hand slowly, and the three of hearts is seen in its position at the bottom of the pack, while immediately following it is the missing three of spades.

A Feat of Divination:

A pack of cards that has been shuffled by the performer is handed to one of the audience with the request that he cut it several times. He is then asked to divide the pack into a number of piles or heaps, to place them near one another on the table and cover them with a borrowed handkerchief. The heaps are laid face up. During these preparations the performer stands with his back to the table. When everything is in readiness he turns and asks some one to touch one heap. Picking up this heap, still covered by the handkerchief, the performer holds it against his forehead, and immediately proceeds not only to call out the names of the cards in the heap, but also the order in which they follow. The heap, as yet uncovered, is handed to one of the audience, who examines the cards and verifies what the performer has told.

The prearranged pack is again brought into use.

The performer gives the cards a false shuffle and then allows them to be *cut*, as often as desired, as that does not disarrange their order. After the heaps have been covered and one heap is selected, the performer picks this up with the handkerchief around it, and drawing the latter tightly over the top card is able to see the card through the meshes of the linen. He then proceeds to call off the cards in the order of the formula. A quick glance at the heap next to the one selected tells him the bottom card of those he is reading.

It may heighten the effect of the trick if, before calling out the names of the cards, the performer pretends to weigh the cards in the handkerchief and tell how many are in the heap. Of course, that is a simple matter with this pack.

To Tell in Succession all the Cards in a Shuffled Pack:

A pack of cards is shuffled and returned to the performer, who at once names the top card. Taking it from the pack he shows that it is the card he named. He does the same with the next card, and the next, and the next, as often as he and his audience may please, and in a very simple way.

When the shuffled pack is returned to him, he quietly turns a corner of the top card and sees what it is, by a glance at the index. As his audience have not been told what he intends to do, this is a very easy matter and does not excite suspicion. The pack is resting in the palm of his left hand, the thumb at one side, the second, third, and little fingers at the other, while the forefinger is in front at the top of the pack. This finger presses the cards a little towards the wrist, causing them to overlap just a trifle. When the performer has called out the top card, he picks it up with his right hand, his thumb at the end of the pack toward his wrist, his fingers on top of the pack. Instead of picking up the top card only, he also lifts the second card just a little so as to see its index, as shown in Fig. 77. The over-

Fig. 77

lapping position of the cards makes that easy. He lets go the second card, however, and slides off the top card, showing it and throwing it on the table. The card that will now be on top, he knows, and he has only to repeat the procedure above described as often as may be necessary. The several movements are perfectly natural and can not be detected if proper care is taken.

To Call Out the Names of the Cards While the Pack is Behind the Back:

A prearranged pack, "four benign kings," etc., is concealed in a pocket behind the performer's back. To show the trick he hands out another pack, with the same back, and has it thoroughly shuffled. This he exchanges for his arranged pack, and with that the work of calling off the names of the cards is a simple matter.

In case he attempts the trick with a borrowed pack the backs are carefully kept out of sight, as that might lead to the exposure of the trick.

Another Method of Discovering Every Card in a Shuffled Pack:

When the audience have thoroughly shuffled the pack, the performer places it behind his back and begins to call out the name of a card. To convince his audience that he is right he skims the card toward them, so that they may see for themselves. Another card follows and another, and still another, until the audience are satisfied. Any pack may be used for the trick as there is absolutely no preparation of any kind. Before beginning the trick the performer gets a sight of the top card of the pack. As soon as he places the cards behind his back he "palms" one card in his right hand—any one—and then taking the top card holds it lightly between the first and second fingers of the right hand. Bringing that hand in front of him, half-closed, with the back toward the audience, he moves the hand toward the shoulder and then with a short, quick jerk sends the card that is between his fingers flying into the audience. This movement enables him to see the card that he has palmed, and that card is the next one to be called out. So he proceeds, as long as he pleases, palming the cards and throwing them to the audience.

To Call Out the Cards While the Pack, With the Faces of the Cards Toward the Audience, is Pressed Against the Forehead:

In this trick a small convex mirror, about the size of

a dime, is concealed in the right hand and reflects the face of the card. When the pack is handed out to be shuffled, the pack is held with the back of the hand uppermost, so that the mirror may not be seen. A convenient way to hold the mirror is to attach it to the larger side of a shirt stud by a bit of adhesive wax. The button part of the stud is held between the second and third fingers, and is thus perfectly secure. If the pack is held at one end with the thumb on one side and the forefinger on the other, the front card of the pack will be visible in the mirror, as the pack is being placed against the forehead. As the name of the card is called out, the card itself is taken away with the left hand. The pack, of course, may be shuffled at any time during the course of the trick.

The Choice of a Card:

The performer gives a euchre pack of 32 cards to some one to shuffle, with the request that afterward it be placed on the table, faces down, in four heaps of eight cards each. One of these heaps is then selected by the audience for the trick. Picking up that heap the performer divides it in two. Taking a part in each hand he requests the person who is assisting him to think of a card that is in either of the packets. When the selected packet is pointed out to him the performer places the other four cards on top of it, and then one of the three packets that lie on the table on top of the eight cards in his left hand and the other two at the bottom. This he does quickly so that the audience may be in doubt whether the heaps went on top or on the bottom. If the performer is expert at making the "pass" it will be better for him to place all three heaps on top, and afterward pass two to the bottom. The performer himself now places the pack on the table in four heaps of eight cards each, by first making four heaps of two cards taken from the top of the pack. Then he. places one card from the top on each heap and repeats this. After this each heap will consist of four cards. Of the remaining sixteen cards he puts four on each heap, "to shorten matters," he says. Picking up one heap he fans out the cards and asks the person who thought of a card whether his card is there. If it is not he lays the packet on the table and shows another until he has the packet that contains the sought-for card. Then the fan is closed and the packet is laid on the table. The performer now picks up the packets, apparently, at random, but really is careful to get the packet that contains the card on top. At this point the "pass" may be used with advantage. The selected card is now the fifth from the top. A false shuffle may be introduced here, taking care not to disturb the five top cards. The performer ruffles the cards, and lays out in a row three cards taken from different parts of the pack, taking care that one is the fifth card from the top, and this he places between the other two. The gentleman who assists in the trick is now asked to touch one card. The chances are in favor of his touching the middle card, especially if the performer carelessly points to it. Should one of the other cards be touched, however, the performer coolly picks it up and remarks, "Now, two remain. Which do you select?" No matter which is touched, the performer leaves the thought-of card on the table. "What was the card you thought of?'' he asks, and when the answer is given, he continues: ''Turn up that card, please. That is your card, is it not? Thank you, you did that trick as well as I could do it.''

The Reversed Cards:

The performer has a card selected and then replaced in the middle of the pack, which is opened bookwise to receive it. Before closing the pack the performer pushes the card with his left thumb a little to the right so that it rests on the tips of the left hand fingers, which draw it out still further until it protrudes about a half-inch on the right side. As the thumb of the right hand is at one end of the pack and the fingers at the other, the card is hidden by the right hand. The cards are now sprung from hand to hand as explained on page 28, and during their passage the pressure of the air on the protruding card will reverse it. The pack is then spread out fanwise, when the selected card will be found staring in the face the one who drew it. To carry the trick further the performer announces that he will repeat it, but this time with four or five cards. Several cards are drawn and replaced in the pack in different positions; all are pushed home and the cards are squared up. They are then sprung from hand to hand, and when they are spread out on the table, the selected cards will be found with their faces turned skyward.

The method employed in this form of the trick is altogether different from that followed at first. As soon as the cards are selected and before they are returned to the pack, the performer slips the top card to the bottom of the pack, reversing it on its way. He then turns the pack in his hand, so that what was the top of the pack now rests on his palm. This is not perceptible, as the top card, which is face downward, covers it. The drawn cards are now replaced in the pack, care being taken not to open it, as that would at once expose the trick. The cards are now reversed. The top card is slipped back to its original position and the pack is turned over secretly. The cards are again sprung from hand to hand and when they are spread out on the table, the selected cards are seen to be reversed.

A Subtile Touch:

After a pack has been thoroughly shuffled by the audience, the performer asks for twelve or fourteen cards. Spreading these out fanwise, faces down, he requests some one to touch any one of the cards. He then explains that he will take away with his left hand this card and the cards below it, thereby dividing the pack in two parts. He shows the bottom card of the upper packet, which is, let us suppose, the seven of hearts. He then shuffles the cards again, taking care to bring the seven of hearts to the bottom of the entire packet. He then announces that he will again spread out the cards fanwise, and asks the person who is assisting him to touch another card, assuring him that his fingers will be involuntarily led to the same place in the pack that they went at first. "Try it, sir; it's a very curious thing and has attracted the attention of the most eminent psychologists, who are at a loss to explain it." The gentleman tries it again, and, strange to say, when the bottom card of the upper packet is shown to him, it proves to be the seven of hearts.

The reader need scarcely be told that there is no psychology about it, but the whole secret depends upon bringing the desired card to the bottom of the pack. When once there and the fan is made, the fingers of both hands, which are under the fan are enabled to move the bottom card to any place in the pack that the performer wishes.

The Sense of Touch:

The performer hands out for examination a euchre pack with the request that it be counted and then shuffled carefully. That done, he takes it back. ''This experiment,'' he says, ''depends almost exclusively on the sense of touch, which I have developed to a remarkable degree. In proof of this, I place the pack which you have just shuffled in my pocket,'' placing it in his left breast pocket. ''Now,'' he continues, ''if you will kindly name any card of the thirty-two, I will at once produce it simply by the sense of touch.'' Let us suppose the Queen of Hearts is called for. ''The Queen of Hearts,'' he says, ''very well.'' Thrusting his right hand into his pocket he produces the right card. ''I could do that,'' he continues, ''with my eyes shut. Strange, isn't it?'' He places the card with its face toward the audience, against a goblet, which stands inverted on the table, so that every one may see it.

Taking the pack from his pocket, he presents it to a lady with the request that she will draw one card. It proves to be, let us suppose, the nine of spades. The name of this card he calls out, and then holds it up, so as to satisfy the audience. Then he stands the card, with its back to the audience, this time, against a second goblet.

Borrowing a handkerchief, he picks up the Queen of hearts with his right hand, and places it under the handkerchief, holding it there with his left hand. To convince the audience that it is really there, he lifts the handkerchief for a moment with the right hand and shows the card. "Mark, what I shall do," he says; "the card taken from the pack, which is standing against the goblet, shall, at my command, change places with the card that is under the handkerchief. Go!" He turns the card which is resting against the goblet, and lo! it proves to be the Queen of hearts, and lifting the handkerchief he shows the nine of spades.

For this very pretty deception sixteen double-faced cards are used, that is, two different cards are pasted back to back, so that, for example, one side of the card represents, say, the Queen of hearts, while the other side is the nine of spades.

The cards are arranged as follows:

The Ace of hearts is backed with the seven of spades.
The King of hearts is backed with the eight of spades.
The Queen of hearts is backed with the nine of spades.
The Jack of hearts is backed with the ten of spades.
The Ten of hearts is backed with the Jack of spades.
The Nine of hearts is backed with the Queen of spades.
The Eight of hearts is backed with the King of spades.
The Seven of hearts is backed with the Ace of spades.

The Ace of diamonds is backed with the seven of clubs.
The King of diamonds is backed with the eight of clubs.
The Queen of diamonds is backed with the nine of clubs.
The Jack of diamonds is backed with the ten of clubs.

The Ten of diamonds is backed with the Jack of clubs.
The Nine of diamonds is backed with the Queen of clubs.
The Eight of diamonds is backed with the King of clubs.
The Seven of diamonds is backed with the Ace of clubs.

As will be seen the highest card of hearts or diamonds is backed by the lowest card of spades or clubs, and this arrangement is followed with the whole pack, proving a great help in remembering the order. To prepare these cards, they are soaked for about an hour in *cold* water, after which they are split apart, and the faces are then pasted (not glued) together, back to back, and put in a press to dry.

A holder is then made by taking two letter envelopes of heavy manilla paper in which the cards will fit easily. These are cut to the proper length, which is a little less than the length of a card for one and a trifle shorter for the other. They are sealed and the flap sides are pasted together. In one envelope group No. 1 of cards is placed and group No. 2 in the other; when ready the holder is placed in the inside breast pocket of the coat. With very little practice it will be found an easy matter to produce any card.

Everything being ready for the trick, the performer hands out a fair pack to be shuffled, and when it is returned he puts it into his pocket alongside the holder with its prepared cards.

When a card is called for, say, the Queen of hearts, he thrusts his hand into his pocket and produces it, taking care that the reverse side is not exposed, and stands it against the goblet, with the Queen of hearts facing the audience. When the performer takes the unprepared pack from his pocket he runs over it rapidly and finds the card that is back of the prepared Queen of hearts, and forces it on the lady who is to take a card. While she is looking at it, the performer shows that the cards are all different, and while doing so, finds the unprepared Queen of hearts and places it on top of the pack. When the nine of spades is returned to him by the lady who draws it, he shows it, by holding it aloft, and then exchanges it for the top card (the unprepared Queen of hearts) and stands it, with its back to the audience, against the second goblet.

As he lowers the handkerchief, after showing that the Queen of hearts is really there, he gives the prepared card a turn, so that the nine of spades will show when he removes the handkerchief.

At the close of the trick, both cards are placed on top of the pack, the prepared card at the very top, and this the performer palms, so that if, required, the pack may again be examined.

A Mathematical Problem:

To pick out from a pack in one's pocket *the card thought of*, without asking a question.

This is one of the most brilliant and most incomprehensible tricks ever invented. Moreover, it requires little skill on the part of the performer, being the result of a cleverly devised mathematical formula. All that is necessary for its successful performance is to follow out the instructions found here. A euchre pack of thirty-two cards is used; the deuce, trey, four, five and six being laid aside.

Before beginning the trick, the performer arranges as

follows, eight hands of four cards each, placing them face uppermost on a table:

Hand 1 consists of an Ace, a King, a Queen and a Jack.
Hand 2 consists of a 7, a King, a 9, and a Jack.
Hand 3 consists of an 8, a Queen, a 9 and a Jack.

In these hands the suits should be as varied as possible. "Hand 4" contains four indifferent cards.

Hand 5 contains two hearts and two spades, regardless of the spots.
Hand 6 contains two diamonds and two spades, regardless of the spots.

Hands 7 and 8 are made up, each, of four indifferent cards. When all are laid out, hand 2 is placed on hand 1; hand 3 on hand 2, and so on to the end, so that hand 1 will be on top of the pack, when it is turned over. Hands 4, 7, and 8, have no bearing on the trick, but are merely intended as a blind.

Hands 1, 2 and 3 have a certain *spot* value, as shown in

Table   I: Hand No. 1, has for *spot value,* 1
Hand No. 2, has for *spot value,* 2
Hand No. 3, has for *spot value,* 4

These numbers show the *spots* of the card thought of, as explained further.

Table II: Hand No. 5 has for *suit value,* 1
Hand No. 6 has for *suit value,* 2

and determine the *suit* of the card thought of.

Eight cards are arranged *mentally* so that the highest card is followed by the lowest, as appears in

Table III:
1. Ace	5. Queen
2. Seven	6. Nine
3. King	7. Jack
4. Eight	0. Ten

The order of the *suits* is that shown in

Table IV:
Hearts	= 1	Spades	= 3
Diamonds	= 2	Clubs	= 0

A formidable list, the reader may say, but one easily remembered, if studied carefully. The pack being arranged, as explained, and the tables memorized, the performer is ready for the trick. To do away with any suspicion of prearrangement, the performer begins by giving the pack *a false shuffle,* so that the order of the cards is not disarranged in the least.

One of the audience is now requested to think of a card, and, so that there may be no question after, to write the name of it on paper and keep the paper.

The performer, sitting at a table with the one who thought of the card, deals out the four top cards with the request that the other shuffles them, without allowing anyone to see them, and then selects and puts aside any and all cards, no matter of what suit, that have the same *spot value* as the card thought of. This is repeated *four times* until *sixteen cards* are dealt out. The performer, in the meanwhile, quietly makes a mental note of the "hands" from which the cards are selected. Of course, it is only the first three "hands" that he watches, the "fourth hand," as has been said, having no bearing on the trick.

If the card was selected from the "first hand," he recalls, mentally, Table I, and at once knows that this hand has a value of 1; then referring to Table III, he finds that No. 1 is an *ace,* and he knows that the thought-of card is an ace. The suit he does not know yet.

Should the selected card be in the "second hand" only, he finds by consulting Table I that the value of the "second hand" is 2, and Table III tells that the card is a 7.

Should the card be selected from the "third hand," Table I tells that "hand three" has a value of 4, and Table III that 4 is an eight.

Should the selected card be in two different "hands" or in the three "hands," the performer simply adds the values of the several "hands" as found in Table I, and referring to Table III, at once knows the card.

For example: If the selected card is in "hands one" and "two," by turning to three in Table III=a *King.*

If in all three "hands," No. 7 in Table III=*Jack.*

If in "hands two" and "three," the value being 6= *Nine.*

Should there be no value corresponding to the thought-of card in any of the three "hands," No. 0 in Table III shows that to be a *ten.*

To learn the suit, the performer watches "hands five" and "six." In dealing "hand five" he requests that any and all cards of the same *color* as the suit of the card thought of, without regard to the *spot* value, be put aside. This he repeats with "hands six," "seven," and "eight," but pays no regard to the last two.

Then he refers to Tables II and IV. Should the suit be in "hand five" only, which has 1 for value, Table IV shows the suit to be a *heart.*

If the suit is "hand six" only, it has a value of 2

and 2 in Table IV=a *diamond*. If in "hands five" and "six" the united values being 3, Table IV shows it to be a *spade*, and should the suit not appear in either "hand five" or "six," the suit shown by Table IV is a *club*.

It must be borne in mind that all references to the several *tables* must be done mentally.

While these instructions may appear complicated, a little thought will show them to be very simple, and the practice spent in memorizing them will be well repaid by the brilliancy of the trick.

Now for the wind-up of the trick. The performer requests that the cards be brought together, be thoroughly shuffled, and then returned to him. When he receives them he places the pack in one of his pockets, and then, putting his hand in, brings out the thought-of card. Wonderful as this seems, it is the easiest part of the trick. In each of four pockets, the performer has eight duplicate cards, arranged in order from 7 to Ace, Jack, Queen, and King; each pocket containing one suit only. When the pack is returned to him, he puts it in the pocket that contains the thought-of card. Then it is but a moment's work to locate the card wanted.

The Reunion.

The performer forces the Queen of hearts on some lady in the audience. When it is returned the pack is shuffled and a rubber band is put around it lengthwise. It is then momentarily placed aside while the performer explains the situation. "I noticed," he says "that in replacing the Queen of hearts, which was drawn, the lady took no pains to put her side by side with the King. That is wrong. They should be together, and we must try to remedy the wrong.''

He turns now to get the pack, but instead of taking the one just used he substitutes for it a prepared pack. From this the King and Queen of hearts have been removed, after which a fine, small rubber band is placed, lengthwise, about the pack. The pack is then stood on

Fig. 78

one end on a table, opened in the middle, bookwise, and laid flat as shown in Fig. 78. The King and Queen are now laid, faces down, over the rubber band, and the part with the faces upward is folded over. Two or three cards are placed top and bottom of the pack and another rubber band is put around it, lengthwise, to keep the cards in place. Turning to his audience with this pack, he says, ''Let us hope that their exalted highnesses have met. Will your Majesties kindly make your appearance?'' Removing the outside rubber band, but holding the pack tightly pressed together, the performer slightly relaxes his hold, when the two cards will rise slowly from the pack. ''Ah, that is well,'' exclaims the conjurer. ''And now for a trip in an aeroplane,'' saying which he relaxes the pressure entirely when the two cards will go soaring into air.

Dr. Elliot's Variation in the Rising Cards:

A pack of cards after being shuffled is divided in two parts by one of the audience who is requested to choose one packet. From this three cards are selected and shuffled into the packet. This is now placed in a goblet, when the selected cards will rise one by one from the glass, on command.

The better to understand this, let us suppose that the cards to rise from one packet are three aces and from the other, three Kings. At the start these cards lie on top of the pack, first the three Aces and on top of these the three Kings. A false shuffle is made without disturbing the six top cards, and after the shuffle the three Kings are passed to the bottom: The pack is now cut in two by some one who selects one part. Taking the chosen packet, the performer makes the ''pass'' and brings the three Aces or the three Kings, according to which packet is chosen, to the middle and forces them on three different persons. After the cards are noted they are shuffled in the packet to be afterward placed in the goblet.

Before they are placed in the goblet, however, a threaded packet containing duplicates of the forced cards is added; this is lying face down on the table, concealed by a handkerchief, which is used to wipe the goblet, while the packet is placed on the prepared cards. To insure that the Aces or the Kings as may be desired, will rise the cards are threaded as hereinafter described. Looking at the illustration, Fig. 79, let us suppose that A, B, and C represent the Aces, and D, E, F, the Kings, and the dotted line the thread. If the Aces are to rise, the half-pack of cards are to be placed directly on D, the thread being pushed aside and going over the half-pack, and in this way is placed in the goblet, with A, B, and C uppermost. If, on the other hand, the Kings are to rise the half-pack is placed on D, but the thread is kept between the threaded cards and the half-pack, and the packet is reversed when stood in the glass, D, E, F, being uppermost. As explained elsewhere, a concealed assistant pulls the thread to make

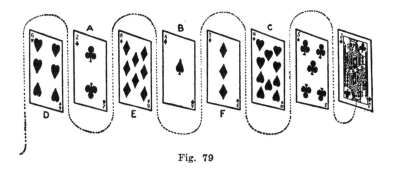

Fig. 79

the cards come up. In order that the cards may not become disarranged and also to insure that the cards rise straight a notch should be cut in the bottom of each card, as shown in the De Kolta Rising Cards.

To tear a pack of cards in two:

While frequently presented as a feat of strength—and it does require some strength—there is a little secret connected with it that enables the conjurer to do what most athletes can not. The illustration, Fig. 80, shows how to hold the pack, and if this is studied and our directions are strictly followed, we believe that most of our readers will be enabled to include this in their pro-

gramme.   Hold the pack so that one end lies in the palm
of the left hand with the two upper joints of the fingers
grasping the end, and the right hand holds the other
end in the same way.   In this position the second-joint
knuckles of one hand rests on the wrist of the other.
The heavy muscles at the base of the thumb are opposite

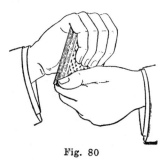

Fig. 80

each other.   With the pack held in this way the hands
twist in opposite directions.   Bracing the left hand
against the upper part of the leg is of considerable help.
A cheap "Steamboat" card tears more easily than a
better card.   As a conclusion, the halves may be torn in
quarters.

II. WITH COINS

Palming:

When one begins to study piano-playing there are certain exercises that must be mastered in order to gain proficiency as a performer. So it is with conjuring. No one can ever be an expert conjurer who has not learned and mastered the elementary exercises.

For tricks with coins, and many others as well, one must be able to *palm*, that is to conceal a coin, ball, or other article in the hand. It need not be hidden in the palm, though from the name one might infer that to be necessary. Any method by which an object is concealed in the hand is *palming*.

There are many ways of palming, good, bad, and indifferent, and from these we have chosen those which we believe are the best.

Many of the sleights here described are used when a performer is supposed to make a coin or other article disappear from the hand in which it was, apparently, placed but a moment before. Let us suppose that the right hand holds a coin. As that hand moves toward the left, which is open, the coin is *palmed* by the right. The moment the two hands meet the tips of the right hand fingers are placed in the left hand palm and that hand closes instantly. Then the right hand is *drawn* away, leaving the coin, supposedly, in the left hand.

Now, for the *palming* itself.

1. The Palm Proper.—The coin is held by the tips of
the forefinger and the thumb of the right hand. The
second and third fingers are brought back of the coin

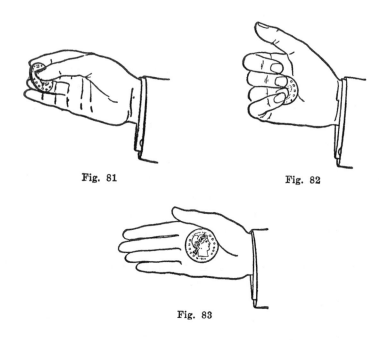

Fig. 81   Fig. 82

Fig. 83

and the forefinger is withdrawn, the pressure of the
thumb holding the coin in place, as shown in Fig. 81.
Next, the thumb is raised slightly, and the second
and third fingers, guiding the coin along the thumb from
tip to base, bring it into the hollow of the palm, as in
Fig. 82. Here the muscles of the ball of the thumb pressing against one edge of the coin force the opposite edge
into the part of the palm almost directly below the third
finger, where it is held firmly, as shown in Fig. 83.

With a little practice it will be found that the coin
may be thrown by the fingers straight to the desired
spot in the palm without the aid of the thumb to guide
it.

A new coin with a sharp milled edge is the best to use
when practicing *palming*.   Both hands ought to be exer-
cised in *palming*, as it is often as necessary to use the
left hand as the right.

2. *The Finger Palm, No. 1.*—The coin should lie on
the second joint of the second finger, with the forefinger
overlapping about a quarter of an inch.   Then the forefinger is lifted a trifle and clasps the coin, as in Fig. 84,

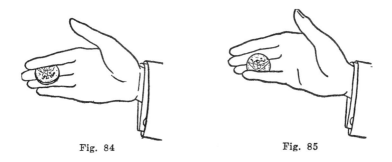

Fig. 84   Fig. 85

which is pushed through by the thumb between the first
and second fingers to the back, where it is held.

3. *The Finger Palm, No. 2.*—The coin lies on the second joint of the third and the second fingers.   The
little finger is raised slightly and laid on top of the
coin, which is held between the little finger on top and
the third finger beneath the coin, as in Fig. 85.   The
first and the second fingers are now moved over in front
of the others until they can clip the coin between them,

as in Fig. 86, when they are brought back to their normal position, and hold the coin by its edges at the back

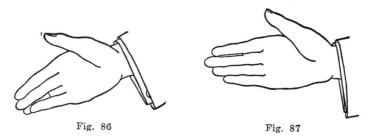

Fig. 86   Fig. 87

of the hand, projecting between the first and second fingers as in Fig. 87.

4. Thumb Palm, No. 1.—Hold the coin between the tips of the first finger and the thumb, as shown in Fig. 88. By means of the first finger slide the coin along the thumb till it reaches the base, where it is held as shown in Fig. 89.

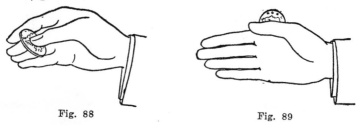

Fig. 88   Fig. 89

5. Thumb Palm, No. 2.—Lay the coin on the top joint of the second finger. Lift the first and the third fingers till they press the edges of the coin, steadying it with the second finger at its back. Move the hand toward the left and at the same moment move the thumb rapidly over the face of the coin till the first joint passes over its upper edge; then bend the thumb and between its first joint and the junction of the thumb with the hand hold the coin, as in Fig. 90. Three or four coins may

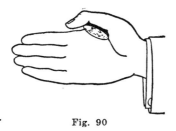

Fig. 90

be held securely in this way and not be seen as long as the back of the hand is toward the audience.

6. *The French Drop.*—The coin is held between the thumb and forefinger of the left hand, with the palm upward, as shown in Fig. 91. The right hand now ap-

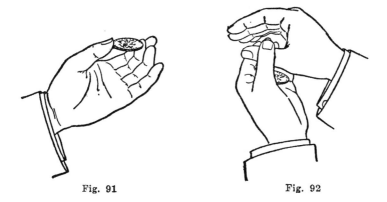

Fig. 91   Fig. 92

proaches the left, and the right thumb goes under the coin, while the other fingers close over it, apparently. See Fig. 92. Just at this moment, however, the coin is dropped into the left palm, where it is held. The left hand, turned slightly toward the body, must remain stationary and be held half-open. The right hand is moved away, the eyes following it, and the result will be that the audience will believe the coin is in that hand. In the meanwhile the left hand drops to the side.

7. *A Deceptive Sleight.*—Place a coin in the extended left palm, and let it be seen there plainly, *without calling special attention to it*. The open hand is raised until nearly level with the breast, and the fingers of the right hand apparently pick up the coin, but really only touch it and leave it on the left palm. The right hand is closed at once and moves away. It will appear as if it held the coin, and shortly after may be shown empty.

Other coin sleights will be described when they are necessary for the proper accomplishment of a trick. Now we shall pass to the description and explanation of some tricks in which the sleights described may be used.

The Miser:

This, if properly done, will deceive the keenest and most sharp-sighted onlooker. To begin, the performer goes among his audience and asks for "a black gentleman's hat or, rather, a gentleman's black hat," remarking that while he prefers a tall hat, rather than no hat at all, a derby will do. Having secured one, he announces that he will use it as a sort of bank of deposit for the money he expects to gather visibly from the air, where, just at present, it lurks invisibly. He returns to his stage or, if in a drawing-room, to the place reserved for his exclusive use. Then, showing his hand empty, he begins to pick from the air piece after piece of money, tossing each coin as he gets it into the hat. Finally, when twenty, thirty, or may be fifty pieces are thus collected, they are turned out on a plate and the hat is returned to its owner.

There are several ways of doing the trick, but we shall explain the method followed by the original Herrmann— Carl Herrmann—who introduced it to this country in 1861, and has never been surpassed in the performance of it.

Let us preface the explanation by saying that Herrmann acted out the trick in a very melodramatic manner, and this greatly heightened its effect.

When the performer goes into the audience to borrow the hat he has *one* coin, say, a silver dollar in his right hand, and as an excuse for keeping the hand closed he carries in it his wand. In his left hand he has twenty-five or thirty coins and that hand grasps the lapel of his coat. The moment he receives the hat, he passes it to his left hand and immediately thrusts that hand into it in such a way that the fingers press the coins against its side, while the thumb, resting on the outside, clasps the rim. Turning the hat crown upwards and still clinging to his wand the performer boldly extends his arms, and requests one of the audience to feel them, so as to be convinced that nothing is concealed there. This examination being made—and it ought not take more than a second—the magician turns toward his stage and, as if to prepare for his work, throws his wand ahead of him. At the same time he drops into his sleeve the coin which is in his right hand. Facing his audience he shows his empty hand, front and back, without uttering a word. Suddenly, he clutches at the air and eagerly peers into his hand. There is nothing in it. This action he repeats once or twice, and then, as if in despair, presses his hand to his brow and afterward drops it to his side. This movement causes the coin in his sleeve to glide into his hand, where he holds it *palmed*. When he again grasps at the air he seems to catch a coin, and shows it to his audience. This coin he tosses fairly into the hat. Instantly, however, he takes it out, looks at it fondly, kisses it, and, apparently, throws it back into the hat. In reality he *palms* it and drops a coin from the left hand into the hat. As the right hand is withdrawn from the hat its back is toward the audience and the *palmed* coin is not seen.

Sometimes the performer pretends to pass the coin into the hat by pushing it through from the outside. This is done by palming the coin just before the fingers reach the hat, or the "Finger Palm, No. 1," may be used. At the moment the tips of the fingers are pressed against the body of the hat, a coin is dropped from the left hand, and the effect is perfect.

When the stock of coins in the left hand is exhausted, the coins are turned out on a plate. Sometimes, however, the performer goes among his audience, and, as if to show that the coins are really in the hat, he picks up a handful and lets them drop back into the hat. In doing this he retains a few, and these he shakes out of a lady's handkerchief, or pulls from a man's beard.

In performing this trick the careful performer varies his movements, substituting for the usual hand palm the Finger Palm, No. 1. The advantage of this is that the open hand may be turned toward the audience.

When about only five coins remain in the left hand,

the performer may conclude the trick as follows: The palmed coin from the right hand is thrown visibly into the hat, while the hand is held out, as if to rest it, but really so that every one may see it is empty. While this is being done, the few remaining coins in the left hand are held between the left forefinger and the second finger. Then the right hand takes the hat and as the fingers go inside they snatch the remaining coins and the left hand is brought out, and it also is shown to be empty. When that hand again holds the hat the right hand palms all five of the coins. Finally, these coins are produced one by one and thrown deliberately and visibly into the hat.

The Peripatetic Coins:

Even with a more simple name, this would be a remarkably good, clever trick. So good and so clever that it has puzzled a number of professional conjurers.

To begin it the performer borrows four silver dollars, and a man's silk hat, or, on a pinch, a derby. The coins are thrown visibly and beyond question into the hat, which is held in one hand, while in the other is a drinking glass. In spite of the distance between these the performer causes the coins, one at a time and invisibly, to pass from the hat into the tumbler. That the coins are the same is susceptible of proof, for they may be marked in any way the audience may choose, so as to be readily identified.

Very little preparation is needed for the trick. To begin, the performer has a fifth coin of his own. In this a tiny hole is drilled just near the edge, and into this hole is tied one end of a piece of fine sewing silk about 20 inches long, more or less, according to the length of the performer's arm. To the other end of this silk is attached a small, black pin, bent about the center so as to make a hook. This is fastened to the outside of the coatsleeve under the left arm, near the arm pit. The coin is tucked away in the waistcoat pocket until needed.

While the performer is borrowing the coins from the audience, he has every opportunity to take out the prepared coin and hold it, unseen, in his closed left hand. The borrowed coins he collects in his right hand, and, when he has four, transfers them to the left hand. Then the two hands are brought together. The forefinger of the left hand goes under the top coin, and with the help of the left thumb the piece is pushed into the hollow of the right hand, where it is "palmed."

Let it be said here, parenthetically, that tricks with coins and with cards may best be understood by following the directions of the several moves with the coins or other articles in the hands.

The coin in the palm, as here described, may be held easily without being detected, if the back of the hand is kept toward the audience and the whole hand is held as if relaxed, which is its natural position.

The other four coins are spread fanwise in the left hand. The right hand now picks up the hat by the rim, while the left hand throws the four coins deliberately into the *hat*. In doing this, it is well to begin with the prepared coin, letting it drop from as great distance as the thread will permit. The three other coins may be tossed in the air, one at a time, and allowed to drop into the hat, the better to deceive the audience.

As soon as all the coins are inside, the hat is transferred to the left hand, the fingers inside and the thumb on the brim, care being taken that the thread comes between the fingers. The audience may even be allowed to look into the hat, but in this case its lining must be black, otherwise the thread might be seen.

The hat is now held away from the left side, and this

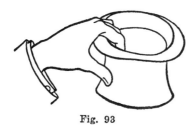

Fig. 93

movement will draw the prepared coin up under the fingers, where it is held against the sweat band.

The performer now picks up a goblet, and holding it so that the palm of the right hand is directly over its mouth, he cries "Pass!" and relaxing the muscles of the thumb, the coin drops into the glass.

The money in the glass is thrown out on the table, and three coins are taken out of the hat, which is held, mouth toward the audience, to show that it is empty.

The hat is placed on the table, and the dollar which has passed is replaced in the goblet.

Taking the three coins from the table in his right hand, the performer, as before, transfers them to the left hand, "palms" one, and goes through the routine already described. In this way he continues until only one coin remains.

This coin the performer picks up with the tips of his second and forefinger and thumb of his right hand, and as that hand moves toward the left the second finger closes down on the coin and leaves it resting on the right hand palm, held, as already told, by contracting the muscles of the ball of the thumb. Almost at the same moment, the tips of the fingers and thumb come together, and are placed in the left hand. They are instantly withdrawn, the fingers wide apart, and the left hand is opened, showing the prepared coin. The audience will believe it to be the coin seen a moment before in the right hand fingers.

The prepared coin is thrown in the hat; again the hat is taken up with the left hand and made to "pass" to the goblet which holds the three coins.

The coins are carried to their owners who identify them, and the performer, who, in the meantime, has pocketed the prepared coin, retires, bowing his acknowledgments of the applause he has earned.

The Walking Coin:

Simple as this little trick seems it is very deceptive. Attached to the lower button of his vest the performer has a hair or, if at some distance from his audience, a piece of fine black sewing silk. At the other end of this hair or thread is a little pellet of wax, which is stuck to another button of his vest. Asking for a small coin, a dime or a cent, the performer secretly gets hold of the wax and sticks it on the coin. Then he takes a tumbler or goblet in his left hand and drops the coin into it. Shaking the glass and at the same time extending his arm, he causes the coin gradually to creep higher and higher in the glass until it reaches the fingers of the right hand held out for it. The wax is quietly removed and the coin is returned to its owner. By taking care to shake the glass continually, the *modus operandi* of the trick will be completely concealed.

The Wandering Coins:

Though old, the following trick may be used to introduce another that is not generally known. The performer places both hands on the table, palms upward, and about eight inches apart, and requests some one to lay a quarter or a half-dollar in the palm of each hand. The hands are now turned down, so that the palms rest on the table, and when they are raised it is seen that two coins are under one hand, while there is nothing under the other. The trick is very simple and easy of execution. In turning the hands down, the left hand moves somewhat slowly, while the right moving a little toward the left is turned quickly and with a throwing motion, causing the coin to be shot from that hand under the left. With but little practice, the transit of the coin is imperceptible.

Having shown this trick successfully, the performer announces that he will repeat the trick, with a slight variation and his hands further apart. He asks for two more coins, as for this version of the trick, it is imperative that he shall have four coins of equal value. Taking a coin in each hand, he rests the back of his hands on the table, at a much greater distance apart than in the first trick, and then slowly closing them, he asks that of the two remaining coins one be placed on the finger-nails of each of the closed hands. In each hand there are now two coins, one inside, the other outside. Announcing that he will cause one coin to pass from one hand to the other, as in the first case, he turns his hands over, but alas! the trick proves a miserable failure, for two coins fall on the table. These the audience, naturally, imagine are the two that were on the finger nails, but such is not the case. When the performer turned his wrist he quickly opened his left hand for a moment, and allowed both the coins, the one *in* and the one *on* that hand, to roll out on the table. Just before the right hand was turned, the fingers were opened a trifle, just enough to allow the coin that rested on them to slip inside the hand. Both hands are again rested on the table and the two coins on the table are placed one on the nails of each hand. Under pretence of taking unusual care this time, the performer with his eyes measures the distance between his hands, moves them a little closer, then further away, and, finally, suddenly turns them over, and as he does so opens the fingers slightly so as to admit a coin in each hand. He opens his hands deliberately and in the left hand is seen *one* coin, while in the right there are three.

The Disappearing Coin:

A borrowed coin, say, a quarter or a half-dollar is placed in the palm of the left hand, the fingers wide apart. The right hand is then placed over the left, the coin being between the hands, which are held perfectly motionless. The hands are then slowly opened, and shown to be empty; the coin has gone. Later it is produced from some man's beard or found elsewhere.

What became of the coin? To one side of a metal

disc, about the size of a cent, is soldered a piece of hard wire, one end of which is bent upward and ends in a very small knob. The other end is twisted into the shape

Fig. 94

of a little ring, and the whole is painted black. To this is attached a fine elastic cord. This goes up the right sleeve, and is fastened to a back button of the trousers on the left side. On the other side of the disc is a piece of adhesive wax. The disc is held in the right hand by the knob, which passes between the first and second fingers. When the right hand is laid over the left, which holds the coin, the waxed side of the disc is pressed on it. The palms are opened a trifle, the fingers release the disc, and the coin flies up the right sleeve. The reproduced coin is, of course, a duplicate.

How Money Attracts:

The performer borrows a ring and a half-dollar, and lays them on his table, about nine inches apart. Then he orders the ring to go to the coin, seize it, and bring it to him, which command is at once obeyed in a most mysterious and amusing way.

To carry out this little trick, the performer provides himself with a piece of fine black sewing silk, about 30 inches long. One end he fastens to the top button of his waistcoat; the other end, to which is attached a little pellet of wax, is stuck on the nail of a finger of the left hand. As he takes the borrowed ring, the performer puts it, for a moment, on the finger to which the waxed end of the silk is attached. Then with his right hand he removes the ring and with it the silk. Both of these he lays on his left palm, and transferring the waxed end of the silk to the right thumb, he presses it on the borrowed coin. Going to his table, which must be covered with a dark cloth, he lays the ring and the coin down, as already told. Then tapping the table gently with his fingers, he gives his order to the ring, and raising his body slightly, the silk becomes taut, and the ring slides along it to the coin. Then the performer lays the back of his open hand on the table, and gently drawing away his body, the ring and coin will move toward the hand and climb into it.

All that remains to be done, is to remove the wax from the coin and return it and the ring to their respective owners.

Some performers substitute a hair from a woman's head for the silk, and for those who learn to handle it properly it is much to be preferred.

To Pass Five Coins from One Tumbler to Another:

Two glass tumblers are used for this trick: one is without preparation of any kind, but the other has the bottom cut out. The performer borrows five half-dollars, and substitutes for them five of his own. In each of these is drilled a tiny hole, near the edge. A black silk thread is tied to one coin and the thread is then passed through the holes in the others. To the free end of the thread is a bit of wax. The wax is held between the roots of the fingers, and the coins, stacked up, are between the finger tips. The coins are dropped, one at a time into the unprepared tumbler, and when all are in the wax is stuck on the back of the glass. The glass is covered with a handkerchief; the bottomless glass is also covered with a handkerchief. The coins are now ordered to leave one glass and go to the other. Taking hold of the handkerchief on the unprepared glass and at the same time of the thread and dislodging the wax, the performer removes handkerchief and coins, the latter concealed in the folds of the former. Picking up the bottomless glass, which is still covered, he places it on his left hand, in the palm of which the borrowed coins are concealed. Pulling off the handkerchief, he shakes up the coins in the glass, and then pours them out into his right hand, and placing the glass on the table, carries the money to the audience to show them that it is entirely unprepared.

The Penetrating Coin:

For this trick a shell coin, either a half-dollar or a dollar is used. The shell coin is a highly useful piece of apparatus. It is made by cutting out one side of a coin until nothing but a complete shell, one side and the edges, is left. When this is hollowed out, a second coin is cut down in its circumference till it will fit inside of the shell; its edges must be remilled. When the trimmed coin is laid inside the shell, the two will appear like an ordinary single coin. Provided with such a coin, the performer is ready for his trick. Laying the shell coin on a table, he covers it with a borrowed hat and says he will pass the money from there into his hand, or, better still, he will remove it from its position under the hat, cause it to leave his hand, and go back to the hat. He puts his hand under the hat and brings out the shell, leaving the trimmed solid coin behind. He shows the good side of the shell, palms it, lifts the hat and shows the coin there.

A prettier trick, however, is the following:— The performer stands an empty goblet on the table and places a breakfast plate on top of it. On the plate he lays two coins, the solid coin and its shell, the shell overlapping the other. Over these he places a tumbler. Picking up the goblet with his left hand and holding the tumbler with his right, he moves them about in a circle, gradually crowding the shell over the solid coin, until, at last, it slips over and covers it completely. At the moment the one coin disappears it is heard and seen to drop into the goblet, as if it had passed through the plate. The last effect is brought about by secretly placing an extra coin between the rim of the goblet and the plate; the weight of the latter holding the coin in place. Just as the shell covers the solid coin, the performer moves the plate forward a little, or tilts it a trifle by means of the tumbler, which he controls with his right hand, and causes the concealed coin to drop into the goblet.

A Coin and a String:

A coin, about the size of a half-dollar, with a small hole drilled in the center, is passed out for examination and marked. After this the performer runs a string, about two feet long, through the hole, and requests two of the audience to hold the ends. The coin, which hangs from the middle of the string, is then covered with a handkerchief. "Now," says the performer, "if I remove the coin from the string, and these gentlemen keep hold of the ends of the string, I think you will admit that it will be impossible to put the coin again on the string. Yet that is what I shall try to do.'' Showing his right hand empty he puts it under the handkerchief and taking hold of the coin draws it to one end of the cord, until it comes in sight. The person who holds that end of the cord is asked to let go for a moment, until the coin is removed. Then the string is taken hold of again. Wrapping the coin in a piece of paper, which is held high up that every one may see it, the performer orders the coin to leave the paper and go back to the string. The paper is torn up and thrown on the floor. The coin has gone! Pulling off the handkerchief, the coin is seen, spinning on the cord.

For this trick a shell-coin is used. Having such a coin, the performer has a hole drilled through both coin and shell, and is then ready for the trick. When the string is through the coins and the ends of the cord are held, the handkerchief is called into play to conceal the method of working the trick. The performer removes the shell, taking care to keep the open side out of sight. The marked coin is still on the string, covered by the handkerchief. The performer now proceeds to wrap the shell coin in a piece of paper. The paper, which is ordinary writing paper, is about five by six inches. It is folded not quite in half, but so that one side is about an inch longer than the other. Taking the coin in his right hand, the performer places it between the folds, as shown in Fig. 95. Holding the paper with the shorter side toward him, he folds the sides away from him (see Fig. 96). Finally he turns down the inch of paper, gained in the first fold, over the side folds, when, to all appearances, the coin will be tightly enclosed (see Fig. 97). Appearances, however, are frequently deceiving,

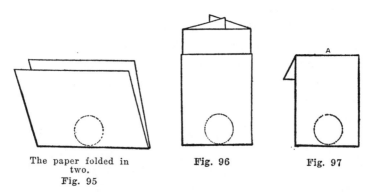

The paper folded in two.
Fig. 95

Fig. 96

Fig. 97

and never more so than in this case, for the top A is open, so as to allow the coin to slide out, as will be found by any one who will fold a piece of paper, following these instructions. Taking the packet at A in his left hand, the performer taps the coin with his wand, so as to convince the audience that the coin is still inside. Then he turns his hand, bringing the end A behind his fingers, when the coin will slide into his hand, where he holds it palmed. The paper is torn up; the coin has gone. The performer snatches the handkerchief away, and to the surprise of all, the marked coin is seen spinning on the string. To add to the effect, the coin may be wrapped in flash-paper, which may be touched off instead of being torn.

When the trick is finished, the performer announces that he will repeat it in a "slightly different way," so that the audience will see more clearly. He hands out

for examination a large metal ring, calling attention to
the fact that there is no joint or secret opening in it.
Taking a piece of tape he has it tied around his wrists,
an end to each wrist, and has the knots sealed, if the
audience so desire. His wrists are about two feet apart.
Picking up the ring, he apologizes to the audience and
turns his back for a moment or passes behind a screen.
When he faces about the next minute, the ring is hanging on the tape between the wrists, as shown in Fig. 98.

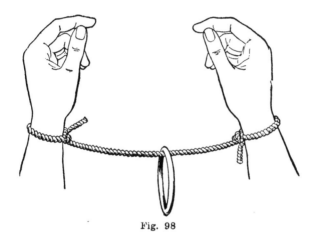

Fig. 98

Of course, while the tricks are similar, the *modus
operandi* is entirely different. Two rings, exactly alike
and each large enough to slip over the hand, are used.
The audience, however, have no idea that more than one
ring is used. Before beginning the trick, one ring is
concealed about the right forearm, inside the coat-sleeve.
After his hands are tied and he has picked up the one
ring, he thrusts it under his vest, as he turns his back,
and lets the other slide down over his wrist and hand on

to the tape. When he faces his audience, they wonder how the trick is done.

To Pass a Coin Through a Hat:

As generally exhibited this is a very old trick, but the following method will be new to most of our readers. The performer borrows eight or ten half-dollars, and places them in a row on a table, preferably one with a marble top. One of the audience is asked to choose one and mark it, and afterward to pass it to several others, with the request that they examine it carefully and also mark it. In the meanwhile the performer is blindfolded. The coins then are put into a hat and shaken up, but when the performer puts his hand into the hat, he at once brings out the marked coin. The secret is that the coin selected in passing from one to the other becomes quite warm and is easily found, the others being, compara-

Fig. 99

tively, cold. In this form the trick is rather flat, but it may be made quite mysterious. When the performer finds the coin he palms it, and then pretending that the trick has failed, takes his hand out. In doing this, under cover of the hat, which is in his left hand, he pushes the

coin between the outside of the hat and the silk band
that is usually around it, where it will be perfectly
secure. In an offhand manner, but without calling attention to it, he manages to show that his hands are
empty. He holds the hat with both hands, fingers inside
and the thumbs outside, as shown in Fig. 99. "Let us
see whether we can shake the coin through the hat," he
says. He shakes it up and down and at the same time
his thumbs press the hat in, near where the coin is concealed. The piece of money will quickly be released and
fall to the floor, giving the impression that it has passed
through the hat. The illusion is all that can be desired.

A Coin, a Card, and a Candle:

This is an unusually good trick, and as it can be done
anywhere and without an assistant, it is especially suited
for the amateur conjurer.

It requires some previous preparation, but will well
repay the trouble in making ready.

The "properties," so-called, are:

1. A Jack of Clubs that has been soaked in cold water,
and then split apart. When it is nearly dry a marked
dime is placed in the center and the card is then pasted
(not glued) together again, put in a press, and left to
dry perfectly. The press is made of two oblong pieces
of half-inch hard wood, about four inches long and three
wide; in the center of one piece is bored a hole a trifle
larger in circumference than a dime; this will allow of
the card being pressed flat. These boards are held together by strong, tight rubber bands or by a weight
placed on them, or still better by a thumb-screw at each
end to keep them together tightly.

2. A second dime, marked like the one in the card, of the same date, and in every way as like it as possible.

3. A pack of cards, with three or four extra Jacks of Clubs on top and on top of these the prepared Jack.

4. A leaf of cigarette paper, folded in half, with the *second dime* lying between the folds.

5. A piece of candle, one-quarter the size of a whole one. From one end of this the wick is cut out, leaving a hole about an inch in length and of sufficient width to admit easily half the cigarette paper when rolled up. This piece of candle is placed inside the handle of the knife hereafter described, the hole toward the lower end.

6. A sharp knife, like an ordinary kitchen knife. On the lower end of the wooden handle is a piece of brass tubing, large enough to hold the piece of candle. The whole handle is painted black or dark brown, and must look like one solid piece.

7. A candle in a candlestick.

8. A box of matches.

9. An unpainted inch-and-a-half board, twelve inches long and six wide. From end to end, the longer way, near one edge is cut a narrow groove, in which a candle will lie, half-way down, without rolling off. About the center of the board is hollowed out a cavity, into which the piece of candle will lie easily, without showing above the surface.

10. A piece of flash paper, the size of the cigarette paper. In it has been wrapped a dime, and the impression of the coin is still to be seen, though the paper is empty, but folded as if it still held the dime. This paper may be bought from a dealer in conjuring tricks

or be prepared by any chemist. (Full instructions for making this paper will be found at the end of the book.) Its peculiarity is that it burns instantly on touching a light and leaves no ash or other trace behind; it is held in a clip under the performer's waistcoat, where he can get it easily.

To begin the trick, the performer goes to a lady with the pack of cards, and as he approaches her he cuts the pack, letting the little finger of his left hand, in which the pack rests, come between the two parts.

"Take a card, please, madam," he says, and he runs over the several Jacks, so that she is sure to take one. While she is looking at the card she has drawn, the performer again cuts the pack, bringing the prepared Jack to the top. "Let me have your card, please. Ah, the Jack of Clubs. Very good. Suppose we put it where every one may see it."

He walks to his table, and stands the card resting against the candlestick. "Keep your eye on it," he says. As he went to his table, he deliberately exchanged, by means of the "Top change," page 16, the card drawn for the prepared Jack, and it is that card he places against the candlestick.

As he lays down the pack, he picks up the cigarette paper, in which is the second dime. Then going to some gentleman in the back of the audience, he asks for a dime. "Will some one lend me one?" he asks. "Ah, you, sir. Be good enough to mark it so that it may be unmistakably identified."

While this is being done, he lets the second coin drop into his hand from the cigarette paper, and holds it concealed between his right forefinger and thumb. The borrowed dime he takes in the same fingers, and as he brings it up toward his face, as if to examine it, he slides one coin over the other, and gives the second dime to some one seated at a distance from the owner of the borrowed coin and nearer the stage, with the request that he will examine it carefully and keep it for a while.

Going to a third person, the performer hands the cigarette paper to him and asks him to write a word across the length of the paper, then to tear the paper through the middle, to keep one half, and to give the other to the performer.

When he receives it he returns to the person who holds the second dime, and taking that he wraps it in the paper, and then takes them to his table. On his way there he drops the borrowed dime into his hand, rolls the paper into a small, compact plug, and takes the flash paper from under his waistcoat. This he rests against the card which is standing against the candlestick, and lays, for the moment, the borrowed coin on the table.

"Now let us have some light on this," he remarks, as he lights the candle. "'How far that little candle throws its beam,' as Portia says.

"Let us see how we stand. Here is the card that was drawn before the dime was borrowed. In this half-sheet on which the gentleman has written, is wrapped the borrowed dime. Now watch the sequel."

Picking up the flash paper, he touches it to the flame of the candle, and in the twinkling of an eye it is gone. Taking the card and getting the borrowed coin at the same time, he goes to the gentleman to whom the second dime was shown, and hands the card to him, saying,

"Please look at this card, and tell us if you see anything unusual about it. There seems to be something in the center? Can you take the something out? No? Then tear the card in two and tell us what you find. A dime! Is it the one you saw a few moments ago? Yes? Thank you.

"The very dime the gentleman saw. Who gave me the coin?"

As the performer goes to the owner of the dime he exchanges the coin taken from the card for the borrowed one, which is at once identified by its owner. The other coin he pockets.

Going back to his table he takes the candle from the candlestick, first blowing it out, and lays it on the groove of the board. Then he takes up the knife, allowing the piece of candle to drop into his hand. Pointing with the knife at the candle he says, "Now I am going to cut up this candle," and lays down the knife. "Because," he continues, "I wish to find that bit of paper which is still missing."

While talking, he inserts the plug of paper, which he has held between two of his fingers, next to his palm, into the hole in the piece of candle. Taking up the knife again, he inserts the piece of candle into the handle, and proceeds to cut up the candle: First he cuts off the burnt end and then divides the candle in two. He lets the audience decide which piece he shall use, and putting the other aside, cuts the selected piece in two. Again he gives the audience their choice. This time he picks up the selected piece, draws it toward him across the board, covering it with his fingers, and allows it to drop in the cavity of the board, holding up the piece that was in the knife handle, and which he had dropped into his hand when he asked the audience to select the piece he should use.

Going to the one who wrote on the paper, the performer cuts through the candle with a pocket-knife until he reaches the paper plug. This, he requests the gentleman to take out, match it to the other half, and identify the writing. All of which is done.

III. WITH BALLS AND EGGS

To Pass an Egg from a Tumbler Into a Hat:

For this a celluloid or a blown egg is needed. To it is attached a fine black silk thread, that has a small hook on the free end, which is fastened to the lower part of the performer's vest. The egg is stowed away under his vest or in a vest pocket. When ready for the trick a handkerchief and a soft felt hat are borrowed and laid on the table; near them are an egg and a goblet. The latter are handed out for examination, and as he goes back to his table the performer exchanges the real egg for the imitation one. Facing the audience, he drops the egg visibly into the goblet. Picking up the hat he stands it behind the goblet, brim up. Taking the handkerchief by two corners he spreads it out, as if to cover the goblet. While the latter is thus screened, the performer moves back a trifle, which causes the egg to rise up out of the glass and drop into the hat. The handkerchief is covered over the glass. Taking the hat in one hand and the glass in the other, the performer orders the egg to leave the glass and go into the hat. Seizing the handkerchief between his teeth he drags it off and shows the glass to be empty. The next moment he pours the egg from the hat into the glass. As he turns to put away the glass he unhooks the thread. Finally he returns the borrowed articles, thanking the owners.

161

It may be mentioned here that a simple and secure way to attach a piece of sewing silk to an egg is to tie one end of the thread to a piece of broken match, about three-quarters of an inch in length, then make a tiny hole in the shell of the egg, about the center, and push in the bit of match. The thread may break but will not pull off.

To Pass a Billiard Ball from One Goblet to Another:

A billiard ball placed in a goblet and covered with a cardboard cylinder mysteriously disappears to reappear in a second goblet, which is also covered.

The necessary properties for the trick are: 1. A wooden or celluloid red billiard ball, to which is glued a small bit of red cloth, a quarter of an inch by half an inch in size. The ends, only, of the cloth are to be glued to the ball. 2. Two glass goblets. 3. Two thin, dark-colored cardboard cylinders, to go over the goblets. Each should be about two inches higher than the goblet and one must fit loosely over the other. 4. A fine black silk thread, with a loop at one end large enough to go over the performer's thumb; it should be about one and a half times longer than the height of one of the cylinders, and at one end have a tiny fishhook, with the barb filed off.

The goblets are on the table, some distance apart, with the cylinders and the ball by them. Picking up the cylinders the performer holds them so that the audience may see through them, and then covering one with the other drops them over one goblet. Then with his left hand he takes up the ball, being careful to conceal the bit of cloth. At the same moment he gets hold with his right

hand of the thread, which he has stuck on the right side
of his trousers or on his vest, and transferring the ball to
that hand, inserts the hook in the bit of cloth and gets the
loop over his thumb. The ball is then dropped through
the cylinders into the glass. To convince the audience
that it is there, the performer lifts both cylinders, taking hold of them near the top. As the thread is longer
than these covers, he can readily do this, showing the
ball in the goblet. Once more he lowers the covers,
and taking hold of the outer one near the bottom, which
will draw the ball inside of it, removes that cover and
places it over the other goblet. At the same time he
lets the loop of the thread slip from his thumb, which
lets the ball land in the glass.

When both covers are removed, the first goblet will be
found empty, while in the second is the ball.

The Changing Ball and Flag:

A billiard ball held in one hand and a silk flag in the
other change places. The requirements for the trick
are: (1) A hollow metal ball, japanned red and measuring about one and three-quarter inches in diameter, with
a hole or opening in it, about one inch in diameter; (2)
A half-shell, of metal, also japanned red and measuring
about one and seven-eighths inches in diameter, so that it
will fit easily over the ball. Inside this shell at its
lowest part is soldered a loop of stiff wire, one and seven-
eighths inches long, the lower parts of the loop about an
inch apart. The loop must be painted flesh-color, see
Figs. 100, 101, 102; (3) Two flags of very thin silk, about
twelve by eighteen inches, each. One of the flags is
folded in plaits or flattened flutings, so that it will ex-

pand at once when released and placed in the wire loop, which it must fill entirely; it may be doubled up, but must slide easily into the ball. The loop is pushed into the ball, so that when the half-shell closes the opening and the ball is held with the shell-side toward the

The hollow ball.

Fig. 100

The hollow ball covered by the half-shell.

Fig. 101

The half-shell showing the wire loop.

Fig. 102.

audience there will be no appearance of preparation. Flag and shell being in place the performer begins his trick. Holding the second flag in his right hand and the ball in his left, he shows them to the audience. Then he places the ball in the right hand behind the flag and shows the left hand empty. With that hand he takes the half-shell away from the ball, being careful that the flag conceals the ball. The half-shell is held between the thumb and fingers toward the audience, who imagine it is the ball. Extending his arms away from his body, the performer announces that he will endeavor to make the ball and flag change places. With an up and down movement of the right hand and the help of his fingers, he works the flag into the hollow ball. He keeps his fingers well closed and is careful not to show the ball. When the flag is entirely inside the ball he closes his hand, so that it appears as if he had the flag there, well crumpled up. In the meanwhile the second finger of the left hand is placed in position to push the flag from the loop. For this purpose, the tip of that finger must be at the lower part of the loop. At the word "Go," he releases the flag by pushing it out. The loop will fall over the second finger, which throws the half-shell to the back of the hand, a little upward motion and the sudden appearance of the flag concealing the operation. The flag is held between the first finger and the thumb, and the inside of the hand is toward the audience. The flesh-color of the loop prevents the audience seeing that it is over the finger. At the same time the performer opens the right hand and shows the ball, the hole being concealed by the palm of the hand. The half-shell is got rid of under cover of the flag.

Novel Effect With Billiard Balls:

This pretty little combination is performed· with billiard balls of different colors which appear, disappear, and change from one place to another in a most mysterious manner. Three solid balls, two red and one white, and a red shell are needed for the trick. The "shell" is a hollow half-ball that fits exactly over one of the red solid, and when of the same color and finish can not when in place easily be distinguished from the ball itself.

The performer borrows a hat and lays it on its crown on the table. Near it he lays the white ball. Taking one of the red balls, which is covered with the shell, he places it between the thumb and forefinger of his left hand, the shell toward the audience. Then he puts the other red ball between the first and second fingers of the same hand, as shown in Fig. 103. His right hand being now in front of the lower ball, he removes the solid ball from the shell with his third and little fingers and palms it (to make this perfectly clear the inside of the right hand is shown in the illustration), the shell only remaining between the thumb and forefinger, as shown in Fig. 104, but the audience imagine that two solid balls are still

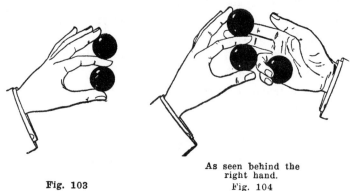

Fig. 103

As seen behind the right hand.
Fig. 104

there. The right hand, in which the red ball is palmed, picks up with the tips of the fingers the white ball and puts it into the hat. The moment, however, that the hand is inside the hat, the red ball is left there and the white one is palmed in its place. "Please note just how matters stand," says the performer addressing the audience. "Here in the fingers of my left hand are the two red balls, while in the hat is the white ball. But if you will watch me closely, you will see, or rather you will not see, that by my magic power and these long fingers of mine that were made on purpose, I shall cause one of the red balls to change places with the white ball that is in the hat. See." With a little motion of the hand the performer with the second finger of the left hand slips the solid red ball into the shell, and to the audience it will seem as if the ball had suddenly and mysteriously disappeared. Then grasping in the air with his right hand, he allows the palmed ball to appear at the tips of his fingers. This he places between the first and second fingers of the left hand. Picking up the hat with the right hand, the thumb on top of the brim and the fingers below, he tilts it over to show the red ball inside. At the same time the left hand is placed on the brim, as if to show that all three balls are there. The thumb and forefinger of the left hand are now immediately over the right palm, and, under cover of the hat, the red ball is released from the shell and palmed. The balls are now disposed of as follows:—One red ball is in the hat, the other is palmed in the right hand. The red shell is between the thumb and forefinger of the left hand and the white ball is between the first and second fingers of the same hand. "Now," says the performer, "I will send the white ball into the hat and take the red out, both invisibly." As he says this he slips the white ball into the shell and shows that it has gone. Clutching at the air, he produces the palmed red ball. "So," he continues, "we have here once more the two red balls," and while placing the red ball, which he has just, apparently, caught in the air, between the first and second fingers of the left hand, he removes the white ball from the shell and palms it. Dropping his right hand into the hat, and taking it out again he shows the white ball between the tips of the fingers. He puts the ball into the hat again. "And now to finish the peregrinations of these spheres, which I (s)fear may bore you, I shall send the red balls to join the white one in the hat, one visibly, the other

invisibly. See!'' Bringing the solid ball behind the
shell he commands it to ''go,'' and to show that it has
obeyed, tilts over the hat, in which are seen a white and
a red ball. Taking the remaining ball, which is half
covered by the shell, he drops it visibly into the hat,
palming the shell and getting rid of it.

The Changing Billiard Balls:

A red billiard ball is wrapped in a small red silk handkerchief and placed in a goblet, as shown in Fig. 105.

The ball in the handkerchief
dropped into the goblet.
Fig. 105

Showing ball palmed.
Fig. 105a.

A green billiard ball is wrapped in a silk handkerchief
of its own color, and that is placed in a second goblet.
When the handkerchiefs are pulled out of the goblets it is
found that the balls have changed places. For this trick
three balls are needed, say, two red and one green, though
the audience imagine that two balls only are used. Be-

sides these there are the two handkerchiefs and the goblets. When the performer begins the trick he has a red ball palmed in his right hand. Picking up the green silk, he spreads it over the open left hand, which is held palm upwards. With his right hand the performer picks up the green ball and apparently puts it in the green handkerchief. In reality the red ball goes in the handkerchief and the green ball is palmed. This substitution will not be noticeable if a slight throwing movement is employed accompanied with a little upward motion of the hand. At almost the same moment the left hand throws the handkerchief over the ball, while the right hand in which the green ball is now palmed wraps the handkerchief around the red ball and puts both in the goblet. The red handkerchief is now spread over the left hand and the same routine, as used with the first ball, is followed. The palmed red ball is slipped into a pocket or otherwise got out of sight. Of course, when the handkerchiefs are slowly drawn out of the goblets it will appear as if the balls had changed places.

The Patriotic Billiard Balls:

Three borrowed Derby hats are placed in a row on the table, and in front of each hat are three balls on a small plate. On one plate there are three red balls, on the second, three white, and on the third, three blue. They are handed out for examination before beginning the trick, which may be done without fear, for there is no preparation about them. The performer begins by putting a red ball into the first hat, a white ball into the second, and a blue ball into the third. This he repeats twice, and naturally, each hat should contain three balls of one color. Instead of that, such is the perverseness of the conjuring tribe, each hat contains a red, a white, and a blue ball. And yet it is so simple, as will be seen if these explanations are carefully followed. Let us call the hats A, B, and C.

1. A red ball is taken up and apparently put in A. The ball, however, is palmed, a filip with the finger against the inside of the hat giving the impression that the ball was dropped into the hat.

2. With the same hand a white ball is taken up and apparently put into the hat B, but instead, the red ball goes in and the white is palmed.

3. A blue ball is taken and this is supposed to be put into C, but instead the white ball goes in and the blue is palmed.

4. A red ball is now supposed to go into A, but the blue takes its place, and the red is palmed.

5. A blue ball is picked up, but palmed and a red is put into C.

6. Another white ball is apparently put into B, but it is palmed and a blue ball is dropped in.

7. A red ball is picked up and put into A, and the palmed white one goes into the hat at the same time.

8. A white ball is put into B.

9. A blue ball goes into C.

As the hand is empty after the seventh move, the audience ought to be given an opportunity to see this, without calling attention to it in words. This may be done by simply moving the hats a little, as that will show the hands are empty. As there is no palming in moves 8 and 9, the performer ought to make the most of this, as it will go far to convince the audience that the same procedure has been followed in every move. When the hats are finally emptied on the plates, it will be found that in each there is a red, a white, and a blue ball.

The trick requires address, good palming and little else. The following tables will make everything clear:—

1	Red	apparently dropped in A, but palmed.		
2	White	apparently dropped in B, but palmed.	Red	dropped in.
3	Blue	apparently dropped in C, but palmed.	White	dropped in.
4	Red	apparently dropped in A, but palmed.	Blue	dropped in.
5	Blue	apparently dropped in C, but palmed.	Red	dropped in.
6	White	apparently dropped in B, but palmed.	Blue	dropped in.
7		A,	R. & W.	dropped in.
8		B,	White	dropped in.
9		C,	Blue	dropped in.

Condition after each move.

	A	B	C
1	0	0	0
2	0	R.	0
3	0	R.	W.
4	B.	R.	W.
5	B.	R.	W. & R.
6	B.	R. & B.	W. & R.
7	R. W. B.	R. & B.	W. & R.
8	R. W. B.	R. W. B.	W. & R.
9	R. W. B.	R. W. B.	R. W. B.

The Egg Ching Ching:

About the year 1866, Colonel Stodare, a very skillful English conjurer, introduced a little trick with an egg and a handkerchief to which he gave the above title. It proved very successful and Carl Herrmann exhibited it some years later at his first performance in New York; and afterward his successor, Alexander Herrmann, often included it in his program. In its first form, an egg was placed in a glass goblet, over which was thrown a large handkerchief. Standing at a distance, the performer picked up a small square of red silk, which he began to gather into his hands.

When it was completely within his hands they were opened, and it was seen that the silk square had disappeared—if that is not a bull—and in the hands was an egg—presumably the one placed in the goblet. On removing the handkerchief from the goblet, the silk square was seen in the glass, but the egg had gone.

The explanation of the trick is simple: the egg that is placed in the goblet has been blown, that is, it is nothing but an egg-shell, the egg itself having been cleaned out by means of two holes, one at each end. By blowing in one hole the contents of the egg comes out at the other. It is not a pleasant job to prepare such an egg, and for that reason many performers use a wooden egg or, what is much better, one of celluloid, which is made specially for conjurers' use. When the performer is about to place the egg into the goblet, it is lying on the large handkerchief, which is spread over his left hand. A fine black silk thread about four inches long attaches the egg to the center of the handkerchief, and between the two is the silk square which is folded into as small shape as possible and concealed in a half-fold of the handkerchief. To fold this properly it is plaited back and forth until it is one long strip, and then the strip is plaited in the same way until it is about an inch and one-half square. Folded in this way, the natural resilience of the silk will cause it to open out when released.

As the performer is about to cover the goblet with the handkerchief after the egg is in, he relaxes his hold of the silk square and drops that in, also. Back of the second square of silk, which is on a table, is concealed a hollow metal egg, with an opening on one side. The silk square and this egg are picked up together, and as the square is drawn into the performer's hands, he works it into the hollow egg, which he finally shows to the audience, who suppose it to be the egg that was placed in the glass. Going to the goblet, the performer lifts up the handkerchief and with it the hollow egg, and shows the square of silk, which has, apparently, passed invisibly into the glass.

In place of a hollow *metal* egg, the performer often prepares a real egg. This can be done by soaking the egg for some time in strong vinegar. After a while the shell will become so soft that it may be cut, without splintering, by driving a sharp pointed penknife in with gentle taps. When the piece is out, the contents are scooped out, and the egg is washed out with a weak solution of carbolic acid, and then lined with a thin coating of plaster of paris. Prepared in this way, it is infinitely better than any imitation.

Another and better method:—An improvement on this trick is to use a drinking-glass, the bottom of which has been cut out. This must be done, of course, by a glass-cutter or engraver. He should be instructed to leave a narrow rim around the bottom, that is, the bottom should not be cut close to the edge.

Provided with such a glass, the performer may use a real egg and dispense with the duplicate handkerchief, as only one is needed. Besides the egg and the handkerchief a piece of rather stiff letter-paper is required. This is rolled into a cylinder which will fit easily over the tumbler, as a cover, and is fastened together with a small pin.

This method of presenting the trick was planned out by the junior editor of this book, and has long been a puzzle to many professional conjurers. It is now properly explained for the first time.

Everything being ready, the performer, with an egg concealed just under the lowest part of his waistcoat, advances to his audience, and begs for the loan of an egg. Addressing one of the company, he asks, "Will you, sir, accommodate me with a fresh egg?" extending his open left hand at the same time. "Thank you; lay it here, please." As the performer leans forward to receive it, his right hand goes, naturally, to the bottom of his waistcoat and gets hold of the egg. At the same time the closed hand moves to the gentleman's mouth, and the concealed egg is allowed to show itself at the tip of the fingers. It appears as if the egg were taken from the mouth. The egg is placed on the table alongside a goblet.

In the next move the performer obtains the handkerchief. This he produces "magically," by means of a false finger or any one of the many ways.

He now inverts a glass goblet, placing it mouth down on the table, and on the bottom of this he stands the bottomless tumbler. "I place this here," he says, "so that it may be seen easily, and in it I put the egg which the gentleman has lent me." In putting this in, the performer is careful to have it rest on the rim which is left at the bottom of the glass. "I hope you all can see the egg." As he says this, he picks up the tumbler with his right hand and places it on the extended palm of his left hand. "I will shake the glass so that you may hear the egg as well as see it. Listen." In shaking it thus the egg is dislodged and rests on his hand. With the paper cylinder, which is ready, he covers the tumbler and in front of it, on his fingers, he throws the handkerchief; then picking up with his right hand the empty tumbler, still covered, he replaces it on the bottom of the inverted goblet. The egg is now in his left palm, but the handkerchief conceals it. He turns the hand with its back toward the audience, and bringing his two hands together begins to roll the handkerchief into a compact ball, which he presses into his right palm and holds it there concealed. He then brings the egg to the tip of his fingers and shows it. "See!" he exclaims, "here is the egg, and in its place in the glass we find the handkerchief." As he says this the performer allows his right palm to come over the top opening of the cylinder, into which he drops the handkerchief, which passes into the tumbler. At the same moment he lifts the tumbler cover, showing that an actual change has taken place.

A Spherical Paradox, Not so Clear as It Seems:

This was a favorite trick of Robert Heller's, and in his hands was a gem. The "properties" needed for its successful accomplishment are:

1. A rectangular board measuring, say, twelve inches from side to side and nine inches from top to bottom, and standing with a tilt, somewhat like an easel. See Fig. 106. It is hinged at its lower front edge to a second board of its own width, but not so high, which lies flat. Two straight, narrow legs, hinged at the back, support the upright board at any desired angle. The face of the

board is covered with black velvet and ornamented with a narrow gilt braid, which divides it into diamonds and also forms a frame round the edges, as shown in the illustration. At the points A and B are holes cut through the board. These holes are large enough to admit the largest ball used in the trick to pass in and out easily. The edges of these holes are carefully covered with the velvet, and back of each is a deep pocket of the same material. At C and D, are cavities in the board; these are loosely covered by the velvet, so that a ball will stand on one without rolling off. In addition, there is a semicircle of pins or "brads" under each cavity, as a rest for a ball. Hanging at the back of the board, near the top, is a wire holder of the shape shown in

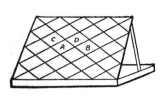

The velvet board.
Fig. 106

The wire holder, with
a safety pin at the top.
Fig. 107

Fig. 107. This holds a ball firmly and yet allows it to be taken away by a mere touch of the fingers.

2. A clear glass decanter. In the bottom of this a hole is cut, and in it is inserted (and cemented with white lead) the inverted bowl of a wineglass, large enough to hold the ruby glass ball, described below. The stem and base of the wineglass are cut off. This forms a "kick,"

that is, the hollow usually found in the bottom of a molded glass bottle.

3. A solid ivory or wooden ball, an inch and a half in diameter and stained red.

4. Two thin brass shells in the shape of a half-ball, each large enough to admit a little more than half of the solid ball. These are japanned red; they are made like a box and its lid, so as to shut together closely and yet not be too tight to open easily. A tiny bit of chamois leather glued on the inside center of each shell deadens any sound that might be heard when the solid ball is placed inside.

5. A clear glass or crystal ball, an inch and three-eighths in diameter.

6. A ruby glass ball of the same size as the crystal ball.

7. A small, clear glass ball, half-an-inch in diameter.

When the performer begins the trick, the velvet board is standing, slightly tilted, on the table; the large crystal glass ball is in the wire holder at the back. The two shells, one over the other, are under the front of the performer's waistcoat at the right of the center. The ruby ball and the small glass ball are each in a separate little pocket sewed on the back of the trousers leg, where the right hand can easily reach them. They are hidden by the coat tails. The solid wooden ball is in the right sleeve.

The decanter, which stands on a second table, is filled with a solution of extract of logwood.

The performer holds one end of his wand in his right hand, the other end resting lightly in his left palm. Addressing his audience, he says:—"I have here my wand," holding it up, "which many imagine is only for show. I assure you that is a mistake. When I want anything I squeeze the end of this magic stick, and I get what I want." As he says this, he holds up the wand with his left hand, and, simultaneously dropping his right, the ball in his sleeve drops into his palm, where it is held concealed. Then bringing that hand, with the back toward the audience, to the wand, he slides the thumb and fingers along the stick to the other end and at the same time rolls the ball with his thumb to the finger tips, so that just as the end of the wand is reached the ball will come in sight, making it appear to the audience as if he had just taken it out, as shown in Fig. 108. "See,"

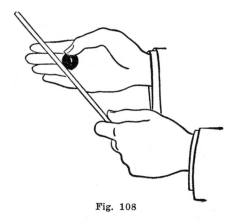

Fig. 108

he continues, "a solid ball. Examine it, please." When it has been examined to the satisfaction of the audience, the performer takes it back with his right hand, and as he returns to his stage his left hand reaches under his vest and takes out the two shells; then his hands are brought together and he inserts the ball into the lower shell.

When he reaches the stage he faces his audience. "See," he says, "I take this ball, and by a simple movement break it in half, as you see, for both balls are the same size." As he pretends to do this, the performer moves his hands from side to side, lifts off the top shell with his left hand and encircles it with the thumb and forefinger, holding the convex side of the shell toward the audience. The right hand takes the second shell, with the solid ball still inside, and holds it in the same position as the first shell. They look like two solid balls. "See," he says, "what one may come to, if handled properly. Again, another twist, and a third will come forth." Once more moving his hands from side to side, he gets out the solid ball and holds the three together in a triangular shape. "This position," he continues, "suggests the symbolic sign, *My Uncle*. Again, pass one this way and one that way, and we have only the original ball remaining." As he moves his hands right and left in front of his body, he slips the solid ball into one shell and then, bringing the two shells together, closes them. "I will stand this here," he says, as he places the ball at C. "Can you see it distinctly?" he asks. "Let me tilt the board more." As his hand goes behind the board, he grasps the large glass ball and holds it concealed. "Again I take this solid ball, and squeezing it just a little, produce this ball of solid crystal." Here he lets the glass ball come in sight and replaces the shells containing the solid ball on the board, at C. "It is as though the ball had wept and this were a tear. I will stand it here." He places the glass ball on the board at D, and turns to his audience.

"So far," he says, "everything has gone along all right. Now for another effect. I take this ball in my left hand and close the hand around it." As he pretends to do this he drops the shells with the ball into the hole at A. "The crystal ball," he continues, "I place on top of my fist over the other ball," suiting the action to the word, "and opening my hand a little, I allow the crystal ball to pass down into the other. You naturally imagine that the larger will absorb the smaller. On the contrary, the crystal ball has swallowed the other. Just the reverse of what you expected." He shows the glass ball and his empty hands.

"On this table," he says, pointing to the side table, "I have a decanter of port—the real Ottoman Porte, you've read about. The wine inside is proof that the decanter is perfect. No traps in that. I now propose to show you how to make one solid body pass through another; the crystal ball through the neck of the decanter into the wine." While the attention of the audience is directed to the decanter, the performer takes the small glass ball from his back pocket and holds it concealed in his right hand, just at the root of his second and third fingers, by slightly closing those fingers. He picks up the large glass ball. "Ah, it is too large," he says: "I will break off a piece." He pretends to do so, and shows the small ball. "Ah, I fear the sphere is now too small. I can not keep the piece. I shall put it back." Palming the small ball in his right hand, he presses his finger tips on the larger one, and as the small ball has disappeared the audience imagine it has gone whence it came.

"Ah, that is better," he says as he places the glass ball on the board at D. Picking up the decanter as an excuse for so placing the ball, he merely moves it. "And now to pass the ball into the decanter." He apparently takes the glass ball from the board, but as his left hand covers it, he lets it drop into B. Placing his closed, but empty, hand over the mouth of the decanter, he exclaims, "Pass!" All eyes are on the decanter, and this gives him an opportunity to get the ruby ball from his pocket. "Yes, there it is," he says, "blushing with the life-blood of the wine. Come out, I say." Lifting the decanter with his left hand, his right goes to the bottom of the bottle and inserts the ball, shaking the decanter so that if a sound be heard the audience will imagine it is caused by the ball inside. As he rattles the decanter, he allows the ball to drop. "What further proof do you want?" he asks. "None, of course. I introduce this trick, first, because it is pure sleight-of-hand, requiring years of practice, and, secondly, because the ball and the decanter being of clear crystal you can see through them, and I flatter myself there is nothing else to see through." [1]

---

[1] The board is on the plan of the so-called " Black Art Table," which within a year or so was introduced as something new. Heller used this board forty years ago. The little wire arrangement for holding the ball was invented about 1865, by Robert Nickle. Verily, there is nothing new under the sun!

IV. WITH HANDKERCHIEFS.

To Make a Handkerchief Disappear from the Hands:

In this little trick the handkerchief that is to disappear is seen up to the last moment. The requisites for the trick are very simple, merely a small silk handkerchief and a little piece of the same silk, which is held concealed at the root of the thumb and forefinger of the left hand. In exhibiting the trick, the performer pulls up his sleeves, folding over the left sleeve so as to form a sort of pocket. Taking the handkerchief by one corner he rolls it into a ball, which he pretends to put in his left hand, but really palms in his right At the same time he takes the little piece that is concealed at the root of the thumb and brings it up above the thumb and forefinger of his closed left fist. The audience will suppose they see the corner of the handkerchief. Then under pretence of adjusting his left sleeve he slips the balled handkerchief under the fold of the sleeve and leaves it there. The hands are now brought together and after rubbing them together for a moment the little piece which is now rolled into a tiny ball is replaced in its hiding place. Then the hands are shown, back and face, apparently empty. This is a very pretty and deceptive trick.

The Stretched Handkerchief:

Let us suppose the two upper corners of a handkerchief, when held up before one, are marked A and B,

and the lower corners C and D. Taking the handkerchief by the upper corners the performer folds it in two,
thus bringing C to A and D to B. He holds A and C
with the thumb and second finger of the left hand, the
forefinger being between the fold. The right hand holds
B and D in the same way. Then, twirling the handkerchief around and around he forms it into a sort of rope.
When it has assumed this shape, the second finger of
the left hand releases A, while the thumb and forefinger
grasps C. Then D is dropped and the thumb and forefinger of the right hand take hold of B. The handkerchief is now held by diagonally opposite corners. The
performer begins to pull and the handkerchief to stretch.
Every little while the performer gives it an extra twist,
and so continues to pull and to twist, till it is stretched out
to an, apparently, inordinate length.

The Handkerchief With Seven Corners:

"Will some lady oblige me with a handkerchief that
has seven corners?" asks the performer. None being
offered he steps back to his table and picking up a large
silk handkerchief or scarf, announces that this will
have to answer his purpose.

"Just for the moment you may see only four corners,"
he says, "but the others will soon be visible to all."

To begin he ties two corners of the handkerchief together, and covers them with the rest of the handkerchief, and asks some lady to hold the knots. Then he
ties two other corners, puts those under the body of the
handkerchief, and asks the lady to keep her hands on
those, also. Then he calls attention to the fact that
although he has tied four corners there are still two

others remaining. These he ties and puts them with the four. "You have six now, as you can feel," he says, addressing the lady who holds the knot, "and yet here is a seventh." This he asks her to take hold of, but requests that she drop it when he counts *three*. "Here goes," he says, "one, two, three!" She drops it, and as the magic spell is broken by her action, the handkerchief resumes its original form.

A large handkerchief is necessary for this trick. To begin, the performer ties two corners with a slip knot. In this he really ties the end of one handkerchief *round* the other and does not tie them together. This so-called knot may be made very tight, and even when one end is withdrawn the folds of the other will be preserved and if felt through a handkerchief will seem to be a genuine knot. In the trick now under consideration just as the lady is asked to hold the knots, the performer draws out one of the corners, and the lady will hold only the semblance of a knot. Three corners will be left, and the performer takes two, knots them in the style of the others, and puts them under the handkerchief to be held. In doing so he again releases one corner. The audience believe that four of the corners are now held by the lady, while there are only two, and two corners are hanging down, which the performer calls numbers five and six. He again goes through the same operation, and still leaves one corner hanging down. "Ah!" he says, "here is the seventh." Of this he takes hold and counts as described; the lady lets go, and he shows the handkerchief with its original four corners.

For a description of the Slip Knot see Appendix.

The Mysterious Knots:

First Method. Three silk handkerchiefs are thrown over the back of a chair. Picking them up, one by one, with the left hand and transferring them to the right,

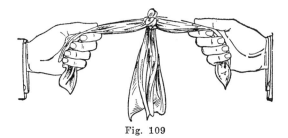

Fig. 109

the performer throws them in the air, and when they come down they are knotted together, as shown in Fig. 109. To fasten these together a tiny, thin rubber

Fig. 110

band is slipped around a corner of each handkerchief before the three are thrown in the air. Again they are bunched together, the rubber band is quietly slipped off, and when they come down the second time they are separate. In order to have the rubber band in such position that it may be easily and readily slipped on the handkerchiefs a little piece of apparatus, as shown in Fig. 110, will be found very useful. It consists of a little brass plate, measuring one and one-half inches square, having four arms, an inch in length, one at each corner, and it is over these arms that the band is stretched. On the reverse side of the plate are four strong pins, so that it may be stuck on the back of a chair, as near the top as possible. The handkerchiefs are thrown over the back of the chair, and as the performer picks them up, his first and second fingers go into the band and after that his thumb also is put inside, and he is now prepared to slip the band on the corners of the handkerchiefs at any moment.

Second Method. Three handkerchiefs of different colors are tied together with a slip knot, made as follows: The corners of two handkerchiefs, A and B, are taken between the thumb and first finger of the left hand,

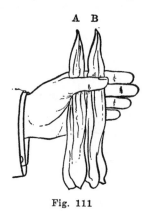

Fig. 111

as shown in Fig. 111. With the right hand the corner B is turned down so that it hangs between the first and second fingers of the left hand. It is then turned to the left, and the first finger is withdrawn from the loop

thus formed.   Corner A is now turned to the right, and
when the corners meet again at the other side of the loop
(nearest the body) they are tied together.   The knot so
formed may be undone with a slight pull.   When the
three handkerchiefs are tied together in this way, they
are laid on a table with the knots in position, as shown
in Fig. 112.   They are then placed close together.   The

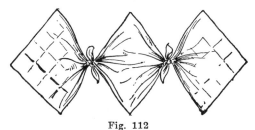

Fig. 112

audience, of course, know nothing of these preparations.
The handkerchiefs lying on the table, as in Fig. 112,
are picked up with the left hand concealing the knots;
the ends being entirely free gives them the appearance
of three unconnected handkerchiefs.   They are rolled
into a ball and thrown in the air, and when they fall,
it is seen that they are tied together in a long string.
Then they are crumpled up once more, the knots are
released by a slight pull, and when they are again
thrown in the air, they come down separately.

The Transit of Old Glory:

This brilliant little trick has the great advantage that
it is as well suited for the drawing-room, that is for
exhibition in a private house or at a club, as for the
stage.   The performer comes forward with half a sheet
of note-paper in one hand.   ''I have here,'' he says, ''a

piece of paper, the product of that great magician, the paper-maker, who turns beggars' rags into sheets for editors to lie on. There is nothing concealed here, as you may see," he turns the paper, so as to show it back and front. "But see! I roll it up for a moment." Suiting the action to the word, he rolls the paper till it is about the thickness of a finger, "and now, tearing it in two, this little flag appears." He spreads out the flag and crumpling up the paper, throws it aside. "Pretty isn't it? It's small, but it covers a lot of ground." Throwing the flag over the back of a chair, he picks up two silk handkerchiefs, a red and a dark blue, ties a corner of one to a corner of the other, bunches them together, and places them in an empty goblet. "So far, so good," he continues. "Now, let me show you this pocket." He turns out the right side pocket of his trousers. "Empty! like every conjurer's pockets." He puts it back in place, and rolling up his right sleeve, so that nothing can be concealed there, slowly puts the little flag into the empty pocket. "See what I shall do. By simply repeating certain incantations, handed down to us from the days of Nostradamus, I shall cause the flag to leave my pocket and take its place between the handkerchiefs now tied together. And this without hiding the goblet from your sight for one moment. Listen! *Chiddy biddy bee, chiddy biddy bi, chiddy biddy bo.* (And let us say, parenthetically, that when you are versed in these mysteries, other words may be substituted for these.) And now you will please observe that my pocket is empty."

As he says this, he pulls out the pocket, and to his surprise and mortification the flag comes out with it.

"Dear me!" he exclaims, "how very embarrassing. Something has gone wrong. Evidently a misquotation. Ah! how stupid of me. I forgot to give the flag the necessary wherewithal to defray traveling expenses." He replaces the flag in his pocket, and pretending to take a piece of money from his waistcoat pocket he puts it in the pocket that contains the flag. Then with a simple command "Go!" he catches hold of an end of each handkerchief in the goblet, and giving them a sharp jerk and a shake, shows that the flag has taken its place between the handkerchiefs and is firmly tied to them. Again turning his pocket inside out, it is seen to be empty, and the trick is done as promised.

But how is it done? Read attentively and you'll know. First, as to the production of the flag. Taking a piece of saffron-colored tissue-paper, technically known as "Havana color," the performer makes of it a long, narrow bag, as near the shape of a finger as possible, rounded and closed at one end and open at the other. Into this he gently pushes a small sheer silk flag. If this be placed between the second and third fingers of the left hand and the fingers held close to each other it will be a keen-eyed one, indeed, who will detect that the performer has one more finger than he is entitled to. When rolling up the sheet of note-paper, it is folded round the hand and the paper "finger" is left inside. Tearing the note-paper in two, the flag is revealed. The crumpled up paper is then thrown aside for the moment, only to be carefully picked up later, lest some inquisitive body should take a notion to examine it, and finding the yellow paper inside get some inkling of the secret of the trick. A false finger of flesh colored sheer muslin may be substituted for the one of tissue paper, and with it an additional effect may be produced. This finger is rolled in the paper as already described. By giving the paper a fillip with a finger the flag will gradually make its appearance at the open end, crawling up, as it were. When it is entirely out, the performer presses the paper together, keeping the false finger inside. The paper is then crumpled up and disposed of as told. Before the flag is put into the pocket the first time it is rolled into a ball. The second time the performer pushes it with his right thumb into the upper part of the pocket near the band of the trousers, and as far toward the center of the band as possible. The other fingers go down toward the bottom of the pocket. With the flag so stowed away, the pocket may be turned inside out, and will appear to be empty.

Opposite one corner of the blue handkerchief a square

Fig. 113

of the same silk, measuring three and a half inches, is sewed so as to make a pocket, with the opening toward the corner and about two and a half inches from it. A triangular-shaped piece of the same blue silk, five inches long and three inches wide at its greatest width is sewed to the corner A of the flag, while the corner B is sewed on to the blue handkerchief, between the mouth of the

pocket and the corner, as shown in Fig. 113. Into the
pocket the flag is tucked, beginning with the corner C,
leaving the end of the triangular piece sticking out.

When these preparations are completed the trick may
be shown.

Picking up the blue handkerchief with his left hand
the performer holds it so that its folds conceal the pocket
and its contents. Then taking the red handkerchief in
his right hand he, apparently, ties one corner of it to a
corner of the other. In reality, however, the actual
corner of the blue handkerchief is folded back and held
down behind the fingers of the left hand, and in its
stead the triangular piece of blue silk that sticks out
of the pocket is tied to the red handkerchief with *two*
knots; as soon as the first knot is made, the actual corner
of the blue handkerchief is brought up from behind the
fingers and the second knot is tied over it (as shown in
the illustration, Fig. 114), and tied tightly, thus keeping

Fig. 114

The dotted lines represent the corner of the blue handkerchief, which
is folded into the two knots.

the flag securely in the pocket. Then the performer
wraps the two handkerchiefs together and puts them in
a goblet with a corner of each hanging out. At the
proper moment he grasps these corners and giving them

a quick jerk the flag is pulled out of the pocket and is seen tied, apparently, between the two handkerchiefs.

Instead of a prepared handkerchief and flag, as described, some conjurers rely on an exchange of packages, and when skilfully carried out this is much the more artistic way. For such an exchange, a small shelf is hung at the back of a chair. On this lies a package made up of a red and a blue handkerchief with a flag tied between them, care being taken that the flag is concealed within the folds of the handkerchiefs. Alongside the shelf is a small black bag, its mouth being held open by a wire run round it in a seam. In showing the trick the performer deliberately and actually ties the two handkerchiefs together at one corner and rolls them into a package similar to the one on the shelf. The flag used in the trick is lying on the back of the chair, and as the performer picks it up with his right hand, his left, that holds the original package, passes for a second only behind the chair, but in that time it grips the shelf package and drops the original into the bag. There is no hesitation, no waiting, but in the twinkling of an eye the change is made.

A Succession of Surprises by Le Professeur Magicus (Adolphe Blind):

The performer hands out for examination a goblet and a cardboard cylinder large enough to go over the goblet and serve as a cover. When they are returned to him he covers the goblet with the cylinder. Suddenly a red silk handkerchief appears in his hands and just as suddenly disappears. Then the cylinder is removed and the handkerchief is seen in the goblet. The performer takes it out and hands it for examination, and then replaces it in the goblet, which he again covers. A moment later he takes the handkerchief from his trousers pocket, and shows that the goblet is empty. So he continues, causing the handkerchief to leave the goblet and return to it, finding it alternately under his collar, in the pocket of one of the audience, and in various other places. At the conclusion goblet and cylinder are once more handed out for examination.

The "properties" for the trick consist of:—

A. A goblet of clear cut glass, about six inches in height and three inches in diameter. The sides are cut with perpendicular lines.

B. A well of transparent glass, about three inches in height, that fits loosely in the goblet. At the top, which is three inches in diameter, it flares out so that it will rest on the edge of the goblet.

C. A plate of brass, silver-plated and highly polished. This is a trifle shorter than the well and fits it snug at the sides.

D. A cardboard cylinder, three and a half inches in height and three and an eighth inches in diameter. One end is closed, but has a hole in it large enough to admit the performer's forefinger. The other end is open.

The brass plate C is placed in the well B, and a handkerchief is dropped on one side of it. Other handkerchiefs are disposed of in the various places from which they are to be taken afterwards. Then B is placed inside of the cylinder.

When these preparations are made, the performer is ready for his trick. He begins by handing out the goblet. When it is returned, he stands it on his table. Then picking up the cylinder, which is lying on its side, he thrusts his forefinger through the hole in the top, so as to secure the well B, and covers the goblet, remarking at the same time, "This is a little cover for the goblet." Almost immediately he lifts off the cylinder, being careful to have the handkerchief turned toward himself, and continuing says, "Please look at this and assure yourselves that it is not prepared in any way." As he removes D he leaves B in the goblet. The trick is now virtually done.

The first handkerchief is made to appear and disappear by any of the methods described elsewhere. In lifting up the goblet, from time to time, he gives it a half-turn, bringing the handkerchief that is in the well in sight or causing it to disappear. How to make a handkerchief appear or vanish from the trousers pocket has already been explained on page 190.

At the conclusion, B and C are allowed to drop into a padded box at the back of the performer's table, and then cover and goblet are handed out for a final examination.

M. Blind also favors us with another trick which he entitles

The Three Handkerchiefs:

When the performer begins there are on his table three cut glass tumblers and three silk handkerchiefs, a red, a white, and a blue. When the handkerchiefs have been examined, so that the people of the audience may be satisfied they are not double nor prepared in any way, each is dropped into a separate tumbler. The tumbler containing the blue handkerchief is placed on a little pedestal, so that it may more easily be seen, and over the mouth is laid a plain glass disk, just a trifle larger in diameter than the top of the tumbler. On this the performer stands the tumbler that contains the white handkerchief and covers it with a second disk, and on this goes the third tumbler, in which is the red handkerchief. Over this pyramid of tumblers is dropped a cardboard tube open at both ends, and long enough to cover the tumblers completely.

Waving his hands over the pyramid and repeating some cabalistic words, the performer lifts the tube, and to the wonder of the audience it is seen that the tumblers have changed their positions. The one with the blue handkerchief is on top, the one with the red is in the middle, and the one with the white is at the bottom.

The tumblers are now placed in their original positions: the one with the red handkerchief on top, that with the white in the middle, and the third with the blue handkerchief at the bottom. They are covered again with the tube and when, shortly after, it is taken off, the tumblers have changed places again, the white handkerchief is now on top, the blue, in the middle and the red at the bottom.

The glasses are now placed so that the one containing the white handkerchief is at the bottom, the one with the red handkerchief in the middle, and the one with the blue handkerchief on top. Again they are covered with the tube and when it is removed for the third time, another change has occurred. The glass that was on top is now in the middle, the one that was in the middle is now at the bottom, and the one that was at the bottom is on top. To conclude, the glasses are arranged so that the blue handkerchief is on top, the red in the middle and the white at the bottom. For the last time the tube is slipped over them and when it is taken off the glasses are seen to be in their original positions.

As our readers may guess, each of the tumblers has a polished, plated brass partition like that described in the preceding trick, the edges being concealed by the pattern cut on the glass. Behind the mirror that is to hold the red handkerchief is concealed a blue handkerchief; back of the partition in the tumbler intended for the white handkerchief is a red one, and back of the third tumbler, a white handkerchief.

The tube is without preparation, but the pedestal on which the tumblers stand has for its top a disk that revolves on a pivot. A black silk thread operated by a concealed assistant causes this to make a half revolution, in this way turning the tumblers just as the performer is covering the tumblers with the tube.

With a little study the ingenious conjurer may arrange the pedestal so that he can turn it himself and dispense with the aid of an assistant. A pedestal might be made to resemble a box, which would be a very natural thing for a performer to use. The revolving disk might be arranged where the lid would be.

A Silk Handkerchief Placed in a Cornucopia Disappears, and is Found Tied Around a Candle:

A candle and candlestick, entirely without preparation, are shown for examination, and, afterward, the candle is placed in the candlestick, which is stood upon a table.

A large handkerchief is then thrown over the candle.

A piece of thin wrapping paper, in size about fifteen by twenty inches, is twisted into a cornucopia; a small red silk handkerchief is placed over one end of the performer's wand and is pushed into the cornucopia, which is then closed, and handed to one of the audience to hold, with the request that he assists in the trick.

A pistol is fired and when the assistant is asked to tear open the cornucopia, he finds, to his surprise, that it is empty. The large handkerchief is taken off the candle, and the missing handkerchief is seen to be tied round the candle.

For this novel trick the following "properties" are needed:

An unprepared candle.

A candlestick, also unprepared.

A small pin.

Two red silk handkerchiefs, each about fourteen inches square. Exactly in the center of one of these is sewed a little patch of the same silk, about the size of a quarter-dollar.

A piece of brass tubing, one and an eighth inches long, that fits easily over the candle. It is covered on the outside with a piece of the same silk as the red handkerchiefs. Around this tubing is tied the handkerchief that has no patch on it.

A piece of thin wrapping paper, fifteen by twenty inches large.

A wand, that consists of two parts; one part is a piece of thin brass tubing, nine-sixteenths of an inch in diameter and about sixteen inches long, one end of which is closed. The other part is a heavy, stiff wire, wound around with black tape; at the top is a small piece of

wood, painted black; at the bottom, the wire is fitted into
a pear-shaped piece of brass, that goes into a piece of
brass tubing, three-quarters of an inch long, the same as
used for the first part of the wand. This tubing is closed
at the lower end. When the wire is placed inside the
long tube, and the whole is pushed close, it resembles an
ordinary wand. See Fig. 115. Every part of it is
black, the outside of a mat or dull color.

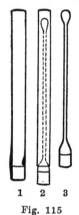

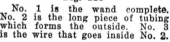

Fig. 115

No. 1 is the wand complete.
No. 2 is the long piece of tubing
which forms the outside. No. 3
is the wire that goes inside No. 2.

Fig. 116

On one side of the candle, at about the center, is stuck
the pin,·so that it projects about a quarter of an inch.
Around the silk-covered piece of tubing is tied the red
handkerchief, as seen in Fig. 116. The loose ends are
brought up and tucked inside the tubing at the top, as
shown in Fig. 116. The candle and candlestick, together with the wand, the piece of paper, the red silk
handkerchief, with the patch, and the large handker-

chief, that is to cover the candle are on a table. Behind the latter and hidden by it is the prepared piece of tubing. This large handkerchief ought to be about eighteen inches square, and of thin green silk with a colored pattern running through it. A white handkerchief is apt to show something of the red handkerchief around the candle, but with the green it is invisible.

The Cornucopia.

To begin the trick, the performer shows the candlestick and the candle, without allowing them to be handled, being careful to hide the pin. Then he puts the candle in the candlestick, which he places on a table.

Picking up the green handkerchief, he simultaneously palms the prepared tubing in his right hand. The large handkerchief is shown, front and back, and is then thrown over the candle. In doing this the performer's thumbs are about six inches apart and are on top of the handkerchief, with the fingers underneath. See Fig. 117. Under cover of the handkerchief, he seizes the prepared tubing, in the right palm, with the first and third fingers of the left hand, his right hand fingers helping him to

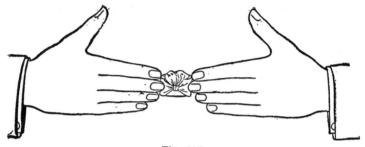

Fig. 117

Showing the tubing held between the fingers, with the ends of the handkerchief projecting at the top.

hold it. He is careful to keep the tubing erect, with the part into which the ends of the red handkerchief are

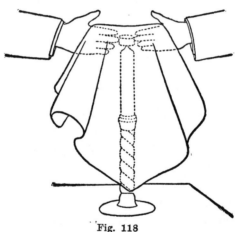

Fig. 118

Showing how the piece of tubing is held when about to slip it over the candle.

tucked at the top. As he covers the candle, he slips the tubing over it. See Fig. 118. The ends of the tucked-in handkerchief are thus pushed out and freed, and the tubing slides down of its own weight, until its lower edge rests on the pin. Then he twists the paper into a cornucopia; when properly made it should be eighteen or twenty inches long, with the open end about four inches in diameter. He turns up the lower end a few inches.

Picking up the wand, he rattles it inside the cornucopia, as if to show that it is empty. As he does this, his left hand takes hold, from the outside of the cornucopia, of the lower end of the wand, so that it will remain inside, when the outer part of the wand is pulled out. So that the two parts may separate easily, the fake end may be drawn out a trifle beforehand, and, as the whole wand is black, that will not be noticed.

The performer lays the cornucopia on the table and as he places it with the top toward the audience, the fake is not seen.

Picking up the red handkerchief, he lays the patch on the open end of the wand and holds it in place with his right hand. Taking the cornucopia in his left hand, he pushes the handkerchief into it in such a way that the end of the wire fake will enter the open end of the wand. He presses the wand down a little way, which causes the handkerchief to enter the tubing, and at the same moment he releases his hold of the handkerchief. It will now expand and fill the top part of the cornucopia, completely concealing the wire fake. At this point the open side of the cornucopia should be toward the audience. The performer's left hand, which is holding the lower end of the cornucopia and keeps the wire fake in position, is far away from his body. He presses the wand down slowly, thus working the handkerchief further into it, and, finally, turns the open end of the cornucopia upward and presses the wand down all the way, close on the fake. As the handkerchief is now out of sight, he removes the wand from the cornucopia, which he closes, by folding over the top, and gives to some one to hold.

Then follows the firing of the pistol, as already described, the tearing apart of the cornucopia, and the revealing of the red handkerchief, apparently tied around the candle, as shown in Fig. 119.

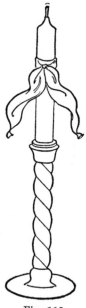

Fig. 119

The effect of the trick may be heightened, by allowing the audience, at the beginning of the trick, to select a handkerchief from a lot of four, each of a different color.

The selection is made by the cast of a die, as explained on page 31.

A correspondent of *L'Illusioniste,* M. Caroly's interesting little magazine, suggests an improvement on the "wand" used in his trick, which commends itself by its simplicity. It consists of a tube of black hard rubber, or other material, of the size of the ordinary wand used by the conjurer, with ivory or silver-plated ferrules or caps at the ends, so that it may look as much like a wand as possible. One ferrule is closed at the end, the other is open, giving free access to the interior of the tube. In the center of the closed end is a tiny hole, through which runs a fine, black silk thread about one yard and a half in length, leaving equal lengths at each end of the tube. The end of the silk at the closed end of the wand is fastened to the front edge of the table; the other end is tied to the center of the handkerchief that is to disappear. Both handkerchief and tube lie on the table. When the cornucopia is formed, the performer standing back of the table drops the handkerchief into it, so all may see it, and as if to push it further in he picks up the wand and inserts the open end in the mouth of the cornucopia. Then holding it up with one hand and the wand with the other he walks backward a step or two, when the end of the thread that is fastened to the table will, naturally draw the handkerchief up into the tube.

SOME AFTER-DINNER TRICKS

An Adhesive Nut:

When the nuts are brought on the table after dinner, the performer picks up a walnut and holding it between his thumb and the second and third fingers, with the forefinger on the top, he rubs it up and down on his sleeve for a few minutes in order, as he says, to generate electricity. Then he removes all but the forefinger to which the nut is seen to adhere. The reason is plain. The rubbing on the sleeve was, as may be supposed, merely a ruse to give the performer an opportunity to separate the two shells at the top. It is into this opening that the performer presses the skin of the forefinger, and thus holds the nut suspended, as shown in Fig. 120.

Fig. 120

Should there be an opportunity it is well to separate the shells slightly at the top before attempting the trick, as some nuts do not give way readily except under very strong fingers.

An Elusive Ring:

The performer has in his pocket a handkerchief to the center of which is fastened the two ends of a short thread, thus forming a loop. Hanging from this loop is a cheap finger ring. When he is called on for a trick, he selects a small goblet and a napkin, with which to show his deftness. Borrowing a ring from a lady, he pretends to put it under the handkerchief, but keeps it and in its place puts the hanging ring, which he holds through the handkerchief by his fingers on the outside. Giving the goblet to a second lady he asks her to hold it. Then he puts the handkerchief over it so that the bowl is completely covered, asks her to keep hold of the bottom of the glass with one hand and with the other to hold the ring (always from the outside). Getting the borrowed ring between the tips of his thumb and first and second fingers, he picks up the napkin and shows it is empty, holding the ring concealed at one corner. Then gathering the corners of the napkin together, so as to make a bag into which he lets the ring slide, he hands it to a third lady, with the request that she holds the corners tightly together. Taking a table knife, he approaches the lady who holds the hanging ring, and says: "When I say three, be good enough to drop the ring into the glass. Now, one, two, three." She drops the ring as requested, and every one hears it strike. Then he taps the glass with the knife, lifts off the handkerchief, and shows that the glass is empty. The third lady is asked to open the napkin, and to her surprise she finds the ring inside. "I am sorry to trouble you, madam, but will you kindly hand the ring to the owner, so that she may identify it. Thank you!"

A Borrowed Bank Note that is Destroyed by Tearing or Burning is Found Imbedded in a Lemon:

This trick is frequently exhibited at a dinner party or in some public place where a lemon may be procured. The performer has the nail of his right thumb quite long and trimmed to a sharp edge. With this he cuts a hole in one end of a lemon, and in it he thrusts his forefinger. To do this without being seen he puts the lemon into his trousers pocket, while some one of the audience is taking the number of the borrowed bank note, so that it may be identified readily. As the performer is looking on, his hand goes into the pocket and does the cutting. As he takes the lemon out, which has been marked in some way at the beginning of the trick, he brings with it an imitation bank note (professionally known as "stage money") folded up. The lemon he lays on the table, and as the real bank note is returned to him he joins the imitation note to it, and folds it till the two notes look alike. Then he places the dummy note alongside the lemon and palms the original. Picking up the lemon, he applies a lighted match to the stage money, and while he watches it burn, his hands naturally go behind his back, which enables him to push the genuine note into the lemon. By this time the other note is destroyed. Gathering the ashes, he rubs them on the lemon, and then proceeds to cut it open at the perfect end. As soon as the bank note is seen he goes to its owner and asks him to take it out and identify it, reading aloud its number.

Some performers use an imitation bank note that is printed on flash paper. This disappears the moment it is lighted.

Instead of a lemon a *small* apple may be used. In this case two apples, alike in size and general appearance, are used. In one of these a hole is cut, large enough to admit the borrowed note. This apple is in the trousers pocket. Under the performer's vest or under his coat lapel is a small packet of flash paper. The perfect apple is on a table. When the performer borrows the bank note he wraps it in a piece of tissue paper and getting hold of the flash paper packet brings the two packets together and exchanges one for the other. The flash paper he asks some lady to hold. As he goes for the good apple his hand is thrust into his pocket and the bank note packet is pushed into the cut apple. The good apple is then handed out for examination. In the meanwhile he palms the other, and as he goes back to his table, ostensibly for a knife, he puts the good apple under his vest and lays the prepared one on the table. Then he returns to the lady who holds the flash paper. Taking it in his fingers, he lights it. Whiff! it is gone. Hurrying to his table, he cuts open the apple, beginning to pare it at the perfect part. As soon as the bank note appears, he takes it out, holding it at arm's length so that the audience may see it is not exchanged, and hands it to its owner. The apple he crushes and lays on a plate, which he carries off as soon as possible.

Each form of the trick has its advantages. The one in which the lemon is used is the more brilliant, as the lemon may be marked for identification; while in the use of the apple, the bank note is not soiled by lemon juice, which is sometimes objected to.

A Disappearing Knife:

While seated at the table after dinner, the performer picks up a knife, and wraps it up in a handkerchief, part of the blade projecting from below. See Fig. 121.

Fig. 121

Holding the packet in his right hand, and standing up, he calls attention to the blade. With his left hand he pushes the blade up into the handkerchief until it can no longer be seen. Then taking hold of the two upper corners of the handkerchief, he shakes it, and shows both sides. The knife has vanished.

The handkerchief is double, that is, two handkerchiefs, exactly alike, are sewed together around the edges. On the inside of one is a pocket, with the open side toward the edge of the handkerchief. In this pocket is hung part of a knife-blade, in the upper part of which is drilled a hole through which a strong thread runs, the ends being fastened to the bottom of the pocket. The thread is of such length that the blade will be drawn entirely inside the pocket when the upper ends of the handkerchief are held. See Fig. 121. To hold the real knife there is a black bag long enough to conceal it. The bag hangs on the performer's back between the vest and the coat and reaches nearly to his waist. The mouth of this bag is held open by a wire ring (a large key-ring will do perfectly) and attached to this are two elastic cords.

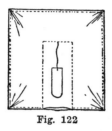

Fig. 122

These go over the performer's shoulders through the arm holes of the vest, and the ends are fastened to the front suspender buttons of the trousers. Before beginning the trick, the performer, seated, gets this bag between his legs and holds the ring between his knees. When he has covered the knife with the handkerchief, he draws the packet near the edge of the table and allows the knife to slide into the bag. The suspended blade which now projects below the handkerchief holds the attention of the audience and deceives them. When the performer stands up the elastics draw the bag up under his coat and all that remains for the performer to do is to stretch the handkerchief by the two corners, and thus draw the blade into the pocket.

A duplicate knife, which the performer has slipped into some one's pocket may then be produced, and shown as if it were the original.

A Match Trick:

This is a good after-dinner trick. Showing his hands empty, the performer takes a few matches from a box, and wraps them up in a handkerchief. The next moment he shakes the handkerchief and the matches have vanished. They are afterwards produced from the pocket or inside the coat of one of the audience.

The secret of this pretty little trick is a tiny rubber band. It is stretched over a box of safety matches. On the label of these boxes there is generally a heavy black line at each end. Where there is not, the performer marks it with ink, and it is over one of these lines that he stretches the rubber band. The band ought not be fresh, but one that is dark from use. The match box may lie on the table without attracting notice. The handkerchief, also, ought to be on the table. As the performer picks up the box, his right thumb rests on the top, at one end, and the first and second fingers push in the end so as to open the box. See Fig. 123. As the

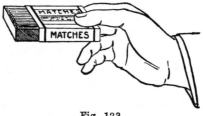

Fig. 123

left hand takes out some matches the right thumb rolls the rubber-band backward so that it encircles the two fingers, which are then closed in on the palm to conceal the band. Laying down the box, the performer picks up the handkerchief with his left hand and spreads it over the right. Under cover of the handkerchief the right thumb joins the fingers inside the rubber-band. See Fig. 124. The left hand now stands the matches upright in the center of the handkerchief, and the right hand grasps them. The handkerchief is then turned over, and, at the same mo· ment the band is stretched over the matches, through the handkerchief. The left hand takes hold of one corner of the handkerchief and shakes it. The matches do

Fig. 124

not fall to the floor. They are gone! Before beginning the trick the performer, who is sitting down, conceals a second lot of matches in a fold of his trousers leg. These he gets hold of, and apparently takes them out of a pocket or from inside the coat of some one in the audience.

The Moving Ears:

No little fun may be created with this trick. Back of each ear is stuck a small piece of flesh-colored court·plaster; to each piece is fastened a piece of black silk thread, the ends being tied together at the shoulders. By tugging at the thread the ears will move, or one ear only may be moved. The trick proves most effective if done when seated in company. Attention ought not to be called to it, as it will soon be noticed. Of course it is more a joke than a trick.

The Talking Glass:

The performer gives out a flint wine-glass, a silk thread about sixteen inches long, and his wand. One end of the thread he ties near one end of his wand, and the other end of the thread to the stem of the wine-glass. While the wand is in the performer's hand, the glass will ring out an answer to questions, tell the number of spots on a drawn card, and the suit, by ringing twice for "yes" and once for "no." Considerable fun may be made, all depending, of course, on the wit of the performer. All that is necessary for this trick is to roughen the wand somewhat, just enough to catch the thread slightly. It is also well to rosin the thread. When the performer wishes the glass to ring, he turns the wand a trifle in his fingers; the thread will go with it a little way, but the weight of the glass pulls it back again, and this jerks the glass slightly, causing it to ring.

The Suspended Glass:

Either a tumbler or a large wine glass may be used for this trick and preferably one of thin glass. Keeping his hand perfectly flat the performer lays it over the mouth of the glass, and when he lifts his hand, to the great surprise of the company the glass is seen to cling to it without visible support. To prove that it is not the result of air pressure, a playing card is passed between the glass and the hand, and the glass still remains suspended. The secret of the trick lies in the fact that the rim of the glass is clipped between the thumb and forefinger. When the flat hand is laid over the glass it is pressed down, letting the lower joint of the forefinger sink into the glass as far as may be. The thumb on the outside presses against the glass. The passing of the card between the mouth of the glass and the hand while tending to heighten the effect of the trick is simple. When properly done the trick is not easily detected.

The Tilting Goblet:

Picking up a wine-glass, a little more than half full of water, and tilting it to an angle, the performer makes mysterious passes over it, and then shows it, still at an angle, carefully balanced on its edge. Others of the company are invited to try it, but every one fails. And the reason is plain, for no one has taken the precaution to *place a match under the table-cloth,* so that the goblet actually rests on it. Care must be taken that the goblet is dry, for should the table-cloth be wet, the match, as well as the trick, will be seen through it. And this brings to mind another trick.

A Broken Match:

The performer spreads a handkerchief on the table and on the center of the handkerchief lays a borrowed match. The handkerchief is folded over it two or three times, and then, picking up the match through the folds of the linen, the performer breaks it into four pieces. Every one is satisfied that there is no deception about this; the match is unmistakably broken. Yet on opening the handkerchief, the match is found to be as sound as at first. Nor is it to be wondered at, for *in the hem of the handkerchief the performer has concealed a second match,* and this it is he breaks.

MISCELLANEOUS TRICKS

Paper Tearing:

The amateur conjurer of twenty-five years ago who was called upon to "do a trick" frequently responded by tearing up a sheet of cigarette-paper, rolling the pieces into a tiny ball, and then reproducing the sheet intact a few minutes later. This was done by substituting a whole piece that was concealed between the fingers, for the torn pieces, which, in turn, were hidden in the mouth when the performer pretended to wet his finger so as to open out the crumpled-up sheet.

The trick was almost forgotten, when it was revived a few years ago by a public performer, in a shape more suitable for stage presentation. Instead of a sheet of cigarette-paper a strip of red tissue-paper was used. This was about an inch in width and a yard or so in length. Baring his arms and opening wide his fingers, to show that nothing was concealed there, the performer in question tore the paper in two, then, folding the pieces together, he tore them in four, and so continued until no one piece was more than two and a half inches in length. These were gathered together, rolled up, and finally pulled out in one entire piece, as it was at first. At no time had the performer's hands come near his body.

How the man who revived this trick did it we cannot say, positively, for he never told us. We have heard that he used what is known as a ''hold out,'' a delicately constructed steel lazy-tongs which, concealed in the sleeve, enables the man who cheats at cards to introduce a desired card into the hand or take out an undesirable one.

It is worked by a lever controlled by the one who uses it and is an expensive affair. We have never tried this method, and cannot answer for it, but there is a way of doing the trick that we can recommend.

The Torn and Restored Strip of Paper:

This is one of the best forms of an excellent trick, and the necessary preparations for it are well repaid by the pleasure it gives an audience.

The properties are :—

1. Two metal caps, each about an inch and a quarter long, made to fit the end of the performer's thumb and painted so as to resemble, as closely as possible, the tip of the thumb.

2. Five strips of tissue paper, each eighteen or twenty inches long and one inch wide. Three of these pieces are plaited in the fashion shown in Fig 125, and then compressed and folded in two.

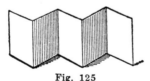

Fig. 125
How the paper is plaited.

One of these strips is placed in each thumb cap; the third lies on the table with the two straight pieces of paper. Behind these is one of the thumb caps; the other is on the performer's right thumb. Picking up one of the straight pieces, the performer holds it between his thumbs and forefingers in such a way that it covers the thumb cap.

Now he tears it up, until it is in pieces about two or three inches long. Taking off the cap, he holds it in his left hand, takes out the plaited piece and, compressing the torn pieces into as small compass as may be, puts them into the cap, which he replaces, on the right thumb. This done, he pulls out the plaited piece and shows it to the audience as the restored strip.

"Let me show you, how simple this is," he says. Turning to his table, he picks up the third plaited piece, drops the cap from his thumb and replaces it by the second cap. Facing the audience, he shows the plaited piece.

"Two pieces of paper are used," he says. "This piece I hold in my palm." As he says this, with his left hand he places the plaited piece in his right palm. Holding his hands up, so that all may see them, he keeps the strip of paper in place by the tip of the third finger of his right hand, taking care to conceal his thumb behind the left hand. Turning to his table again, he picks up the remaining strip of paper with the left hand and proceeds to tear it, as he tore the first piece. When torn to the desired size, he packs the pieces away in the thumb cap, first taking out the plaited piece. The cap he replaces on the thumb. He has now two whole strips in his hands, but the audience imagine he has the torn pieces and one whole strip.

Without any attempt at concealment, he changes the

pieces. "Now, ladies and gentlemen," he says, "I simply open out this piece, as you see," here he opens one strip and drops it on the floor, "and these pieces." As he says this he pulls one end of the remaining strip, and continues to pull until its full length is shown. "Ah, well, I see you know just how the trick is done."

Just a word here as to the manipulation of the cap. When stretching a strip between his fingers the performer may easily, even at close quarters, show that there is nothing in his hands except the strip of paper. When running the strip through his fingers, the thumb with the first and second fingers of the left hand may remove the cap from the right thumb. This off, that thumb may be shown, incidentally, empty. By repeating this move the cap may be replaced.

A popular and clever London conjurer, Selbit, suggests the following substitute for the metal thumbpiece, which, as he truly says, is clumsy: Provide yourself with a nicely fitting ring of thin, flat brass that will pass over your thumb down to the first joint. Next, get at a druggist's a thumb stall of thin flesh colored rubber; Fig. 126, put it on the thumb and push the ring down

Fig. 126

over the outside of the stall. Just above the ring toward the closed end of the stall, apply some rubber cement, turn back the open end of the stall so as to cover the ring and the cement will stick the rubber together, leaving the ring hemmed in between the two parts. When it is dry,

cut away the loose ends of the stall. To use it, place the
duplicate slip, plaited closely, against the flat end of the
left thumb and pull the stall over it, as shown in Fig.
127. To exchange the duplicate slip for the torn pieces,

Fig. 127

place the latter against the tip of the left thumb and
hold them there by pressing with the right thumb; then
with the first and second fingers of the right hand, take
hold of the ring and pull it over the right thumb, as in
Fig 128. The result is that the torn pieces are concealed

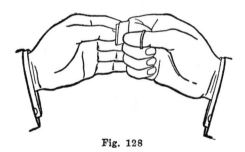

Fig. 128

and the duplicate strip is in your hands, which may be
shown, apparently empty.

Another Method. In this method four strips of tissue,
each thirty inches long, are used. Red tissue is prefer-

ably the best color and shows to the best advantage, but, unfortunately, most of it rubs when wet, so if a fast red can not be had, white will answer. Two of these strips are pasted together, making one strip about sixty inches long. This serves as the duplicate. This is plaited zigzag and, finally, is doubled. To plait the paper easily one end of the strip is laid on a playing card, near the edge, another card is laid on top of this, the strip is folded over this card, and then it continues over and back between cards until the entire strip is plaited in even folds. It is then taken from between the cards, pressed tightly together and doubled. It will make a little parcel about an inch and a quarter long. On the outside end a bit of white tissue paper is pasted, so that the performer may find it when he wants it. A

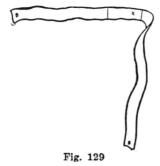

Fig. 129

band of the same tissue paper measuring two by two and a half inches is now wrapped around the folded strip A, and the ends of the bands are pasted together. The strip A is now in a sort of envelope. A pencil mark is made on one end of this envelope directly over the spot where the bit of white tissue lies. Two of the remaining

thirty-inch strips BB, are taken and an end of each is
pasted to an end of the envelope to prevent it opening
and to make a continuous strip as shown in Fig. 129.
Everything is now ready for exhibiting the trick.

The performer shows his hands back and front, the
fingers wide apart. Picking up the strip BB he hangs
it over the right hand, with the "envelope" part on the
inside of the hand, as shown in Fig. 130. The "envel-

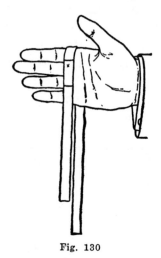

Fig. 130

ope" is now taken with the left hand and the right hand
tears the strip BB just at the point where it is pasted
on the envelope. The envelope might now be opened,
but for the present it is not. Holding the two half strips
together, and allowing them to hang down between the
forefinger and the thumb of the left hand, the performer
brings the four ends together and proceeds to tear the
strips first in two, then in four, and finally in eight
pieces. These he holds between the thumb and the fore-

finger of the left hand, with the "envelope" which still contains A, behind them. While in this position he passes all from hand to hand to show, apparently, that there is nothing there but the torn pieces. With a twist of his right hand he brings the ends of these into the left hand, and squeezes them into a compact wad. While he is doing this his thumbs, at the back, open the "envelope," take out the strip A, and hold it next to the wad between the fingers and the thumb of the left hand. The performer now covers the wad with the tip of his left forefinger while the right hand takes hold of the loose end of A, and draws it out a few inches, the piece of white tissue making this easy. Bringing it toward his mouth he blows away from him the end as it makes its appearance. He continues to draw it out a few inches further, and as his fingers touch his mouth for an instant, a perfectly natural movement, he pops the wad into it.

The trick is really done, but the performer continues to pull out the strip and blow on it till the full length is revealed. This form of the trick constitutes a problem which several professional magicians tried in vain to solve.

A trick akin to this paper tearing is that of apparently tearing a borrowed bank-note in pieces, and restoring it whole to its owner.

Although only a little trick, this will test to the utmost the ability of the performer. Mr. Francis J. Werner, a prominent member of the Society of American Magicians, makes a specialty of this, and in his hands it serves to illustrate the saying, "It is not the trick but the man."

Before beginning the trick the performer folds up a bank-note of his own, and conceals it in the fold of his sleeve at the bend of the left arm. When he borrows a bank-note (taking care that it is not frayed about the edges), he holds it gingerly in his right hand fingers so that everyone may see he has nothing hidden in his hands. Then he pulls up first his right and next his left sleeve and as his hand goes to the latter he seizes the note concealed there between the first joint of the second and third fingers. Taking the borrowed note between the fingers of both hands, he catches the upper right-hand corner between the thumb and finger of the right hand and gives it a quick, sharp, downward jerk toward his body as if tearing it. As he brings the corner down he retains it with the third and the little finger of the left hand. At the same moment he permits the duplicate note, which is between his fingers, to be seen. Crumpling the two bills together, he pulls them apart, allowing the audience to get a mere glimpse of them. Again and again he brings them together and separates them, rubbing one against the other, which will give the impression that they are being torn. Each time that they are separated the hands must be parted so that a bill may be seen in each hand, and finally the hands are held out toward the audience, who seeing the two bills will believe them to be one in many pieces.

In concluding the trick, the hands are brought together and the borrowed note is opened out and held so that all may see it; the duplicate bill is palmed in one hand and as the borrowed bill is held out in the other, the palmed bill is dropped into the trousers pocket. In exhibiting the trick Mr. Werner is here guilty of a bit of magician's audacity. He works more rapidly than at first. Crumpling up the borrowed bill he repeats with the one bill almost the same motions used with the two bills. He rubs the right thumb against the rumpled bill, making a sound as if tearing it, and as the audience believe they saw the separate pieces in the first instance they imagine they see them again. Finally he opens out the bill, which has been rolled into a ball, shows that it is whole, and returns it to the owner.

The Cigarette-Paper Trick:

There is a way of doing this trick, which is referred to on page 214 that will puzzle many of those who know the old method. Before beginning, the performer rolls a sheet of cigarette paper into a tiny ball and with a little bit of wax sticks it on the nail of his right thumb. He can now show his hands, seemingly empty. Taking a fresh sheet he tears it to bits. These he rolls into a ball and bringing the thumbs and forefingers together takes the whole piece from the thumbnail and for it substitutes the torn bits. It is a simple matter then to open the whole sheet slowly and show the hands with the fingers spread wide open.

A Japanese Trick:

Some years ago an Italian who assumed a Japanese name and costume, introduced a little trick which lately has been revived, and has proved popular with the public and the "profession."

Taking some small sheets of tissue paper, red and white, the performer tore them into narrow strips, placed these in a goblet, and poured water on them. With one end of his wand he pressed the paper into the water until it was thoroughly saturated, and afterward fished it out. Placing the wet strips in his right hand, the performer squeezed out the water, and then made them into a little wad. Picking up a fan, he opened it, and beginning to fan the wet wad, a number of tiny pieces of red and white paper flew about in every direction. The wad had disappeared.

The tiny bits of paper, which are of a fairly stiff quality, say, like writing paper, are gathered into a ball and wrapped in a piece of thin, white tissue paper, which is then tied with a bit of thread, as shown in drawing. Fig. 131. Before beginning the trick this little ball is placed under the right armpit.

Fig. 131

In fishing out the wet strips, the performer does so with his left hand; he removes the wet paper with his right hand and squeezes the water out. At the same time he places his wand under his right arm, and in this way gets hold of the little ball. The next move is to pretend to place the wet strips in the left hand, but, in fact, the performer retains them between the second and third fingers of the right hand, picks up the fan, and begins to fan the supposed wet pieces. A little pressure breaks the tissue wrapper, and the tiny pieces fly about like a snow flurry. The wet wad in the right hand is dropped on the table behind a book or a box, when putting down the fan.

The Disappearance of a Glass of Water, by Okito (Theo Bamberg) :

On the center of a small table, the top of which is only twelve inches in diameter and half an inch thick, is placed a glass of water. Over this glass is dropped a cardboard cylinder, open at both ends and double the height of the glass. A second cylinder, a trifle larger in circumference than the first but about an inch shorter and of a different color, is placed over the first, and finally a third, larger in circumference than the second and an inch shorter and of another color goes over the second. The glass is now covered with the three cylinders, A, B, C, as shown in Fig. 132. After some re-

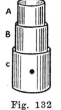

Fig. 132
The three cylinders.

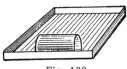

Fig. 133
The tray with cylinder.

marks by the performer, he lifts off the cover C and lays it on a tray, as shown in Fig. 133. Then he takes off B and places it along side C. The cover A he does not touch, but firing a pistol at it the cover drops to the floor. The glass with its contents has disappeared.

For this trick a table, D. Fig. 134, is used that has a

rod running through its leg. At the upper end of this
rod, flush with the top of the table, is a disk of the same
diameter as that of the bottom of the glass, E, Fig.
134. A cord attached to the rod leads off to a concealed
assistant, who pulls it to raise the rod; it falls of its own
weight. The covers A and B are without preparation,
but at one side of C, if a round object has a side, near
the bottom, is a hole large enough to admit the tip of

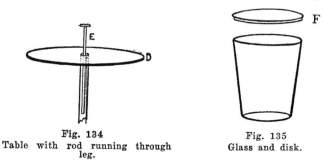

Fig. 134
Table with rod running through
leg.

Fig. 135
Glass and disk.

the second finger. The upper edges of the glass are
ground perfectly flat and in the mouth of the glass is
a disk of clear glass, made with a shoulder, so as to
insure its fit, as shown at F, Fig. 135. When this is in
place the glass filled with water may be turned upside
down without spilling a drop.

When the performer begins the trick the glass is
standing on the table. He fills it to overflowing from a
water-bottle and while moving the glass to the center of
the table quietly covers it with the glass disk which he
holds palmed. Then he drops cover A over the glass, cover
B over A, and C over B. He calls the attention of his
audience to the position of the glass and its covers.
"You will notice, ladies and gentlemen," he says, "that

it would be impossible to remove any of these through
a trap, even if I should descend to such a deceitful ex-
pedient, for you would see through it as clearly as you
can see through the glass itself. Suppose we try a
more simple way." Taking hold of C he proceeds to
lift it slowly off the other covers. As he does this the
tip of the second finger enters the hole in the side of
C, and at the same moment the concealed assistant pulls
the cord that raises the rod in the table and lifts the
glass well into C. The performer presses against the
glass with the tip of the second finger and against the
opposite side of the cover with his thumb, thus holding
the glass tightly in place. Then he lifts off glass and
cover together, as shown in Fig. 136, and lays them care-

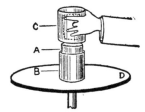

Fig. 136
Lifting glass and cover together.

lessly on a tray, as shown in Fig. 133. No one will suspect that the glass is removed, as no water runs out.
Cover B is then slowly lifted off, and as the performer
is about to lay it alongside C he (?) accidentally drops it
on the floor. Afterward he is about to lift A, but apparently changes his mind and merely moves it so that
a part of the lower edge rests on the edge of the disk
in the table. Picking up a pistol, he fires at A, and at
the same time the assistant jerks the cord, the edge of

the disk strikes the edge of A, which is knocked off on to the floor, and, to the astonishment of the audience, they discover that the table is bare—the glass of water has disappeared

A Second Method.—This is better suited than the foregoing to the needs of the average amateur from the fact that it may be done without the aid of an assistant.

The glass used for this trick is made with a tube blown in the center. It is open top and bottom and runs from the bottom of the glass nearly to the top, and is the shape of a truncated cone, as shown in H, Fig. 137.

Fig. 137
Glass with glass tube.

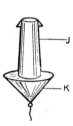

Fig. 138
Wooden plug.

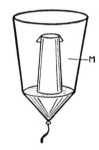

Fig. 139
Wooden plug fitted into glass tube.

Into this tube fits a wooden plug. The lower part of this plug somewhat resembles a top with a screw-eye fastened in the pointed end. (See K, Fig. 138.) To the screw-eye is attached a strong elastic or other pull. (For the description of a pull, see the end of the book.) In the end J of the upper part, are two pieces of steel that drop down when the plug passes through the tube and prevent it from being withdrawn, as shown in M, Fig. 139.

Before beginning the trick the performer fills the glass with strong, black tea to hide the tube. Picking up the glass with his right hand, in which is palmed a glass cover, similar to that described in the first form of the trick, he quietly lays the cover over the mouth of the glass. Then he stands the glass on his left hand, and throws over it a large handkerchief. Under cover of this he inserts the plug J. K. When it is firmly in place he counts one, two, three. He releases the elastic, shakes out the handkerchief which, as it falls in front of him, conceals the flight of the glass on its way under the performer's coat.

A Temperance Trick:

The performer spreads a newspaper on a table, so that there may be no suspicion of a trap or opening of any sort, and on it sets a glass of wine. Over this, for a moment, he throws a borrowed handkerchief. Then, picking up the covered glass, he exclaims in the language of Horace: "Nunc est bibendum," and, snatching away the handkerchief, shows a glass of water, which he drinks.

Inside the glass, and dividing it like a partition, is a piece of transparent celluloid stained of a wine color; to this is attached a piece of fine silk thread, which hangs over the side of the glass. On the free end of the thread is fastened a small black button, which enables the performer to get hold of the thread easily and to pull out the celluloid partition when removing the handkerchief.

The drinking of the water is to do away with the idea, that some of the audience may have, of any chemical preparation.

The Chinese Rice Bowls (With Variations by Conradi):

For this great improvement on an otherwise rather mildewed trick the editors are indebted to Herr F. W. Conradi, of Berlin, whose fame as an inventor of clever "magic" is known the world over.

The trick begins by the performer handing out for examination two empty China bowls. When they are returned to him he fills one with rice from a bag, and stands it on a table. Then he places the other, mouth down, on top of the first. A moment later he removes it, and to the surprise of the audience it is found that it, too, is filled with rice which rises in a heap and over-flows the sides of the lower bowl, as shown in Fig. 140.

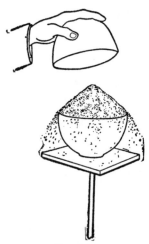

Fig. 140
The bowl with rice overflowing.

This rice is removed till it is level with the brim of the lower bowl which is still full. Then the lower bowl is again covered with the other. Picking up both bowls with his two hands, so as not to disturb their position, the performer holds them for a second, and when he separates them once more, the rice has disappeared and one bowl is overflowing with water, which he pours from one bowl to the other. The audience are again allowed to examine the bowls, which will be found to be without preparation of any kind.

In concluding the performer picks up a metal vase or jar, and pouring into it the water from the bowls covers the mouth of the jar with a piece of paper. Touching a lighted match to the paper it disappears with a flash. Then the performer turns over the jar and it is found to be empty, the water is gone.

For this trick the necessary properties are as follows:—

I. A bowl, about the size of a porridge bowl. The edges of this bowl are ground perfectly flat. Fitting over the mouth is a disc of transparent celluloid about one-sixteenth of an inch larger in circumference than the mouth of the bowl, outside measurement. When the bowl is filled with water and the disc is laid on top, the bowl may be turned upside down without the slightest danger of spilling its contents. The edges of the bowl, however, ought to be moistened beforehand. Careful attention must be paid to this as it is at the basis of the trick.

II. Two other bowls resembling the first in every respect.

III. A bag of stout manila paper, filled with rice. The bottom of the bag is turned in and upward, and although there is no actual partition it is virtually divided into an upper and a lower part. In this way, the lower part forms a space or cavity that is not seen by the audience and is large enough to serve as a hiding place or place of concealment for the bowl, A, which is filled with water and covered by the celluloid disc. In the illustration Fig. 141 part of the side of the bag is removed so

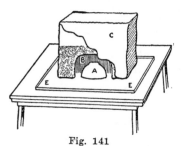

Fig. 141

Paper bag, with side broken away to show bowl underneath.

as to show the view from the back: C is the bag; B the space or cavity at the bottom of the bag; and A, the celluloid-covered bowl. The bowl is resting on the tray, EE.

The bowl of water and its disc are placed inverted on the tray, with a match or coin under some part of the edge, so that the disc does not touch the tray. Without this precaution, should the tray happen to be wet, the disc might stick to it when the bowl is picked up.

IV. A metal vase, as shown in Figs. 142 and 143. This is divided in two parts, A and B, by a partition. If, holding the vase straight, the performer pours into it the water from the bowl it will run down to the bottom and when he turns the vase slowly in the direction of the ar-

row C the contents will flow into the side B instead of
pouring out at the opening, and the vase will seem to be
empty.

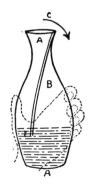
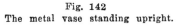
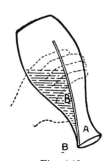

Fig. 142
The metal vase standing upright.

Fig. 143
The metal vase turned upside
down.

V. A shelf, known to conjurers as a *servante* (dumb-
waiter), at the back of the table, as shown at F in Fig.
144.

VI. A piece of flash paper, a nitrate of cellulose,
somewhat like gun-cotton. Precise directions for making this paper will be found at the end of the book.

Before beginning the trick the performer fills the
bowl A with water and covering it with the disc, places
it, inverted, on the tray and stands the rice bag over
it. He places the other bowls on the tray, one on each
side of the bag. The back of the tray must be close to
the edge of the table. The metal vase, also, with the
flash paper near it, is on the table, toward the front.

The performer is now ready. Taking the two bowls
he shows that they are without preparation of any kind,

and hands them to the audience for examination. He then places them, inverted, next to the bag. At least this is what he appears to do. In reality he places only bowl B on the tray and bowl B¹ on the *servante* F. Now comes the part that the performer must servilely follow in order to make the illusion perfect. At the very moment that his right hand places bowl B¹ on the *servante* his left hand lifts the bag.

By this perfectly natural movement the performer shows the third bowl which had been concealed under

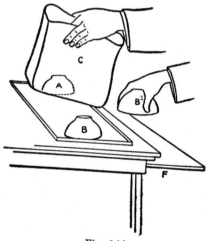

Fig. 144
Showing one hand lifting bag and the other putting bowl on servante.

the bag, as shown in Fig. 144. If these instructions are carried out to the letter the illusion will be perfect and the audience will imagine that they see the original two bowls. Taking bowl B with his right hand he fills it with rice that he pours from the bag, Fig. 145. The

bowl he replaces on the tray, the bag he stands on the
table. As there is more rice on the bowl than it can

Fig. 145

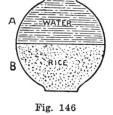

Fig. 146

hold, the performer runs his wand over the surplus
grains and removes them. Then picking up bowl A, always holding it mouth down and in a slightly slanting
position so that his audience may not see the disc, the
performer places it on bowl B, as shown in Fig. 146.

Taking up both bowls and holding them horizontally
before him on about a line with his chin, he turns them
over so that when he sets them on the table again their
positions will be reversed, and the bowl of rice will be
on top. Slowly he lifts bowl B, and the rice falling on
and over the disc will make it appear as if both bowls
were full of rice. With his wand he levels the heap
of rice, still leaving the lower bowl apparently full.
This he covers with the empty bowl. Once more he
lifts the bowls with both hands in a horizontal position,
as before, then turning them upright, he removes bowl
B and stands it on the tray, so as to get rid of the disc,
which he took away with the top bowl. Then he shows
bowl A full of water. Taking the bowl from the tray

he pours the water back and forth from one bowl to the other. Finally he picks up the metal vase and pours the water into it, covering the mouth with the flash paper. Applying a lighted match to the paper, it disappears, and turning over the vase shows that it is empty.

Firing a Girl from a Cannon Into a Trunk:

One of the most popular tricks with professional conjurers is that in which a young woman is fired from a large cannon, standing on the stage, into the innermost of a nest of three trunks that has hung suspended in full sight of the audience from the ''flies'' or upper part of the stage.

The trick is simplicity itself. In the lower end of the cannon—an enormous affair of wood and heavy tin which rests on a heavy gun carriage, is a trap which allows the girl to pass from the muzzle of the gun under the stage. Inside the mouth of the cannon is a revolver, the trigger of which is actuated by a cord in the hands of the girl and is fired at a given signal to heighten the effect of the trick.

When the trunks are lowered to the stage they are empty. The outer one is opened, and pushed aside; then the center one and the innermost one are taken out and placed directly over a trap in the stage. The bottom of each of these trunks is provided with a flap, as shown in Fig. 147, and the girl who is now under the stage is run up into these trunks by an elevator. When she is inside the bottoms of the trunks fall in place of their own weight.

Sometimes the girl who is placed in the cannon re-

mains in it until it is taken off the stage, and a second
girl, made up to resemble the first as nearly as possible,

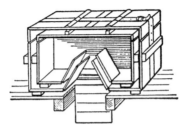

Fig. 147

This illustration shows the bottoms of the two trunks and the trap
in the stage open, affording a passage for the girl.

gets into the trunk, though, as the reader will understand, this is unnecessary.

Of course, this trick is only intended for the stage,
and is explained here merely to gratify the curiosity of
some readers who are desirous of knowing "how it is
done."

A Fruitful Experiment:

Here is a pretty trick for two people. They begin by
borrowing two hats, and then standing side by side they
place the hats in front of them on two chairs that are
turned sideways, so that the backs will not obstruct the
view of the audience. The hats are turned over and
shown to be empty, yet when they are replaced and Mr.
Number One puts his hand in the hat before him, he
brings out a lemon. He holds it up so that all may see
it, and then hands it to his friend on his left, Mr. Number
Two, who takes it and puts it into the hat that is before
him. This they continue, until at least a dozen lemons
are taken from one hat and put in the other. Finally

Number One announces that his hat is empty. "How many have you?" he asks his friend. The latter turns over his hat, and shows—it is empty. Where did the lemons come from and where did they go? Surely they were not "up the sleeve." Certainly not, though they might be hidden there, for *only two lemons* are needed for the trick.

Each of the performers has a lemon under his left arm pit. Before they begin, they hold out their hands to show that they are empty. Then they pull up their sleeves, first the right, next the left. As the left is pulled up the right hand goes, naturally, under the arm pit and takes the lemon from the place of concealment. Keeping the back of his hand to the audience Number One thrusts his hand into the hat and produces the lemon. He pretends to put it in his left hand and give it to Number Two, but keeps it in his right hand, turning the back to the audience. As his left hand meets Number Two's right, the latter allows his lemon to be seen. If properly and carefully done, the two men acting in concert, it will appear to the audience as if one lemon had passed from Number One to Number Two. As soon as Number Two appears to have the lemon, he pretends to pass it to his left hand, but retains it in his right. Then his left hand goes inside his hat, which he taps gently as if he had dropped the lemon, and immediately brings his hand out. These actions are repeated until it seems as if ten or twelve lemons had been produced and stored away, and, finally, the hats are turned over and shown to be empty.

Something from Nothing:

"Let me call your attention to these pieces of tissue-paper," the performer begins, as he picks up three pieces, each ten or twelve inches square, a red, a white, and a dark blue. When these have been duly examined by the audience, he returns with them to the stage. Crumpling the papers together, in a second his hands are filled with tiny flags, which go floating down among the audience like "leaves in Vallombrosa." Should the supply become exhausted, he brings his hands together again, and the flags multiply right under the eyes of the audience. Finally, when but few remain, his hands are once more placed together, and from them come the original red, white, and blue pieces from which the flags sprang.

Wonderful as it seems, the method of this trick is simple. The so-called flags are merely bits of tissue-paper of various colors, about two by three inches each. These are mounted by pasting a small end of each on a twig of broom-corn about four inches long. When ready, about a hundred and fifty are laid one on top of another and rolled together; when bunched up the ends of the twigs are then cut evenly with scissors. The roll is then placed on a piece of *black* tissue-paper. The paper is rolled over them once or twice, then one end is turned in and the rolling is continued. When finished, there will be only one end projecting, and this is to be twisted tightly. Last of all, the turned in end is neatly trimmed with scissors. The result will be a compact package that will hold together well, and yet may be opened easily. Two or three such packages, according to the size of the audience, must be prepared in order to produce the proper effect. Even if the audience is small in number, the performer must show a quantity of flags scattered about to heighten the effect. Before coming before his audience, the performer tucks one of these packages *under* the right lapel of his coat. To secure it there a large black pin is thrust down through the cloth and the lower end is then bent upward so the point stands out, and on this point the package is stuck. In this place it is hidden by the lapel, but a simple upward touch of the hand will remove it. A second packet is fastened in the same way under the left lapel of his coat on a line with the top button hole, and still another under the vest, a trifle above the waistline, in such place that it may be easily reached by the hand that is on the opposite side.

As the performer gathers the original pieces of paper from the audience, he receives the blue first, the red next in his right hand, holding them with the second finger in front and the other three fingers and the thumb at the back. To take the third piece he turns his left side, partly, to the person who holds it and reaches for it with his left hand. This, naturally, brings his right hand against the lapel where the first packet of flags is concealed; the three fingers and thumb instantly seize the packet and hold it behind the blue piece of tissue-paper, where it is not seen.

The performer is careful not to bring away the hand at once, as that would surely attract attention, but when the left hand receives the white piece of tissue, the two hands are brought together. The trick is now, virtually, done. All that remains is for the performer to crumple up the three pieces of paper, break open the packet, twisting the twigs in an opposite direction from that in which they are rolled, and scatter about the flags. As they fall to the ground he lets the black wrapper go at the same time. When the performer has a number of flags in his hand, he sticks one in his buttonhole on the left side, and at that moment takes the packet that is under that lapel of the coat. The original pieces of paper are rolled into a ball and concealed in one hand. It is an easy matter to get the third package from under the vest: the performer need only bow in presenting a flag, and as he bends to offer the flag with one hand, the opposite hand reaches under the vest and secures the package there.

As a conclusion, the performer throws into the air a package which, when it reaches a certain height, bursts open and a shower of little flags falls over the audience. The effect is pretty and the arrangement is simple: the flags are bound together by a band of black tissue paper. Passing under and over one part of this band is a loop of fine black sewing silk. Attached to this loop is a length of the same silk, measuring about thirty feet, the other end being tied to a button of the performer's vest. The thread is pleated and held against the packet by a small rubber band. When the performer wishes to use it he slips off this band and taking the package throws it into the air. The rebound tears off the band and the flags fly about in every direction.

When only a few flags remain in his hands, the performer pulls out the original papers and shows them, but this is not necessary.

Sometimes a large silk flag is wrapped up and concealed under the side of the coat, and the performer seizes this and spreads it out as a finish, and it always brings applause.

The Adhesive Dice:

Two ivory dice are handed out for examination. Then the conjurer places one on top of the other, being careful that the number of spots on the faces are the same. He requests some one to take hold of the top die and, without touching the lower one, to lift them from the table. This the audience find difficult to do, and yet when the conjurer takes hold they both are raised together. The secret is, that while the audience are busy trying the trick, the conjurer quietly wets a finger in his mouth. This he passes over the face of one die, and then the two will adhere. The notion of having similar spots together are like "the flowers that bloom in the spring"; that has no bearing on the trick and is only for effect.

The Antispiritualistic Cigarette Papers:

The effect of this little trick can not be imagined; it must be seen to be appreciated. For it the following "properties" are needed: (1) A book of cigarette paper. (2) A piece of thin cardboard, a little larger than a sheet of cigarette paper, covered on one side with blotting paper. (3) A frame of stiff cardboard, the same size as the thin piece, on one side of which are pasted four pieces of rubber band, as shown in Fig. 148, *a, b, c, d.* A sheet of cigarette paper is laid on the blotting paper and covered with the frame, the rubber side down; the two pieces of cardboard are fastened together with

a small clamp, as shown in Fig. 149. The combined
action of the blotting paper and the rubber will prevent
the paper shifting. (4) Four pieces of colored tissue
paper, say, red, blue, yellow, and green, each about one

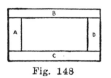

Fig. 148

Fig. 149

and a half by two inches. (5) Four pieces of colored
pencils, of the same colors as the tissue papers. These
are each about an inch and a half in length; so as to distinguish them by feeling they are prepared as follows:
the red is pointed at one end; the blue at both ends;
the yellow pointed at one end, but a notch cut around it;
and the green notched in the same way, but pointed at
both ends. The slightest touch with the fingers will
enable the performer to identify them. The frame with
the cigarette paper in place and the four pencils are
in the performer's trousers' pocket on his right side.
One of the audience is requested to select a leaf of
cigarette paper, to roll it into a ball, to stick it on the
end of a pin and keep it for a time in sight of the audience. Another of the audience is asked to select a
piece of the colored tissue paper, and to keep it for a
moment, while a third one is requested to choose a word
or a number and to announce it, so that everyone may
know it. In the meanwhile the performer has thrust
his hand into his pocket and found the pencil of
the same color as the selected tissue. Then in his
pocket he writes on the framed piece of paper the word

or number that was called out, releases the clip that holds the two pieces of cardboard, and getting hold of the paper rolls it into a pellet. With this concealed between his thumb and forefinger, he takes the ball of paper off the pin and exchanging one pellet for the other places the one from his pocket on the selected piece of tissue paper. Rolling these together and putting both on the point of the pin, he hands it again to some one to hold. Then calling to the spirits from the vasty deep, he bids the one who holds the pin to open the pellet, and when this is done the selected word or number is found on the cigarette paper written in the color of the selected tissue paper.

The Spirit Table (by Germain*):

In selecting the idea here presented from others, perhaps more practical or more original in effect, the writer has acted on his theory that books on conjuring should be composed of suggestions, rather than finished effects, so that it devolves on every performer to work out the details anew, thus in some small measure preventing that apelike imitation which has brought so much discredit on the mystic art. The trick here employed, he has himself used, in two entirely different ways, yet it was for the effect described that the ruse was invented.

The performer places upon a small unprepared table, several tambourines, bells, a slate, a small guitar, etc. Then remarking that a *real* medium can produce manifestations in the light as easily as in the dark, if only he screens his ghostly visitants from profane eyes, he holds a piece of drapery about two feet square as a

* This trick is presented in Mr. Germain's own words.

screen, before the table-top. Immediately sharp raps
are heard to come from the table and answers are rapped
out to the performer's queries. Tambourines and bells
are rattled and rung, and shaken against the cloth, or
the performer's arm, then thrown with great force into
the air and even at the performer. The guitar is played
upon while it is seen to float about; the slate is written
upon; in short, almost any of the usual "spirit" manifestations can be produced. After each manifestation
or racket, the performer quickly lowers the cloth, but
nothing suspicious is seen.

For this trick, the performer needs three arms, and

Fig. 150

fortunately he has them, two are his own, and so is the
third, for he has paid for it, but it is not as valuable
as the other two, for it is made of *papier maché*. See
Fig. 150. It is provided with flexible joints at elbow

and wrist, and a hand modeled and colored as nearly as possible like the performer's own right hand. This false arm is permanently fixed into the right sleeve of a coat he wears especially for this effect. This coat he dons during a moment's exit after his introductory remarks and his arrangement of the table and instruments. His right arm is held behind his back, and, without letting his left hand or his face know what it does, it "assists" the spirits. A stout little rod with a steel hook at the end, enables it to reach all parts of the table-top and to rap and bang the various instruments; the floating and throwing of them is accomplished by engaging the hook of the rod in screw-eyes, with which they have all been provided; the guitar is provided with a music-box which plays while the instrument is "floated" about. Just as soon as an instrument has been thrown or laid down, the little rod is drawn under the coat-tail, and the cloth lowered almost simultaneously. The cloth has a hook in one corner which is hooked into an eye under the coat-lapel. Rather heavy drapery goods works best, and it is advisable to weight the lower hem with shot, that the folds may not cling or stage zephyrs disturb the harmony of the spirit concert. The performer comes on holding the false hand in the real left hand; when he releases it, it will drop with a perfectly natural movement to his side. He then takes the cloth from the table, hooks it onto his coat, and proceeds with the trick. As he cannot turn round, or exit except by awkward side-stepping, the curtain should be dropped on the last manifestation.

A somewhat similar apparatus, but more simple and less cumbersome was described some years ago in *Ma-*

hatma, which we are allowed to reproduce here through the courtesy of Mr. Frank Ducrot, the proprietor of that journal.

For this it is necessary to have a lazytongs of steel or other metal, that may be extended or contracted at will by pressing the knob that is at one end. The other end of the lazytongs has attached to it four false fingers, made in exact imitation of a half closed human hand. The tongs is sewed between two handkerchiefs or other pieces of cloth, at one edge, leaving the false fingers on the outside, as shown in Fig. 151.

Fig. 151

To use this apparatus the tongs is closed and the handkerchief is thrown over the back of a chair, the fingers hanging behind. The performer picks it up with both hands, the fingers of the left hand covering the false fingers. He opens it out, showing both sides, and then spreads it in front of him, allowing his left hand to fall

behind him. He may then ring a bell, shake a tambourine, or cause articles to appear on the table or to
disappear from it. In fact, many wonderful "manifestations" may be worked, to the astonishment of the audience, and the performer is free at any time to turn or
to leave the stage.

The Needle Trick (by Clement de Lion):

The performer shows a number of needles and a piece
of thread about eighteen inches long. The thread is
wound around the needles. Then several pieces of bright
colored sewing silk are offered to the audience who select
one and tie it to the end of the thread that is wound
around the needles. These preliminaries being finished,
the performer puts needles and thread into his mouth,
the bit of colored silk hanging out over his under lip.
Then follow some grimaces as if the performer were
swallowing the needles, and when these cease the conjurer takes hold of the silk, pulls it out and it is followed by the needles *threaded* and about an inch apart.

As our readers no doubt surmise, a duplicate lot of
needles, already threaded, is used; the rest of the length
of thread is wrapped around them, except about three
inches. This bunch of needles is passed under a ring
that is worn on the second finger of the performer's left
hand, and is kept there concealed, as shown in Fig. 152.
A similar number of needles and a thread are now
exhibited. The needles are bunched together and the
thread is wound around them except about three inches.
Then they are put between the thumb and the first and
second fingers of the left hand for a few moments, and
the loose end is, apparently, run between the fingers and

left hanging outside. We say, *apparently*, for in fact it is dropped inside the hand and the end of the other bunch of needles is allowed to show outside. One of the colored threads is now selected and tied to the loose end that belongs to the threaded bunch. When about to "swallow" the needles, the performer takes them, seemingly, with his right hand, but drops them into the left hand and takes those that are under the ring. The

Fig. 152

audience have no suspicion that any change has been made, for they see the colored silk that they suppose was tied to the needles first shown. The needles are put into the performer's mouth, the silk thread dangling outside, and the trick is brought to a conclusion, as described. The points of the needles are ground dull to insure safety in handling them.

The Vanishing Glass of Water:

Like most good tricks there are several ways of doing this. One performer used to present a somewhat similar effect, and while it appeared to be the most simple thing possible, it was really very complicated and suited only for the stage. In the form here offered the trick may be done anywhere, and the necessary apparatus can be prepared by any boy. Here is the effect:

Taking an ordinary glass tumbler, the performer fills it with water and covers it with a silk handkerchief. Then holding it, still covered, by the mouth, he moves it to and fro, from side to side, and finally throws it in the air. Wonderful to relate, the glass has vanished, the handkerchief is empty. The performer's hands have not been near his body, so he could not have concealed it there. There is no trap in the table, into which it might be dropped. Where then has it gone?

With abject apologies, the performer turns his back to the audience, and from his coat-tail pocket takes out the tumbler—or a tumbler—still filled with water.

Some little preparations are necessary for the trick. The pitcher that holds the water has tapering, straight sides and in circumference is smaller at the top than at the bottom. It should be about half as high again as the tumbler, and this latter also should taper, but must be smaller at the bottom than at the top.

Inside the pitcher is a roll of corrugated straw board, such as is commonly used in packing bottles, large enough in diameter to hold the tumbler without letting it fall to the bottom of the pitcher. The roll, in order to hold the tumbler properly, is in the shape of a truncated cone, as shown by the illustration, Fig. 153. Its edges are sewed together, so that it will not break open. A little dab of glue here and there outside the roll, will fasten it to the sides of the pitcher and prevent it falling out. When this is properly in place the pitcher is half-filled with water.

Fig. 153

When about to show the trick, the performer throws the handkerchief *over his left arm. Remember this,* for it is important. In the center of this handkerchief on the lower side is fastened a ring of the same diameter as the top of the tumbler and made of light stiff wire. So that this ring may not, by any possibility, be seen

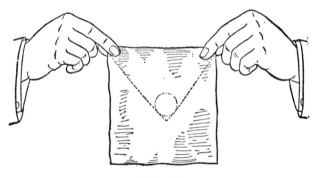

Fig. 154

it is better to place it between a double handkerchief, that is two handkerchiefs of the same pattern sewed edge to edge, and also, so as to form a triangular enclosure,

as shown by the dotted lines in the accompanying drawing. When the handkerchief is held by the upper corners, a slight shake will bring the ring in proper position.

Holding the pitcher by its handle with the second,
third, and fourth fingers and thumb of the left hand,
so as to leave the forefinger free, the performer pours
water into the tumbler, which is held in his right hand.
Both hands are now in use, and as the handkerchief at
this moment must be thrown over the tumbler, the latter
is transferred to the left hand, which with the forefinger
and thumb holds it directly over the mouth of the pitcher.
Artful performer! Taking the handkerchief, he covers
the tumbler and then grasping the wire ring, which the
audience imagine is the top of the tumbler, he lets go
of that vessel and it drops into the pitcher, where it is
caught by the pasteboard cone.

Still holding the ring, the handkerchief is moved away,
supposedly with the glass under it. The pitcher is stood
aside, and all eyes are fixed on the handkerchief. Back
and forth the magician sways it and finally tosses it
in the air, catching it by one end as it falls. The
tumbler has gone!

All that remains to finish the trick, is for the performer
to bring from his coat tail pocket a *second tumbler* partly
filled with water, which has been covered with a little
rubber cap, that is pulled off just a minute before it is
brought in sight.

Should there be any trouble in finding such a cap,
a sheet of thin rubber stretched over the mouth of the
tumbler, and held in place by a stout rubber band will
answer admirably.

Phantasma (by Félicien Trewey):

On the stage is a platform on which stands the framework of a cabinet, as shown at A, Fig. 155. Resting against the wings are five screens, which serve to build up the cabinet. These are fixed in position by means of hooks at the top of four screens; the screen for the top lies flat (Fig. 155). When the performer has shown to

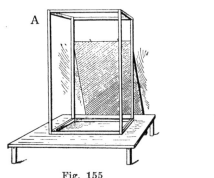

Fig. 155

Fig. 156

the satisfaction of the audience that no one is concealed about the platform, the screens are brought forward and stood, leaning, against the back of the platform. From there they are lifted in place, beginning with the top, followed by the sides, the back, and the front until the cabinet is built up. The front screen is now removed, and a young girl steps out, makes her obeisance to the audience, and bows herself off the stage, leaving the onlookers to guess where she came from.

If we see the trick from the back of the stage, we shall find that the girl is run up through a trap from below the stage and takes a position behind the back screen before it is hung in place. Near the top of this screen is a ring to which she holds and at the bottom is a narrow ledge on which her feet rest. While there, she and the screen are lifted together and the latter is hung in place. That screen is really a door and gives access to the interior of the cabinet. The better to bring the girl in place she is pulled up from beneath the stage by a number of fine steel wires pendant from an overhead bar carried by a counterweight which is led over guide pullies to the back of the stage.

Instead of the rather flat entrance of the girl from the cabinet, as described, the illusion might be worked up to a dramatic situation by having the screens fall away from the cabinet when the performer fires a pistol.

A Traveling Wand:

Before he attempts to exhibit this trick, the performer makes a case of stiff black paper, just large enough to allow his wand to slide in it. It must look as much like the wand as possible and be open at each end. Silver paper at each end, somewhat like the caps or ferrules, generally seen on the ends of a conjurer's wand, add to the illusion. Slipping his wand into this, he tucks both under one arm and comes before his audience. Taking two pieces of thin wrapping paper, each about ten inches wide and four inches longer than his wand, he rolls them in the shape of a tube, and closing the ends of one gives it to some one to hold. Before this, however, he lays both on his table and in doing this (?) accidentally drops his wand on the floor, thus testifying to its solidity, without calling special attention to it. As he picks it up, he pushes it an inch or so out of the case. Then taking one tube he puts his wand inside,

presumably to see that it is the proper length. When
he apparently takes out the wand, he really pulls out
the case, leaving the real wand in the tube, which he
immediately closes and hands to his volunteer assistant.
The imitation wand is put into the other tube and that
he closes. Calling the attention of the audience to the
disposition of the tubes, he says: "The tube that the
gentleman holds is empty, while mine contains the wand.
Now see the result when I cry *Go*." As he says this
he crushes the tube that he holds, affording indisputable
evidence that it is empty, and asks the person who
holds the other to open it, when the wand will be found
inside.

A Mysterious Flight:

The performer shows a canary and announces that it
is about to take an aërial flight. "I trust the aëroplane
will not break down," he says, "for I think a great deal
of this little bird. I call it Wheeler and Wilson, because
it is not a Singer. I was told it could be trained to sing,
but I've trained it over a great many miles, and it can
nary sing." With these few remarks the performer
binds the feet of the bird together. "But," he continues, "as that will not prevent him flying, I shall wrap
him up in this piece of paper. I might add, parenthetically, that this is not a spirit rapping." When
the bird is wrapped up, the package is laid on top of
a soft felt hat. "I shall now load our little traveler into
this pistol," he says, picking up the usual conjurer's
pistol. "You see, the trick is done mainly by concussion,
and this is the concussor. Will you take this weapon,
sir?" he says, addressing one of the audience. "I will

take this sword. When I say *three,* you fire and I'll thrust. Now then, ready! One, two, three!'' Bang goes the pistol! and the same moment the performer makes a thrust with the sword, and there is the bird on the point.

For this experiment, the performer needs: two canaries, nearly alike in size and color; a sword; a pistol with a large barrel; a soft hat; a piece of soft cord; a piece of paper in which to wrap the bird; a dummy packet, resembling the one in which the bird is placed;

Fig. 157

and a table with a padded box at the back, to catch the bird package. The sword is like the well-known card-sword, and in the handle is a spring-barrel on which is rolled the cord that draws the bird, at the proper moment, to the point of the sword. Another style of sword is made with a hollow blade through which runs an elastic cord. See Fig. 157. The bird is pro-

vided with a harness, made of a strip of soft leather,
about three-quarters of an inch in width and three and
one-eighth inches in length. In this are made four cuts,
as shown in Fig. 158. The bird's wings go through two
of these cuts and its feet through the other two. The
ends of the strip meet under the bird's belly and are
sewed together, and at this point is fastened a small ring.
See Fig. 159. To this is attached the cord or the elastic

Fig. 158   Fig. 159

to which the bird is fastened before it is put in the
holder on the hilt of the sword. Care must be taken
when the bird is laid in the holder, to see that its feet lie
next to the inner side of the hilt. If the tension of the
spring-barrel or the elastic is right, neither too strong
nor too weak, no harm can befall the bird as it is
shielded by the leather band, which may remain on the
bird.

In binding the feet of the second bird a soft, cotton
string must be used and be tied loosely. The left hand
takes the bird by its feet, which will cause it to flutter,
and it is at this moment that the feet are tied. The
soft hat is shown to be empty and in going back to his
table the performer drops into it the dummy packet.
The hat is laid, rim down, on the table, and the bird-
packet is placed under it (the dummy packet is already
there), taking care to lift the hat only a trifle. Ad-

dressing the audience the performer says: "Don't imagine that I got rid of the bird when I put it under the hat, but to satisfy you I will place the packet on top of the hat." As he says this, the performer, before raising the hat, draws it toward the back of the table, and as he is about to raise the hat to pick up the dummy, the genuine packet will drop into the padded box. Showing that the hat is empty, he lays it on another table and puts the dummy packet on top of it, as shown in

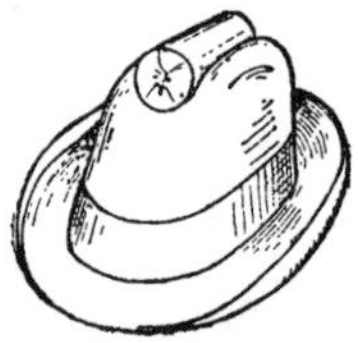

Fig. 160

Fig. 160. Picking up the pistol he loads the dummy packet into the barrel and then hands the weapon to some gentleman with the request that he fires at command. The performer takes the sword, which is already prepared, counts three, and as the pistol is fired thrusts out the sword, releasing the spring-barrel or the elastic, and the bird is seen at the sword's point. The performer is careful to hold the sword horizontally, not pointing upwards. Further, the sword must be held with the arm at full length, and at the moment the spring or the elastic is released, the arm must be drawn back quickly toward the body. This will prevent the forcible impact of the bird against the point of the sword; it will be impossible for any one to see where the bird comes from and it will seem as if it were caught flying in the air. With

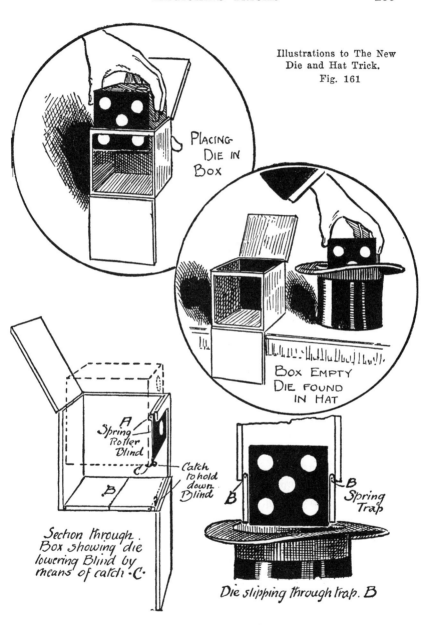

Illustrations to The New
Die and Hat Trick.
Fig. 161

PLACING DIE IN BOX

BOX EMPTY DIE FOUND IN HAT

A
Spring Roller Blind

C

Catch to hold down Blind

B

Section through Box showing die lowering Blind by means of catch ·C·

B

B
Spring Trap

Die slipping through trap. B

proper care the bird will not be injured in the least and may take part in the trick for years.

The dummy packet to be loaded into the pistol ought to be made of flash-paper.

For the explanation of this trick and the diagrams, the editors are indebted to Mr. Ottaker Fischer, of Vienna, an accomplished and ingenious conjurer.

The New Die and Hat Trick (by Will Goldston, London):

Nearly every conjurer has at some time either used or seen the old Die Box, with two compartments. The idea is good, but the trick is old.

The box now to be described is quite new and suitable for the stage or the drawing-room.

The performer borrows a hat, shows that it is unprepared and empty, and places it on a table in full view of the audience. A square box is next shown on all sides, and is opened; a lid in front drops down and one on top opens upward; the box may be shown freely, without allowing it to be handled. A solid wooden die of a size that will just fit inside the box is handed out for examination; then both lids of the box are opened and the die is dropped in at the top, so that the audience see it plainly. Then the box is closed. The performer waves his hand over it and commands the die to leave the box. This is opened at once and is found to be empty. Then the hat is handed to its owner, and to his surprise the die is seen inside of it.

The accompanying illustrations show that the box is fitted with a spring roller curtain A, at the front opening. An eye is sewed to the back of this curtain so that when the die is dropped into the box it lowers the cur-

Illustrations to A Girl produced from Empty Boxes.
Fig. 162

tain. This has the same number of spots painted on it that are on the side of the die presented to the audience as it drops into the box. A hook, C, catches the eye of the curtain at the bottom of the box, and holds it until the performer releases it. The bottom of the box B, which is held over the inside of the hat when exhibiting the trick, has a spring trap which allows the die to drop into the hat, the front lid hiding this. The illustrations, Fig. 161, which Mr. Goldston sends are so clearly drawn that there ought to be no difficulty in following the details of the trick.

A Girl Produced from Empty Boxes (by Will Goldston):

Two large boxes are standing, side by side, on a platform, when the scene opens. The sides, back, and front of each box, together with the lid, are hinged together, and are kept in place by spring catches, and may be opened out flat. Taking one box at a time, the performer spreads it out on the stage. When the audience is satisfied that there is nothing concealed, the boxes are replaced on the platform; the small box is dropped into the large one, and the boxes are closed. Immediately after the lids fly open and a young woman springs out. See Fig. 162.

At the beginning the girl, in a crouching position, is concealed behind the small box as shown in Fig. 163. When the large box is replaced on the platform, after the performer has opened it out for the audience it is stood close to the other which gives the girl an opportunity to pass behind it and to enter it through a trap. The bottom of the small box is of black paper instead of wood, enabling the girl to go through it, as it is dropped

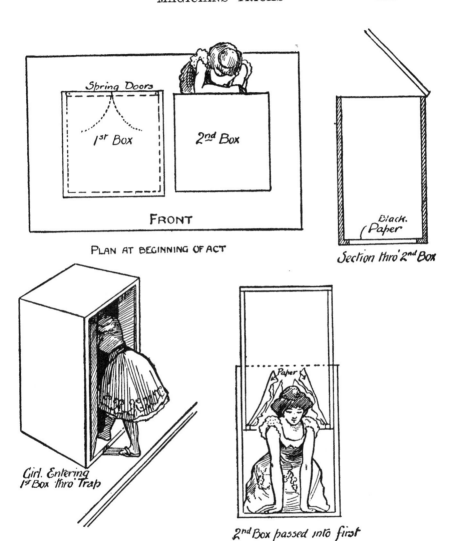

Illustrations to A Girl produced from Empty Boxes.
Fig. 163

into the large box. The trick is very effective and a favorite with some of the best conjurers.

The Nest of Boxes:

On the stage stands a chair with a cane back. This back is lined with a piece of stuff of the same material and color as that of the curtain or screen at the back of the stage.

Hanging on the back of the chair is a bag the mouth of which is held open by a ring of tempered wire that does not bend readily, and lying over the back of the chair is an open newspaper. From the "flies," or the ceiling, hangs a nest of four boxes, the outer one being about 12 x 14 x 20 inches. In the smallest or innermost box is a small, white rabbit. Around its neck is tied one end of a ribbon, six or seven inches long, and on the other end is a snap-hook, such as is used on the end of a watch-chain. In closing the boxes, care is taken always to keep this ribbon hanging outside, so that when the largest box is reached at least two inches of ribbon will remain outside. Fastened to the front side of the box, over which the ribbon hangs, is a small hook. This side is kept away from the audience. Finally, the boxes have small holes bored in many places, so as to give the rabbit air. These preliminaries are, of course, arranged before the curtain goes up, and the audience knows nothing of them.

When the performer comes on the stage, he begins by asking for a watch, and as he steps down among his audience to borrow one, he stops before some gentleman and, excusing himself, takes from under the man's coat a rabbit, exactly like, in size and color, the one in the box.

This rabbit the performer has concealed under the front
of his waistcoat. As he steps up to the man from whom
he is to take it, he seizes the lapel of the man's coat
with his left hand and, stooping slightly, takes the hidden
rabbit with his right hand, thrusts it under the man's
coat for an instant and withdraws it almost immediately,
holding the rabbit high in the air. Then he borrows
the watch, and returns to the stage. When the stage
is reached, the rabbit is placed on the seat of the chair.
Turning toward the audience, the performer comments
on the watch:

"I see our watch is a second-hand affair. Most
watches to-day are made that way." Here he looks at
the watch. "I've seen better—now don't misunderstand
me—I've seen better tricks done with watches than with
any other small article. Now *watch* this." He throws
the watch in the air once or twice, and finally makes a
motion of throwing, but retains it in his hand, holding it
there by clasping the ring between the thumb and forefinger, and as he stands with his right side to the audience, and only the back of the hand is seen, they imagine
it has disappeared. Afterward he slips the watch into
his vest pocket.

"Now for the rabbit," he says. Picking it up by its
ears, he remarks: "Plucky little creature! It never com-
plains, no matter how much you hurt its feelings. An
American, I should say from its pluck. No Welsh rabbit
about that." Standing at one side of the chair, the
rabbit in his left hand, he opens the newspaper over the
back of the chair, and laying the rabbit on it draws the
front of the paper toward the left hand so as to cover
the rabbit, and as he reaches down as if to take up the

overhanging part of the sheet at the back of the chair, the rabbit is dropped into the bag. See Fig. 164. The paper is gathered up in the shape of a bundle, so as to appear as if it held the rabbit, the ends are twisted, and the parcel laid carefully on the seat of the chair. "Now

Fig. 164

for the crucial moment," exclaims the magician. Picking up the bundle he moves it three times toward the box, and then suddenly smashing the ends together throws it on the floor. The box is lowered, and, while the eyes of the audience are fixed on it, the performer takes the

watch from his pocket, and as the box nears the table he
reaches out, as if to steady it, and hangs the watch on the
hook that is on the front side of the box, which is turned

Fig. 165

toward the back of the stage. The boxes are opened and
piled one on top of the other, and when the last one
is reached the watch is taken from where it hangs and
hung on the end of the dangling ribbon. See Fig. 165.

The last box is opened, and as the rabbit is taken out the ribbon is twisted once or twice around its neck. The squirming creature is then carried down to the owner of the borrowed watch, who identifies his property.

When this trick is exhibited on the stage the performer generally ends it in a very striking way. When he returns to the stage he places the rabbit on a large table at the back of which is an open bag or box. Picking up a pistol, he stands behind the table, his right side turned in the direction of the audience. Catching hold of the rabbit, he tosses it twice in the air, and the third time makes a motion as if to throw it, and at the same moment discharges the pistol. The audience are startled by the report, and before they recover from the shock the rabbit has been thrown into the bag at the back of the table. The rabbit has, apparently, disappeared in midair, and the performer walks toward the footlights bowing his acknowledgments of the applause he is sure to receive. The trick is not yet quite done. Suddenly stopping, the performer smiles and points at a man in the audience, some one seated near the stage. "Ah! sir," he says, "you are trying to play a trick on me, I see. You have something hidden under your coat." Hurrying toward the man on whom all eyes are now turned, the performer pulls open the innocent man's coat as if searching for something. Abandoning the breast, however, after a moment, the performer runs his right arm down the neck of the coat. This gives him the opportunity to get close to the man, and as his (the performer's) body is thus concealed he takes with his left hand a rabbit from a large pocket in the tail of his coat, and thrusts it up the back of the man's coat as far as possible. "Will you help me, sir?" the performer asks some one seated near; and as the audience look at the new assistant, the performer reaches down the back of the first man's coat and pulls out the rabbit. It is not very polite to the rabbit, but as for the performer—well, the audience applaud and shout with laughter. Of course, the performer apologizes to the man who has been somewhat roughly handled.

There is another popular form of the Nest of Boxes, which to an audience seems almost identical with the one just described, but is entirely different in its manipulation.

A large box hangs from a support of some kind from the moment the curtain goes up. When the performer reaches the trick in his program, he goes down among the audience holding in his right hand, by one end, a little stick, the wand of the conjurer, and asks for the loan of four or five finger-rings from some ladies. As they are offered he extends the wand with the request that the rings be slipped on it, "so that I do not handle them." When he has borrowed the required number he returns to the stage, and on his way, grasping the other end of the wand with his left hand, he tilts the borrowed rings into it and allows a number of brass rings, which have been concealed in his right hand, to take their place on the stick. These rings he drops on a plate from the stick. The plate lies on the stage near the footlights, and directly under it is a hole. See Fig. 166. The performer immediately picks up the plate with his left hand, and as he stoops to do this he drops the borrowed rings into the hole in the stage, where they are received by one of his assistants, who hurries off to place them in the little box in which they are finally found

Fig. 166

Picking up an old-fashioned horse-pistol,—which he informs the audience was originally a Colt's,—the performer drops one of the rings into the barrel and rams it down. He pretends to find the next ring too large and batters it with a hammer, to the delight of every one in the audience except the owners of the rings. "There, that will go in now," he says, and rams it down. So he continues, until all the rings are in the pistol. Pointing at the box that is hanging in full sight, he remarks, "This is one of my aims in life. Let us hope it will succeed," and bang! goes the pistol. As the barrel of this particular pistol is disconnected from the hammer and the trigger, merely a cap explodes, but that answers every purpose.

While the attention of the audience was directed to the performer during the loading of the rings into the pistol, a small table was run on the stage from the wings. In the top of this table is an opening of a size to admit a small box, which rests on a shelf under the table top. When in position, the top of this box comes flush with the top of the table. When the performer takes down the box at which he fired the pistol, he places it on this table, unlocks it, for effect, and takes from it a second box. So he goes on, taking one box from another until he has three or four stacked up. Finally he reaches *a box that is bottomless.* This he places over the opening in the table top, unlocks the box, and reaching down takes up the box that is in the opening and walks toward the footlights, box in hand. He unlocks this and finds still another box which, when opened, reveals the borrowed rings, each attached to a small nosegay. He carries these to the owners, who identify their property.

Returning to his stage, the performer picks up a champagne-bottle, with the remark: "As some slight return for your kindness in lending me your rings, I am going to ask you to have a glass of wine with me. What shall it be? Anything you please. My bottle here will supply all kinds." Just then he pretends to hear a call from the audience. "What is that? One of the rings has not been returned? Too bad, too bad! But I'll see about it after I have satisfied the thirst of our friends here. Now then, what shall it be? Wine, brandy, whisky, Old Crow, forty-rod, Jersey lightning, instant death? What you like." Holding a tiny wine-glass, filled with water, in one hand and the bottle in the other, he asks the first person he comes to what he will have. Pretending to hear a call for water, he says, "Water? Certainly, sir; pure Adam's ale," as he goes through the motions of filling the glass, but covering the mouth of the bottle with his fingers so that nothing comes out. "The real article, is it not?" and he throws what is left on the floor. He passes rapidly from one to another and gives each one, serving, perhaps, half a dozen, some sweetened whisky—the same to all, no matter what is asked for, but calling out the name of a different liquor each time. He serves only a sip at a time, for it is only the neck of the bottle, which is plugged at the bottom, that contains the liquor. When through with this farce, the performer returns to the stage and, calling for a hammer and a tray, breaks the bottle, and behold! inside is a wriggling little guinea-pig with a ribbon round its neck, to which is attached the missing ring and a tiny bouquet.

For a simple trick nothing is more effective than this one. To prepare the bottle, the bottom is first removed. This may be done by tapping it gently with a hammer or it may be cut off by a glass-worker. In the first case, which is the better, a false bottom of wood or tin is used; in the second, the bottle is cemented together with a little shellac varnish, colored with lampblack. Here and there a hole is drilled in the sides of the bottle to give air to the pig. While the bottom is off, a plug is fitted tightly inside the bottle near the neck, and melted paraffin is poured over it to prevent any leak. It is in the space between this plug and the mouth of the bottle that the liquor is held. In the lower part of the bottle the guinea-pig, with the ring attached to it, is placed by the performer's assistant, who closes the bottle and hands it to the performer.

In a later method of preparing the bottle much time, trouble and expense are saved. The upper part of the bottle, including the neck and about a quarter of the body, is of copper. Inside, a little below the neck, is a solid bottom, and to this is soldered the metal cover of a fruit-preserving glass jar (the kind known as a "Mason Jar"). Through this cover, leading to the outside of the metal bottle, where it ends in a hole, is a metal tube, to afford air to the guinea-pig. Into this cover, the jar itself, which is painted black inside, is screwed. It fits well up into the metal body and completes its form. With a wine label on the outside, its appearance is most deceptive. The pig is put into the jar before it is screwed in place. In exhibiting the trick the jar is broken with a hammer. To replace it is less than half the cost of a champagne bottle, and is no trouble.

A Floral Tribute:

The performer borrows a man's hat and places it on his table; then he asks the ladies to lend him four or five rings. These he ties with a bit of ribbon and hands to some lady, asking her to hold them.

Then he breaks an egg into a tin cup, and going again to the one who holds the rings extends his open left hand and, at the same time, his right hand, in which is the cup.

"Will you, madam," he says, "be good enough to drop the rings in here."

Naturally, the lady drops the rings into the cup.

"No, no, madam," the performer cries, starting back as if in astonishment, "not in the cup! In my hand. However, it is too late now. How shall I get the rings out?"

Returning to his stage, he pours the egg and the rings from the cup into the hat, which is on the table.

"Who lent me the hat?" he asks. "You, sir? Then I shall get you to help me fish the rings from this mess."

Going to the owner of the hat, the performer turns the so-called "mess" on to his head, whereupon, to the surprise and admiration of the audience, there is seen on top of the man's head a lovely wreath of flowers to which are attached the borrowed rings.

When the performer borrows the hat he receives it with his left hand, and takes it to his table, where he lays it on its side. On his way to the table, his back being to the audience, his left hand approaches the left lapel of his coat and opens it a trifle, while he releases with his right hand from under the left breast of his coat, close to the sleeve, a small wreath of flowers which is concealed there hanging from a hook. An excellent hook for this purpose is sold for use on a lady's dress. It has broad, rounded points that will not tear, and at its back is a safety pin. As he takes it out, he brings the hat close to his breast and thrusts his right hand, with the wreath, into it. Should the movement be noticed at all, it will merely appear as if the hat were being passed from one hand to the other. As the wreath drops into the hat, the performer seizes the brim with his right thumb inside the hat, the fingers outside, and holds it stationary till he reaches the table; the left hand drops to his side.

Before he goes to borrow the rings the performer holds concealed in his right hand four cheap, gilt rings, which he takes from a hook attached to his trousers' leg and hidden by his coat tail; under his left arm is his wand, which he has picked up from his table. As he approaches the ladies, from whom he is to borrow the rings, he takes the wand from under his arm and slips the imitation rings over one end, keeping them covered with his hand. As the rings are offered to him he receives them as explained in the second part of The Nest of Boxes.

Putting the fingers of his left hand into the lower pocket of his waistcoat, he leaves the rings there and takes out a piece of bright colored ribbon. With this he ties together the dummy rings, hands them to a lady who is seated at a distance from the owners of the borrowed rings, and requests her to guard them carefully between her two hands.

On his table are the egg and the cup. Returning to the stage, the performer breaks the egg into the cup, and going to the lady who holds the rings induces her, as already told, to drop them into the cup.

This cup is double or, rather, there are two cups one inside the other. In the inner one the bottom is not at the extreme end, but is set up about an inch and a half, as shown by the dotted lines in the illustration A, Fig. 167, so as to leave a space at the lower end, and there is a slight cut there to allow the air to escape. The upper edge of this cup is turned outward so that it will rest on B, and may be easily lifted out.

With the rings, apparently, in the cup, the performer returns to his table, and as he turns the hat over on its crown, drops into it the borrowed rings, which he has

taken from his pocket.   Pretending to measure the depth
of the hat he lowers the cup into it for just a moment,
and, as he does so, leaves B. inside.   This he does in a
half hesitating way, as if uncertain what to do, and then,
as if fully decided, lifts out the cup and pours the contents of A into B, though apparently into the hat.   At

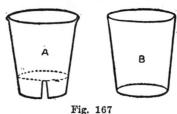

Fig. 167

the last moment as A disappears for a fraction of time,
it is fitted again into B, and the two cups are brought
out together.   As if some of the egg is on his fingers, the
performer pretends to wipe them on the hat, and while
doing so attaches the borrowed rings to tiny hooks or
bits of wire on the wreath.   After this, he hurries to the
owner of the hat, and turns the wreath and the rings
out on his head.

When presenting the trick in a private room or a
small hall it is advisable to have the bottom of the cup
B covered with a thin lining of cork, so as to deaden the
sound made by the rings when they are poured from one
cup to the other.

A Curious Omelet:

One of the best tricks of the old time conjurer was
that in which he baked a cake or a pudding in a hat.   It
always created a laugh—generally at the owner of the

hat—and was, consequently, popular. The trick we are about to explain while much the same is widely different. How they differ may best be told by describing the latest version. The performer begins by borrowing a silk hat, or, as he says, "a tall hat or no hat at all." "I want to show you," he continues, "the most improved method of cooking, without range, gas or oil stove or even a chafing dish. I would especially direct the attention of young unmarried ladies and of bachelors, young and old, to the advantages of this method. For my own part, I am delighted with it. Let me give you an ocular demonstration of what may be done with it, for example, let us try an omelet."

He deliberately breaks an egg and drops it visibly and unmistakably into the hat. This he follows with flour from a dredging-box and salt from a salt-cellar. "Don't forget the salt," he says, "if you would have a palatable omelet." Finally, he beats up the mixture with a spoon, and then, of a sudden, there is a burst of flame from the interior of the hat. Clapping a plate on the opening of the hat, the performer turns it over, and produces—not an omelet, but a large and beautiful bouquet.

The apparatus for this trick is not at all complicated, and if our readers will follow our directions carefully, they need have no trouble in preparing it. It consists of a tin cylinder, four and a half inches in height and five inches in diameter. It is open at both ends, but in the middle there is a partition that divides it into an upper and lower part, as in A and B, Fig. 168. This partition also forms a bottom for both parts, A and B, depending on the position of the cylinder, whether A or B is uppermost. In the center of the partition is a hole, C, an inch and a quarter in diameter, which is crossed by a small bolt, D. Secured to the bottom of A by four upright pieces of spring brass that clamp it at different points, is a tin box, E, Fig. 169, which

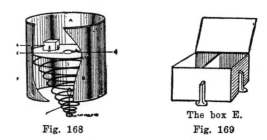

Fig. 168   The box E.
               Fig. 169

has a tightly-fitting hinged cover.* So much for part A. Securely soldered to the bottom of B is one end of a slightly tapering spiral spring, F, measuring four and a quarter inches in diameter at the larger end and four inches and a half in length. The smaller end of the spring is soldered to a disk of strong tin, H, that is three inches in diameter. One end of a stout wire, J, three inches long, is soldered to the center of this disk, and the other end is twisted into a ring. The ring end passes through the hole C in the partition and the bolt, D, is run through the ring, thus closing up the spring and holding it safely. The cylinder inside and out and both sides of the partition are painted a dull black. At three-quarters of an inch below the edge of A, around the edge of the disk H, and around the cylinder at a point in B just below the partition, tiny holes are

* The drawing of this box, E. Fig. 169, is greatly out of proportion, for the original is a very small box.

punched to admit of a needle being passed in and out for sewing. The work on the cylinder being finished, the outside is covered with chints that is printed with designs of bright-colored flowers *on a dark ground.* Good paste with a few strong stitches will do this work. When that is done, the spiral spring, F, is also covered with a bag, made of the same chints, that extends from the bottom of the partition in B to the disk H; this should be sewed on. Finally, on the outside of the cylinder and also on the bag are sewed muslin artificial flowers and leaves, covering every spot, so as to make what will look like a large, handsome bouquet. When the spiral spring is pushed up inside of B and fastened by passing the bolt through the ring of J, a compact package is made that will easily go into a hat, while on withdrawing the bolt we have quite a presentable bouquet.

One more article that is needed is a small iron spoon. This has a wooden handle modeled to look like the metal handle of a spoon and covered with silver leaf. With the spring brought up and fastened in place by the bolt, and the "bouquet" properly fixed the performer is ready to begin his trick. Prior to ringing up the curtain, he sticks part of a wax match in the center of a small portion of red fire, and then wraps the whole in black tissue paper, letting the business end of the match stick through. This little packet he lays on his table where he can put his hand on it. The bouquet is laid on the shelf back of the table. When the performer goes to borrow the hat, he holds in his hand, bunched up and concealed by his wand a large silk handkerchief. He receives the hat with his left hand and bringing it near his face, as if to read the maker's name, his right hand passes over the mouth of the hat and drops the handkerchief inside. Going to his table he stands the hat on it and begins to tell what he is about to do, as already narrated. Passing to the back of his table he picks up the hat with his left hand and looks into it. "Ah," he says, "the gentleman has left something here." He shakes out the handkerchief, pressing his left thumb on some part of it as it falls, so as to half-stop it for the moment, and at the same time his right hand takes up the "bouquet." The mouth of the hat is turned down, and near the top of the table. The performer pushes the handkerchief, that is now out, with the brim of the hat, toward the front of the table. Leaning over as if to look more closely at the handkerchief, the hat is, naturally, drawn toward the back edge of the table for a second, and in that second he claps the "bouquet" into it. If done deliberately, carefully, and not too hurriedly, no one is the wiser. Of course the part B goes in first. On the table stand an empty dredging-box, supposed to contain flour, a glass salt-cellar, filled with white paper, a plate with an egg on it, and a dinner-knife. Deliberately putting a hand inside the hat, the performer opens the box E, then picking up the egg, he breaks it with the knife, and drops it into the box. He again puts his hand into the hat and closes the box, and as he brings his hand out, wipes his fingers, apparently, on the brim of the hat. Then he pretends to shake in flour and salt, and finally calls for a spoon. His right hand rests for a second on the table, and picks up the packet of red fire. Just then his assistant enters with a spoon on a plate. The bowl of the spoon has been held in a gas light till it is almost at a white heat. Taking it by the wooden handle, he pretends to stir up the omelet and laying the red fire inside the box E, touches the head of the match with the hot spoon, and the fire flames up. "That's cheerful," says the performer. "Everyone enjoys that except the owner of the hat, he does not see it in the same light." When the fire burns out, he closes E, carefully draws the bolt D, which causes the spring F to extend, and claps a plate over the mouth of the hat which he then turns over. He slowly lifts the hat, and reveals the bouquet, so that all may see and admire it. Throughout the trick a running fire of jokes and small talk should be kept up. The trick is not difficult, but requires practice to carry it out well and also good acting.

The Coffee Trick:

A trick always popular with the professional conjurer is that known as the "Coffee Trick," though some "highfalutin" title, as, for instance, "Marabout Mocha," is better for a program. It has the advantage, too, of not conveying any idea of what the trick is to be. The trick is as suitable for the drawing-room as for the stage, and may be done easily with a little practice. Remember, *with a little practice*, for, like everything in conjuring, not only a little but sometimes a great deal of practice is necessary if the performer desires to do his tricks with ease and skill and so as to bewilder his audience.

When about to present this trick the performer has on a table three large wooden boxes, a large goblet-shaped glass jar, and two German silver "shakers" or cups, such as are used in mixing the lemon-juice, ice, etc., for a glass of lemonade. In one of the boxes is a quantity of bran, in another some pieces of chopped-up white paper, and in the third a similar lot of blue paper. These, with two pieces of black velvet, each about nine inches square, and a paper cylinder, are all that *appear* to be used in the trick. Picking up one shaker, the performer fills it with white paper, and immediately pours its contents back into the box. Again he dips the shaker into the box, and, with a shoveling motion, fills it and stands it on a table so that everyone may see it. The other shaker he fills in the same way, but with the blue paper. Finally, the glass jar is filled with bran and stood on a table by itself. Over one shaker is spread one of the velvet squares and on top of it is placed a small, round, metal plate. The other shaker is covered with the second velvet square, but without any metal plate.

"Remember," says the performer, "this cup is filled with white paper, and that one with blue"; and pulling the velvet piece off one cup he pours from it into a small pitcher about a pint of milk. "The milk of human kindness, as extracted from the daily press." Removing the metal plate and the velvet from the second cup, he pours from it into the first cup "steaming Mocha coffee. No grounds for complaint." Picking up the paper cylinder, he drops it over the upper part of the glass jar, and lifting it up almost immediately, it is found that the bran is gone and the jar is filled with lump sugar.

It is a showy trick which is generally followed by applause, that sweetest of music to a performer.

In each box of paper is a duplicate shaker, one filled with milk, the other with coffee. Fitted into the mouth of each shaker is a shallow metal saucer, the edges flaring out so as to rest on the mouth of the cup. At one point on the edge of each saucer is soldered a semicircle of stiff wire about the size of a dime, so that the performer may easily grasp it. On each saucer is glued some bits of the paper with which the shaker is supposed to be filled. These shakers stand upright in the box, in such position that the wire piece of the saucer will be toward the performer when he is ready to remove the velvet cover. As he shovels the paper into the shaker he leaves that one in the box, grasps the other filled with milk or coffee, and brings it out, some of the loose bits of paper clinging round the top. These he brushes off carelessly, and in doing so, when necessary, adjusts the shaker so that the wire finger-piece will be in the proper position. In covering the shakers the performer takes hold of the velvet covers so that the thumbs are under the cover and the fingers on top, and with these he catches hold of the projecting finger-piece, lifts up the saucers and draws them off, dropping them instantly into a padded box or a bag fastened at the back of the table.

As the glass jar is transparent it follows that a mere saucer of bran in its mouth would not do, so resort is had to another device. A hollow shape of tin, slightly tapering, that fits loosely in the jar is used. The larger end, which is the top, is slightly larger in circumference than the top of the goblet, and is closed while the bottom is open. Bran is glued over the outside of the shape and some loose bran is spread over the top. The shape is filled with lump sugar, placed inside a second jar and stood inside the box of bran. When the first jar is put into the box, ostensibly to be filled, the performer exchanges it for the second. This he takes out and shows it apparently filled with bran. It is covered with the paper cylinder, which goes on loosely, and in removing this the performer grasps the overlapping top, through the paper, lifts out the tin shape and the sugar falls into the jar. As the shape is taken out, the performer's hand passes carelessly over the box of bran, into which the shape is dropped. At almost the same moment the paper is crumbled up, and tossed into the audience. The trick is so neatly done, and is, withal, so simple, that he must be a bungler, indeed, who cannot deceive even a clever audience.

As a pretty wind-up for the trick we would suggest the following: Have a large cup, in the shape of a coffee-cup, made of tin and painted white so as to resemble china. The inside of the cup is divided in two by a partition. At one side of this partition, in the bottom of the cup, is cut a small hole. The other side of the partition is filled with paper "snow," that is, tiny bits of white paper.

Set the cup in a *very deep* saucer, which may also be of japanned tin. After the performer has produced the coffee, he pours out some for himself, using the trick cup. Of course, the coffee is poured into that side of the cup that has the hole in the bottom. The result is, the coffee runs out into the saucer, but the audience cannot see this. When the cup is apparently full, the performer walks down to the footlights, cup in hand, indulges in a little pantomime to convey the idea that he is about to drink the health of the audience, and then, suddenly, and to their astonishment, blowing into the cup, throws the contents of the cup toward them—and instead of coffee it is only a cloud of little bits of white paper. It is amusing to see the startled look on the faces nearest the performer; and the trick, as we have said, makes a pretty ending to the evening's performance.

A Second Method. In this form of the Coffee Trick the performer introduces a cylindrical vase, A, of polished, not japanned, heavy tin, Fig. 170, measuring from

Fig. 170

its top to the bottom of the base about fifteen inches in height and four inches in diameter. It is entirely without preparation, as may be seen when it is handed out for examination. Accompanying this is a cylinder of embossed leather, lined with heavy manilla paper, to give it a body. It is made to go easily over A, for which it is intended as a cover, and is open at both ends. On a table toward the rear of the stage are two lighted candles in candlesticks.

Before beginning the trick, the performer allows both vase and cover to be examined. Then he stands the cover on his table and proceeds to put some cotton wool from a box into the vase. This done, he puts on the cover for a moment, and on removing it, stoops over and breathes into the mouth of the vase. Instantly the cotton wool bursts into flame and almost as rapidly goes out. Picking up a tray on which there are cups and saucers, the performer pours from the vase fragrant, boiling coffee.

This trick differs in most respects from the first version. The top of the conjurer's table is covered with a black

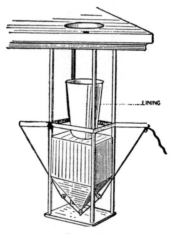

Fig. 171

baize or velvet; about seven inches from the front and six from one end is cut a round hole, four and a half inches in diameter; this is not discernible by the audience as everything below it is of a dull black. Directly under this hole is a sort of elevator, Fig. 171, made of four upright rods, and between these runs a grooved block, which is pulled up and down by a string on pulleys, moved by an assistant behind the scenes or, if preferred, by a simple clockwork controlled by the performer. The top of this block, at the center, is hollowed out to the depth of half an inch, and in this hollow stands a tin cylinder, filled with hot coffee. This cylinder, which is to be a lining for the vase A, must fit tightly in A at the mouth, but the bottom tapers slightly and is rounded, as shown in the illustration, so that it may go into the vase easily. The outside of this cylinder as well as the elevator and block are painted a dull black. Around the inside of the mouth of this cylinder-lining some loose guncotton is fastened by fine iron wire.

When the performer is putting the cotton wool into the vase, he stands the cover directly over the hole in the table, and in the brief moment it is there the lining is run up inside of it. Then he picks up the cover, and with it, the lining, covers A, leaving the lining inside, thus pushing down what little cotton wool is there to the bottom of A. He lifts off the cover and drops it on the floor. All that remains is to fire the guncotton. For this purpose, he has palmed in his left hand a metal disk about the size of a half-dollar, and to the center of this is brazed (not fastened by soft solder) a bit of brass tubing, an inch in length and not larger in diameter than an ordinary leadpencil. Into this tubing is stuck a piece of wax taper. After the vase A is placed on the table and before it is covered, the conjurer moves the candles nearer to the front, as if to get more light. The first candle he picks up with his left hand and as

he changes its position gently blows on the light; as it
flickers, he places his right hand around it as if to shield
it from the draft. The second candle he picks up with
his right hand (his left side must be toward the audience) and repeating his action with the first, shields it
with the left hand, which gives him an opportunity to
light the taper. When he stoops over the vase, to
breathe on it, his open hands naturally go up one on
each side of it, and just a touch of the lighted taper
fires the guncotton. It burns out in a second; he pours
the coffee into the cups and serves it out to his audience.

The Growth of Flowers:

No prettier trick was ever presented to an audience
than this. It was originally introduced in London by
Colonel Stodare, and was brought to this country in 1867
by Joseph M. Hart, better known as M. Hartz, the Man
with "The Devil of a Hat," and later was invariably
included in Kellar's program. In exhibiting this trick
the performer uses two tables draped nearly to the
floor (in the original production three tables were used,
but Kellar used two only). On the top of each is
a circular piece of metal supported on light wire legs.
Attention is first called to a cardboard cone open at
both ends, and positively empty as the audience may
readily see. Besides the tables and the cone there are
two flowerpots, made of pasteboard, to resemble the
common red clay pots. These are filled with sand.
They are placed on the little metal stands that are on
the table, and as there is considerable space between
the top of the stand and the top of the table it does

away with the suspicion that might arise that the flowers came from below. The performer covers one of the pots with the cone and on raising it a bud is seen just above the sand. He covers it a second time and this time when he raises the cone a beautiful bush of flowers is in the pot. The second pot is now placed on a small table, without drapery of any kind, that stands nearer the audience. This is covered with the cone and when that is again lifted the second pot contains a rose bush fully fifteen inches high.

The average layman when asked for an explanation of the trick generally suggests that it is done by a spring. A very natural explanation for, as we all know, Spring brings up the flowers. This case, however, is somewhat different, as our readers will now learn. Besides the cone that the audience see, two other cones play an important part. These fit one in the other, and both, eventually, go into the visible cone. Behind each table, near the point where the drapery ends, there is a shelf. On this shelf stands a plant, covered with a cone that fits inside Cone No. 1. The base of this plant is a moss-covered wooden disk that goes into the mouth of a flower-pot. From this disk a green cord ending in a ring leads up to the top of its cone, where the ring goes over a flat hook inside the cone and near the top. Picking up the cone that the audience have just examined the performer holds it with both hands, one at each end, and covers the first flower pot. As he does this he drops from the top a rose bud that is fastened to a small, loaded spike, so that it will be sure to fall, right side up, into the sand. This spike he takes out of his vest pocket or from his table, and holds between the second and third fingers of his right hand which goes inside the top of the cone, as he is about to cover the pot. Now comes the most important move of the trick. The performer stands with his right side to the table, and lifting the cone to show the bud, he lets it drop in the most natural way over the cone that contains the first bush. Seizing the two cones with his fingers inside, he passes back of the table and stepping out on its right (as it faces the audience) he carries with him the loaded cones in his right hand and the flower pot in his left, to show the bud. This flower pot he replaces on its table. Then he covers it with the cone and releasing the ring inside the second cone, lifts off the two cones, revealing the bush standing in the pot. As he lifts the cones he drops them over the third cone, that is back of the second table, and almost immediately passes back of the table, to the front, carrying the three cones with the second bush. It might seem as if the audience would notice this movement, but it is so natural and the cone is out of sight for such a brief moment, that nine out of ten people in the audience would declare, if asked, that they had not lost sight of it for a second.

Going now to the undraped table on which he stands the second pot, the performer covers that and as he raises the cone he turns the mouth momentarily toward the audience so that they see it is empty. The attention of the audience, however, is so fixed on the second bush, that they hardly give a glance at the cone.

Several attempts have been made to improve this trick, so as to do away with the draped tables. One of these is worth mentioning on account of its ridiculous ending. The performer who attempted this improvement decided

that he would have the flowers run up from below into
the cone, as it rested for a moment on the stage. The
idea proved better than the execution, for on the first
night when the performer gracefully rested the cone
on the stage a trap opened *on the opposite side,* and a
bush was thrust up in full sight of the amused audience.

A real improvement on the trick was devised by that
graceful and brilliant performer, Mr. Karl Germain,
whose retirement from the stage is regretted by all who
have had the pleasure of witnessing his performance.

In his version, a single uncovered flower pot stood
on a table. Standing near it Germain began to fan
the pot, when gradually there appeared to spring from
it a few leaves. These were followed by buds, and then
the plant increased in height until it was fifteen to
eighteen inches above the top of the pot. That the flowers on it were real there could be no doubt, for the performer cut them off and distributed them to the ladies
in the audience.

Before beginning the trick proper, the performer
passes around for examination a flower pot filled with
earth. This pot is in two parts, an inner and an outer
part. The outer is a mere shell, without a bottom. The
inner, which contains the earth, is held in place by two
bayonet catches or in any way that the ingenuity of
the performer may suggest. When he returns to his
stage, he rests the pot for a moment on a side table,
while he turns to speak to the audience. As he stands
the pot on the table he releases the catches and the
inner part sinks, of its own weight, through a trap.
The outer part or shell of the pot the performer finally
places on his center table in a place that is hollowed

out to receive the bottom part, which stands over an opening. Under this table is a tube leading up to the opening in the table top. Inside this tube is the bush fastened to a solid base, and at the proper time it is pulled up into the pot either by clock work or by cords leading off to a concealed assistant. The center table is of the three-legged variety, but is shaped so that all three legs may be seen from any part of the house. It is, in fact, almost a round frame with a triangular shaped top. The space between the legs is filled in with black velvet and back of the table hangs a handsome bright plush curtain, the lower part of which, from a distance of about four and a half feet above the stage, is of black velvet. The result is that the audience imagine that they see under the table. The effect is somewhat similar to that produced by a "Sphinx table," but requires fewer curtains and does away with the danger of breaking expensive glasses.

The Secret of Rope Tying:

Since the days of the Davenport Brothers many conjurers have exhibited rope tying. To shake off the most intricate of these ties is never very difficult, for it is only a matter of bringing a strain on the rope until one hand is free—which is soon done—and then the rest is plain sailing. But it is very different where one allows oneself to be tied tightly with rope, then frees oneself so as to perform seemingly impossible "stunts," and afterward is found tied up as at first. That is what Mr. Kellar used to do. How he did it he never told us, and yet

The Kellar Tie, we firmly believe, is just what is here-

inafter described. The performer asks two of the audience to assist him in the trick. To these gentlemen he
offers a piece of sash cord two or three yards long and
when they have pronounced it strong and perfect, he
extends his left arm and requests them to tie the rope
around the wrist, knotting it on the front of the wrist.
When they have the rope tied in a satisfactory way the
performer requests the gentlemen to stand slightly in
advance of him, one at his right, the other at his left,
and each to take hold of an end of the rope. As
they do this he extends his left arm, the hand open with
the palm upward and the rope on that side passing

Fig. 172

between his first and second fingers, as shown in Fig. 172.
Then the assisting men pull, and when they are satisfied the performer puts his hands behind his back. As

Fig. 173

his left hand goes to his back the fingers on each side
of the rope give it a twist (See Fig. 173) and lays it on
the wrist with the bight of this twist pointing up the

arm. Almost simultaneously the back of the right wrist
is laid on the rope and pressing on it conceals the twist.
The ends of the rope are now hanging down one on each
side of the wrist. These the assistants, as requested, pick
up and tie in a good, hard knot on the front of the right
wrist, as in Fig. 174. The performer has gained his
"slack" and is ready to proceed. He asks the gentlemen

Fig. 174

to stand a little in advance of him and close to him at the
sides. As soon as they comply and thus shield him, he
releases the pressure on the rope, the slack falls away,
and he thrusts his right hand out in front of him. The
next moment he puts it back in the loop of the rope, the
left fingers twist the rope again, and the back of the right
wrist and hand holds it pressed tightly against the left.
With practice this is but the work of an instant.

"That's all very fine," we hear some one say, "but
his left wrist is still tied, and yet we have seen a performer take off his coat, when his hands were tied behind his back and the ends of the rope were fastened,
quite out of his reach, to the rounds of the chair on
which he was seated. How was that done?" In this
case he works in a cabinet or behind a screen so that
he may not be seen. As soon as he goes into the cabinet
he frees himself altogether from the rope, which he con-

ceals on his person or somewhere in the cabinet, and substitutes another rope. This rope is prepared in the manner shown in Fig. 175. A A are two hard overhand knots; B is a strong tie. To get these in the right posi-

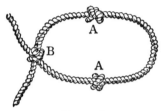

Fig. 175

tions the performer, long before he attempts to exhibit the trick, has his hands tied together loosely. They both point in one direction, but he turns them so that they will be in opposite directions. This will twist the part of the rope that is between the hands and he has the spots where the rope crosses marked with a pencil. Then the rope is untied and taken off his hands. The next move is to tie a hard overhand knot where the two marks are. Then his wrists, both pointing one way, are tied together rather tightly. At this time, the performer twists his hands so that they point in opposite directions and that will bring the knots A A together and show them as if knotted firmly together. The tie on his right hand is an honest tie. With this rope concealed where he can get it easily, he steps into the cabinet, rids himself of the first rope and proceeds to tie the ends of the second to the rounds of the chair so that he could not reach them when seated. Last of all he slips his hands into the loop of the rope, gives it a twist and calls a committee to examine and see that he is securely tied. Then follow raps, bell-ringing and other didoes. Finally, he throws his coat out of the cabinet and calls for "Light!" being careful to tie himself up first. Again his hands are examined and appear to be fairly tied. "Now," says the performer, "will some gentleman hold my coat a moment and place his on my knees?" This is done, the cabinet doors are closed and when they are reopened, almost immediately, the performer has the gentleman's coat on, though his hands are still tied behind him. "This is done," he says, "merely to convince you that a trick coat is not necessary. Now, one more test. I shall ask that gentleman to place my coat on my knees. As soon as the doors of the cabinet are closed, I shall throw out his coat, and I want to see whether he can get into it quicker than I can get into mine." The cabinet doors are closed once more and the man's coat comes flying out, but before he can get it on, *for it is turned inside out,* the performer steps from the cabinet, his coat on and the rope in his hands. It is needless to say that this time it is the original rope, the knotted one being concealed under his coat.

In a magazine article published this year (1910) a gentleman well-known in the field of science describes a seance given by Mr. Fay, at one time manager of the Davenport Brothers. In the course of the seance Mr. Fay was tied up, according to the writer of the article, in such a way as to preclude the freeing of himself and yet he did most marvelous things. Let us assure our readers that Mr. Fay's tie was almost identical with the one we have just described, and depended, as most rope-

tying tricks do, on gaining *slack*. That is the whole secret. Let us add here, that Mr. Fay and Mr. Kellar
were at one time associated in business. *Verbum Sap.*

The Muslin Tie. While entirely different from the
Kellar Tie this is quite as good and just as clever. The
performer shows a number of strips of white unbleached
muslin, each two feet long and two inches wide, and requests a committee from the audience to tie him with
these. A strip is tied around each of the performer's
wrists, and so tightly as almost to stop the circulation.
The ends of the strips, four in all, are then tied together,
so as to bring the wrists together behind the performer's
back. If desired by the audience the knots may be
sewed or sealed with sealing-wax. Two staples are
driven into the door-jamb or into a stationary, upright
post, one about twenty-four inches above the floor and
the other about twenty inches higher, and from each
there hangs a solid iron ring about two and a half inches
in diameter. Seating himself on a campstool, his back
against these rings, the performer has another muslin
strip run through the ring and over and under the
strips that bind his wrists. Still another strip is passed
around his neck, tied and then tied to the upper ring.
To all appearances he sits there unable to help himself
in any way. To secure him still further, a rope is tied
to each ankle and led out among the audience, and a
nickle piece is laid upon each shoe so that he can not lift
his knees without dropping a coin. A tambourine is
placed on his knees and a hand bell is stood inside of it.
A screen is now put in front of him, so as to conceal
him from the sight of the audience. Immediately the
bell is rung and thrown over the screen, the tambourine

is shaken and that, too, goes flying in the air. The
screen is removed, the performer is still seated on the
chair, the knots are undisturbed. The tambourine is
replaced on his knees and a goblet half-filled with water
is stood on top of it. The screen is again placed so as
to hide him, and when removed, the goblet is seen to be
held, empty, between his lips, and is taken away by one
of the committee. Then follow in succession a number
of "manifestations," as for instance, an empty pail

Fig. 176

placed on his knees is found over his head; a piece of
board with a hammer and nails is laid on a wooden-
seated chair that is placed alongside him, the sound of

hammering is heard and a nail is driven into the board; a guitar is thrummed, a horn is blown, and after each manifestation of assistance from some unseen source the knots are examined and in each case are found to be intact. Our illustrations, Figs. 176, 177, show very clearly

Fig. 177

what the "unseen source" is, to wit: the hands of the performer stretched around one side. It hardly seems possible, but the bandage that passes through the lower ring is always tied in five or six knots "to make it secure," the diameter of the ring helps, and so does the length of the staple; the bandage slips up the arm a little, and when the performer is about to reach around his side, he stretches his hands out as much as possible, and then pulls his body to the opposite side of the post, past the lower ring, and is able to reach anything that is placed on his lap. A small waist is necessary, and for this reason, a woman or a child is more successful with the trick than a man: one thing is certain, no one with a ''corporation'' will ever succeed in doing it.

A Knotty Problem:

The performer clasps his hands, and the crossed thumbs are tied tightly together with a strong cord. A man from the audience is asked to lock his hands and the next moment the performer's hands, still tied, are around the man's arm. Then they are ''off again, on again.'' Standing behind the man, the performer's right hand comes suddenly in front, taps the man's face, and goes back again as suddenly as it came forward. Finally, a hoop, which examination has shown to be solid, is thrown toward the performer's hands, and is seen to be hanging on his right arm. Then it is as quickly thrown off. The tie on the thumbs is examined repeatedly and is always found intact.

The secret of the trick is in the position of the fingers. When the performer clasps his hands the left forefinger is on top; next to it is the right forefinger, then follow in this order: the left second finger, the right *third* finger, the left third finger, the right little finger, and, last, the little finger of the left hand. The right second finger, as the reader will notice, in Fig. 178, is free *inside the hands*. When the cord is placed under the thumbs, preparatory to tying them, this hidden finger catches it and pulls it down, holding it firmly. In this way enough slack is gained to enable the performer to

release his thumbs at any moment, and yet to show them
at any time tied tightly. The right finger, as the illustration shows, will not be missed. At the conclusion

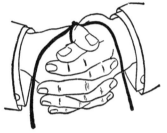

Fig. 178

of the trick the performer pockets the cord, lest the
undue size of the loop might lead to a solution of the
problem.

A Second Method. Two men from the audience are
asked to assist. The performer holds his open hands
before him, about four inches apart, with the fingers
extended at full length and the thumbs crossed. A light
rope or a heavy whipcord, about three yards long, is
then laid under the thumbs, well into the roots, and
each assistant is requested to take hold of an end.
"Now, sir," says the performer, turning to the man on
his right, "please stand as far away as the rope will
allow. And you, sir," addressing the second man, "do
the same." As he speaks to them, the performer nods
his head repeatedly and points with his hands toward
the direction he wants them to go. The audience naturally watch the performer's face and their attention is
taken away from his hands. As the second man moves
away the performer, holding the rope tightly at the
roots of the thumbs, brings his hands together, allowing

the intervening part of the rope to fall between them, where it is held tightly. He now has all the slack he requires. The assistants are then asked to tie the rope tightly. When this is done a soft hat or a Derby is placed over the hands, and the performer is ready to exhibit the "stunts" described in the preceding method.

A Third Method. In this method, known as the Ten-Ichi Tie, the performer uses two pieces of heavy twine, about fifteen to twenty inches in length, respectively. Around each is tightly wound a strip of Japanese pa-

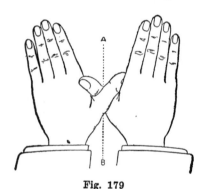

Fig. 179

per, about an inch and a half in width. Both cords are knotted at the ends. Two men of the audience are invited to act as a committee and assist the performer. A cord is handed to each, with which they are to tie the performer's thumbs together. He puts his hands in the position shown in Fig. 179 and crosses his thumbs, the left thumb on top. The tip of his right thumb presses against the base of the left forefinger and the tip of the left thumb goes under the base of the right forefinger. The thumbs are held firmly in place so that the cord can not pass between them and the bases of the forefingers. The longer cord, at the direction of the performer, is now passed twice around the thumbs from A to B, and tied as tightly as the committee desire. The smaller cord is passed between the ball of the left thumb and the base of the right, forming a figure 8 and from there over the right thumb, where both ends are tied together. To release himself the performer brings his hands together, extends his fingers, and drops the thumbs between his hands, as shown in Fig. 180.

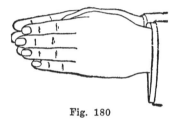

Fig. 180

Then he slightly bends the first joint of the right thumb, when he can easily remove it from the cords—being careful not to pull—and as easily replace it. Then he shows the usual "manifestations," as already described in the foregoing methods. So quickly can he release and replace his thumb that there is no need of covering the hands.

At the close of the trick, the committee are requested to untie the knots, and, if necessary, to cut them. This the performer always requests, as it adds to the effect of the trick.

The Knot of Mystery:

One end of a cord is tied around one wrist of the performer and then the knots are sealed. The other end of the cord is held by one of the audience. Turning his back for a moment or passing behind a screen the performer causes a knot to appear upon the cord. A look at the accompanying illustrations will explain the secret of the trick better than many words. As soon as the cord is secured around his wrist the performer gains slack and makes a loop, as shown in Fig. 181. Taking

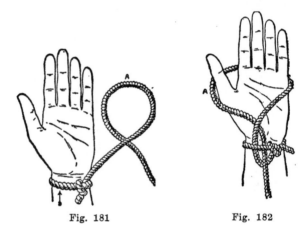

Fig. 181   Fig. 182

hold of the cord at A he pushes it under the cord around his wrist in the direction indicated by the arrow. Pulling it through he brings it over his hand, leaving it in the position shown in Fig. 182. Again taking hold of the cord at A he draws it down and pushes it under the cord around his wrist. The cord will now be in the position shown in Fig. 183. Once more taking hold of the cord at A he brings it up and entirely over and around his hand, and when the cord is stretched it will be found that there is a knot on it, as shown in Fig. 184. This is a double knot, as the illustration shows. To get a single

knot the procedure is slightly different. As will be seen
in Fig. 182 the ends of the loop in the palm of the hand
cross each other. If the cord is so twisted as to form

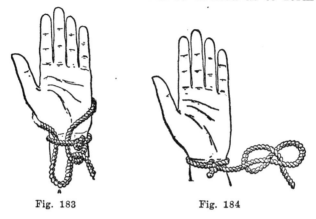

Fig. 183   Fig. 184

a straight loop, as shown in Fig. 185, and the performer
continues in the way already explained, the result will

Fig. 185

be a single knot, as seen in Fig. 186. Instead of having
one end held it may be tied to the other wrist, and in
that case the knot will be on the cord between the wrists.

Two or three knots, one after another, may be made by simply repeating the procedure described and adjusting the space between the knots.

Before the loop is placed around the hand, as shown in Fig. 182, a borrowed finger ring may be tied to the

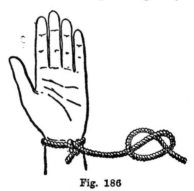

Fig. 186

cord by simply dropping the ring over the loop and proceeding in the manner explained.

The Afghan Bands:

This is a trick that many conjurers, professional as well as amateur, imagine they can do, but if they will read this they will find it a "somewhat different" explanation. The effect of the trick is that three strips of paper, each with its ends pinned together so as to form a ring, are cut around with a pair of scissors. The result is that, in one case, two rings are formed, as is to be expected. In the two other cases, however, although the procedure seems to be identically the same as with the first strip, the result is entirely different, for with the second strip only one ring is obtained instead of two rings, but twice the original size, and with the third strip there are two rings, but linked together.

These effects are obtained in the one case by giving the strip one twist before pinning the ends together, and in the second by giving it two twists. It is just here that the trouble begins, when giving the double twists. Many performers avoid this difficulty by having the strips pinned together before beginning the trick. This is one way, but it is not a good way. The twists may be made without attracting attention. For one twist the strip of paper is taken between the thumbs and fore-fingers, as shown in Fig. 187. Then the right hand is

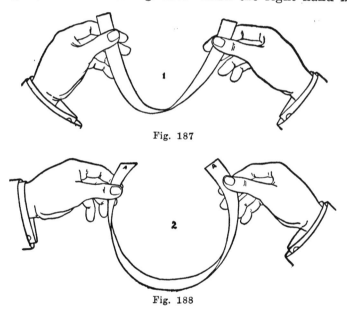

Fig. 187

Fig. 188

brought to the left in order to put the ends together, and as the hands approach the end in the right hand is turned so that the parts marked A A, in Fig. 188, are

laid together.　The left hand must not move.　The ends
are then pinned together or fixed with a "paper fas-
tener."　When this strip is cut in two, lengthwise, it
will make one large ring, double the original size.

To make the two twists is even more simple.　The
strip is held as shown in Fig. 189.　Keeping the left

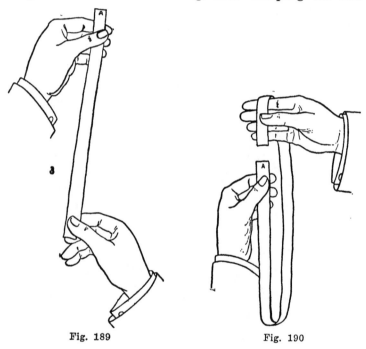

Fig. 189　　　　　　　　　　　Fig. 190

hand in the position shown, the right hand is brought up
and the lower end is simply placed on the end A, held
by the left hand, as in Fig. 190.　The movement is so
natural that no one will suspect any "hanky panky"
work is going on.　When the strip is cut, two rings,
linked, will be seen.　The third strip is simply brought

together in the natural way, and when fastened and cut through lengthwise, two single loops will be the result. Strips cut from a newspaper answer admirably. They ought to be a yard long and an inch in width.

In presenting the trick the performer may begin by handing them to three different persons, and then taking them back fastens them and cuts them, as already described.

Mnemonics as Applied to Conjuring:

While it is not within the province of this book to go into a study of a system of artificial memory, there are certain conjuring tricks frequently presented to the public as "Mental Phenomena," that have a system of this kind for their groundwork, as, for example, the following which depend, mainly, on *numbers,* for their effects: "Second Sight;" the memorizing of a long list of words at one reading; the instantaneous raising of any two numbers to the cube or third power; the memorizing of a pack of cards or a set of dominoes, etc., etc. "Second Sight" can not be considered here, for the trick as exhibited to-day, with its varied codes, would need almost an entire volume to explain clearly, and calls for deeper, longer, and more continuous study than most conjurers would care to devote to it. Some of the other tricks, however, while also requiring some study, will, we believe, prove interesting to our readers.

The first step in this study is to learn so thoroughly that they may be recalled without the slightest hesitation, (1) the Alphabet of Figures and (2) the Table of Fixed Ideas. In the first, the numerals 1, 2, 3, 4, 5, 6, 7, 8, 9, 0 are represented by letters, as follows:

The Alphabet of Figures

T and D represent 1	J, ch, sh, zh, z in azure, g soft as in genius, represent	6
N	represents 2	K, C hard, G hard, and Q represent	7
M	represents 3	F and V represent	8
R	represents 4	P and B represent	9
L	represents 5	S and Z represent	0

As will be seen, all these letters are consonants. The vowels *a, e, i, o* and *u,* and *w, h, y* are merely to form words, as, *nail* (n-l),=25; *chess* (ch-s)=60.

"But," asks the reader, "how shall I remember which consonant represents *three* or which *eight?*" Very easily by bearing in mind that *t* is made with *one* downstroke; *n* with *two* downstrokes; *m* with *three* downstrokes; *r* is the last letter of *four,* which has *four* letters; *L,* in Roman notation is *fifty,* but with the cipher off it is *five; J* looks somewhat like a reversed *six; K,* inverted (ꓘ), is much like *seven; f,* in script, resembles *eight; p* is a reversed *nine; c* is the first letter of cipher and stands for *naught*.

The above are the primitive letters, and in practice each letter is pronounced as if it were followed by *e,* as, *te, ne, me, re, le, je, ke, fe, pe, ce*. Remember it is the *sound,* not the *spelling,* is the guide. The other letters are those that have similar sounds, as, for example, *d,* which sounds like *t* and represents 1; *ch, sh, tch, zh, z* in *azure, g* soft as in *genius,* sound like *j,* and stand for 6; *g* hard and *q* sound like *k* and stand for 7; *v* sounds nearly like *f* and stands for 8; *b* is almost the sound of *p* and represents 9; *s* and *z* sound like *c* in cipher and stand for 0. As proof that these sounds are similar, the foreigner often says *dat* for *that, chudche* for *judge.*

Silent letters, those that are not pronounced, have no value, as, for example, knife (n-f)=28; lamb (l-m)= 53; *gh* in thought; *l* in palm. Double consonants are treated as one letter, as *mummy* (m-m)=33; butter (b-t-r)=914; but if the double letters have distinct articulation, then each letter has its own numerical value, as, accept (k-s-p-t)=7091; bookkeeper (b-k-k-p-r)= 97794. As the cipher never begins a whole number, *s,* which represents the cipher, may be prefixed to any other letter, as *stone* (t-n)=12; *snow* (n)=2.

At first glance it may seem a difficult task to learn these letters and their equivalent numbers, but half-an-hour's careful study will generally prove enough for the greatest dullard.

The next study is that of a table of one hundred words, known as a *Table of Fixed Ideas,* and this will prove to be time well spent, for by its aid most of the conjuring "stunts" are effected. By sounding to one's self the letters that represent the numbers the word may be easily recalled. It is advisable to prepare such a table for one's self, but those who do not care to go to that trouble will find the following good and perfectly reliable. One thing, however, must be borne in mind, that *this Table ought not be changed,* once it is memorized.

TABLE OF FIXED IDEAS. NO. 1.

1 *Tea*	5 *Ale*	9 *Pie*
2 *Noah*	6 *Shoe*	10 *Dice*
3 *Ma*	7 *Key*	11 *Date*
4 *Hare*	8 *Hive*	12 *Den*

13 *Dime*	43 *Room*	72 *Cane*
14 *Door*	44 *Rower*	73 *Comb*
15 *Doll*	45 *Rail*	74 *Car*
16 *Dish*	46 *Rush*	75 *Coal*
17 *Dog*	47 *Rug*	76 *Coach*
18 *Dove*	48 *Roof*	77 *Cake*
19 *Tub*	49 *Rope*	78 *Cave*
20 *Noose*	50 *Lass*	79 *Cab*
21 *Note*	51 *Lad*	80 *Face*
22 *Nun*	52 *Lion*	81 *Foot*
23 *Gnome*	53 *Lime*	82 *Fan*
24 *Nero*	54 *Lyre*	83 *Foam*
25 *Nail*	55 *Lily*	84 *Fire*
26 *Niche*	56 *Lash*	85 *File*
27 *Nag*	57 *Leg*	86 *Fish*
28 *Knife*	58 *Leaf*	87 *Fig*
29 *Knob*	59 *Lip*	88 *Fife*
30 *Maize*	60 *Chess*	89 *Fob*
31 *Mat*	61 *Shot*	90 *Boys*
32 *Moon*	62 *Chain*	91 *Bat*
33 *Mummy*	63 *Gem*	92 *Bone*
34 *Mare*	64 *Chair*	93 *Bomb*
35 *Mill*	65 *Shell*	94 *Beer*
36 *Match*	66 *Judge*	95 *Ball*
37 *Mug*	67 *Cheek*	96 *Bush*
38 *Muff*	68 *Shave*	97 *Book*
39 *Map*	69 *Sheep*	98 *Beef*
40 *Rose*	70 *Case*	99 *Baby*
41 *Rat*	71 *Cat*	100 *Doses*
42 *Rain*		

This Table being perfectly mastered, so as to call *instantly* the letter or word which represents a certain number, the pupil is prepared to learn some of the tricks made possible by a mnemonical system. To begin let us describe one which was introduced to this country by

Cazeneuve, a wonderfully clever conjurer, when he visited us in 1876.

Handing out a pack of cards he allowed several persons in his audience to shuffle it and then to distribute the pack among themselves, as it suited them. He then requested them to arrange their cards in any order they pleased and to keep them in the same order. Going from one to another he rapidly looked at the cards, and retiring to his stage called off the names in the order they were arranged. In like manner he distributed a set of dominoes and some Loto cards, and these he called off after looking at them a moment. Finally he allowed one of the audience to select one of four or five volumes offered, and requesting that it be opened, preferably about the middle, he read off the first three, four, or five lines. The trick made a hit, especially with his audiences, who were mostly educated people.

The cards, dominoes and Loto cards were all done on one principle, and as to explain one is to explain all we shall confine ourselves to an explanation of the cards.

Each card in the pack is represented by a word. The initial letter of this word tells at once the suit, the words representing Spades beginning with S, Hearts with H, Clubs with C, and Diamonds with D. So far it is simple. The other consonant or consonants in the word represent the number of spots on the card, according to the *Alphabet of Figures*, counting the Jack as eleven, the Queen as twelve, and the King, thirteen. As the preparation of these words requires some time and thought we give herewith the card list that we have used for years.

CARD LIST.

1 *Soot*	*Hood*	*Coat*	*Dodo*
2 *Sun*	*Hen*	*Cone*	*Down*
3 *Seam*	*Ham*	*Cameo*	*Dam*
4 *Sore*	*Hero*	*Crow*	*Deer*
5 *Sail*	*Hail*	*Claw*	*Dial*
6 *Sash*	*Hash*	*Cash*	*Douche*
7 *Sock*	*Hook*	*Cook*	*Duck*
8 *Safe*	*Hoof*	*Calf*	*Dive*
9 *Soap*	*Hoop*	*Cop*	*Dope*
10 *Seeds*	*Hothouse*	*Cats*	*Dots*
11 *Statue*	*Hot tea*	*Cadet*	*Deadhead*
12 *Stone*	*Heathen*	*Cotton*	*Dudeen*
13 *Steam*	*Hay time*	King	*Diadem*

King is used as no other word could be found that would as well express the King of Clubs; *Deadhead* may be represented by a *skull;* and as a *Dudeen* may not be a familiar word to some of our readers, let us say it means a short tobacco pipe.

In exhibiting the trick let us suppose that seven cards are taken from the pack at first, as, for example, the nine of diamonds, the deuce of hearts, the seven of spades, the four of spades, the six of clubs, the Queen of diamonds, and the ten of hearts. When the conjurer goes to the person who drew the cards, he asks, "How many cards have you, please?" and when he hears "seven," he at once pictures to himself a *tea*-table with, say, a large *key* lying on it, and remembers (without trying to remember) that *seven* cards have been drawn by the *first* person. Then he connects *tea* (the first word in the *Table of Fixed Ideas*) with *dope*, the nine of diamonds. How does he connect them? In any way, as, for example, by comparing the two words and seeing in what way they are alike, in spelling, in appearance, in characteristics, in color, taste, or what not, or how they differ, or he may make a mental picture of the two *things* (not words), as, for instance, a man refusing a cup of tea because there is some axle-grease (which is *dope*) floating in it. We believe that the latter method, that of making use of a mental picture, will prove the best for most persons. Proceeding he connects *hen,* the deuce of hearts, with Noah, the second word in the *Table of Fixed Ideas,* as, let us say, Noah looking out on the waters of the flood, while a hen is perched on his shoulder. Absurd, the reader may say, but absurd or not it does the work, and, in most cases, the more absurd the mental picture the stronger the impression will be, as he who does this work night after night can testify. For the second lot of cards let us suppose that twelve cards are drawn. The performer says to himself, seven and twelve are nineteen, and he immediately connects eight, *hive,* with nineteen, *tub,* and then the mnemonical name of the first card with *hive,* and so on to the end. Difficult and complicated as this may seem, we assure our readers that in practice it will be found most simple and always reliable.

The reading of a book is very different. *The books are all the same,* but with different title-pages and corresponding titles on the covers. Not only are they all the same, but they are made up of two pages only, repeated over and over. The performer, as will be remembered, asks that a page about the middle of the book be selected, and in that way is assisted by the person who opens the book.

Another trick that makes a good impression on the average audience is that of

Memorizing at One Reading a Long List of Words Suggested by the Audience:

This is a regular exercise with the teachers of Memory Systems, but as a *trick* it was first presented, to the best of our knowledge, by the senior editor of this book. It was introduced later in this country by Ernest Patrizio, a Spanish conjurer, who first appeared in New York in 1878. It is simple and consists merely in connecting the words suggested by the audience with those in the *Table of Fixed Ideas*. When this connection is clearly made there is no difficulty in repeating a hundred words in the order set down, or recalling them backward or telling the number any particular word or words occupy in the list.

A somewhat similar trick, one that has proved something of a puzzle to professional and amateur conjurers, is that commonly known as

Kellar's Cube Root Trick:

As here presented we have substituted other cues for those used by Mr. Kellar, and, we believe, with advantage, but the method is identical with his.

In several system of mnemonics as many as three and four *Tables of Fixed Ideas* are used, and in this cube-root method we use one that differs in most words with Table No. 1.

In presenting this as a trick it is generally offered as something similar to the so-called "Lightning Calculation," and not as a feat of memory. Mr. Kellar prefaced

it with merely a few words in which he announced that
if the audience would call out any one number or two
numbers he would immediately write down the cube on
the blackboard and he did. It will be seen by the following Table that each number is represented by one
word and the cube by a short sentence. These are connected in the performer's mind, in the manner already
described; the moment a number is called out he thinks
of the word that stands for it and that word, if his table
is properly memorized, will revive in his mind the word
or sentence that stands for the cube. The cubes of tens
are not noted here, as they can be recalled instantly by
calling the cubes of units thousands, as, for example,
the cube of 3 equals 27; the cube of 30 is 27,000; the
cube of 7 equals 343; the cube of 70 is 343,000. Now
for the Table itself.

3 Ham	$\overset{2\quad\ 7}{\text{An Egg}}$
4 Rye	$\overset{6\quad 4}{\text{Sherry}}$
5 Lie	$\overset{1\ 2\ 5}{\text{Denial}}$
6 Hash	$\overset{2\quad\ 1\ 6}{\text{On a dish}}$
7 Key	$\overset{3\quad 4\quad 3}{\text{My room}}$
8 Hive	$\overset{5\,1\quad 2}{\text{Wild Honey}}$
9 Bee	$\overset{7\quad 2\,9}{\text{Go Nip}}$
11 Date	$\overset{1\quad 3\quad 3\quad 1}{\text{With my maid}}$
12 Dine	$\overset{1\ 7\quad 2\quad 8}{\text{Take enough}}$
13 Item	$\overset{2\ 1\ 9\ 7}{\text{Note book}}$
14 Author	$\overset{2\,7\quad 4\,4}{\text{Ink hirer}}$

15 *Tell*
3   3   75
Me meekly

16 *Dish*
4 0   9 6
Rose bush

17 *Talk*
4 9   1   3
Ripe theme

18 *Thief*
5 8   3 2
Love money

19 *Daub*
6   8   5 9
Shave a lip

21 Ha*n*d
9 2 6 1
Punched

22 *N*u*n*
1   0 6   4 8
Does show her vow

23 *N*ame
1 21 6 7
A dandy joke

24 *N*ew *Y*ea*r*
1   3   8 2   4
With my fine rye

25 *N*i*l*e
1 5   6 2   5
Dull channel

26 We*nch*
1   7   5   7   6
Took all cash

27 *N*a*g*
1   9   6   8   3
To buy each wife a home

28 K*n*a*v*e
2   1 9 5 2
Neat plan

29 *N*o*b*
2   4 3   8 9
No army fop

31 *M*a*d*
2   9 7   9   1
In a big pout

32 *M*oney
3   2   7   6   8
May now catch a foe

33 *M*y Home
3   5 9   3   7
Home will be Mohawk

34 *M*a*r*y
3   9   3 0 4
May be a miser

35 *M*u*l*e
4   2   8   75
Ruin a vehicle

36 S*m*a*sh*
4 6 6   5   6
Rich jewel show

37 S*m*o*k*e
5 0   6 5   3
Lose a chilly home

38 *M*o*v*e
5   4   8   7 2
Lower a heavy can

39 *M*y *p*ay
59 3   1   9
Help me to buy

41 *R*oa*d*
6   8 9 21
Chief point

		74 0 8 8
42 *Run*	Across a five

		7 9 5 0 7
43 *Rum*	Keep losing

		8 5 1 8 4
44 *Rower*	Awful diver

		9 1 1 2 5
45 *Rail*	A bad tunnel

		9 7 3 3 6
46 *Rich*	Big mummy show

		10 3 8 2 3
47 *Rake*	Hits my wife numb

		1 1 0 5 9 (
48 *Rough*	The head sea will open

		1 1 7 6 4 9
49 *Rube*	To take a chair up

		1 3 2 6 51
51 *Lad*	The man child

		1 4 0 6 0 8
52 *Lion*	Dares chase a foe

		14 8 8 7 7
53 *Lamb*	Drove off a cook

		1 5 74 6 4
54 *Liar*	Idol crusher

		1 6 6 3 7 5
55 *Lily*	Dutch show my equal

		1 75 6 1 6
56 S*louch*	Tackle a schottishe

		1 8 5 1 9 3
57 *Look*	The evil witty poem

		1 95 1 1 2
58 *Loaf*	Double the weight now

		2 0 5 3 7 9
59 S*loop*	When I sell my cup

		2 26 9 8 1
61 S*hod*	An inch by a foot

		2 3 8 3 2 8
62 *Jane*	Name of my new wife

		2 5 0 0 4 7
63 *Chime*	Only uses a rock

		2 6 2 14 4
64 *Chair*	No china drawer

		2 7 4 6 2 5
65 S*hallow*	Niagara channel

		2 8 7 4 9 6
66 *Judge*	No fake rubbish

		3 0 0 7 6 3
67 *Joke*	Amuse a sick chum

68 *Shave*	8 1 4 4 3 2 May draw your moan
69 *Shop*	8 2 8 50 9 Woman feels happy
71 *Goat*	8 5 7 9 1 1 Milk by the day
72 *Coin*	8 7 3 2 4 8 Make men rave
73 *Come*	3 8 9 01 7 Move up a stake
74 *Choir*	4 0 5 2 2 4 Rose Hill nunnery
75 *Quill*	4 2 1 8 7 5 Worn out of gall
76 *Coach*	4 3 8 9 7 6 Remove baggage
77 *Cook*	4 5 6 5 3 3 Relish a oily mummy
78 *Cuff*	4 74 5 5 2 Sore, cruel line
79 *Cop*	4 9 3 0 3 9 Rip a museum up
81 *Food*	5 3 1 4 4 1 Well made arrow root
82 *Fine*	5 51 3 6 8 Loyalty may shave
83 *Foam*	5 7 1 7 8 7 Liquid quaffing
84 *Fire*	59 2 70 4 Albany gas ray
85 *Fall*	6 1 4 1 2 5 Shatter town hall
86 *Fish*	6 3 6 0 5 6 Shame a choice leach
87 *Fake*	6 5 8 5 0 3 Shall a fool swim
88 *Five*	6 8 1 4 7 2 Shaved a racoon
89 *Fop*	7 0 4 96 9 Kiss our bishop
91 *Piety*	75 8 5 7 1 Gloomy lookout
92 *Pony*	7 7 86 8 0 Kick a fish off a hive
93 *Poem*	8 0 4 3 57 Vassar Milk
94 *Bar*	8 3 0 5 8 4 Famous loafer

		8 5 7 3 7 5
95	*Pill*	Vile chemical
96	*Page*	8 8 4 7 3 6 Favoring a mash
97	*Pack*	9 1 2 6 7 3 Beaten each game
98	*Puff*	9 41 1 9 2 Part the bun
99	*Pup*	9 7 0 2 9 9 Big as a nabob

Let us caution our readers to observe carefully the exact sounds of the letters, the variations in sound of the same letter, and the silent letters, as, for example, *g* in *judge* is sounded like *ch*=6; in *baggage*, the double consonants are sounded like a single *K*=7, whereas the third *g* has the sound of *ch*=6; in *chair* the *ch* equals 6, while in *chemical* it has the sound of *K*=7. These several sounds once mastered no further trouble will be experienced and no one, we believe, will regret the time devoted to the study of this branch of mnemonics.

With Apologies to the Audience:

A selected card is torn to pieces, and these, with the exception of one piece, are put into a small envelope which is handed for safe keeping to the one who drew the card. A cigarette is borrowed, but when lighted it will not draw. On examination it is found that it contains the destroyed card, all but the one piece that is held by one of the audience. Then the envelope is opened, and instead of the pieces the tobacco of the cigarette is found inside.

The properties for the trick are not at all elaborate. The performer needs: 1. A pack of cards. 2. An imitation cigarette, made by tightly rolling around a lead pencil a duplicate of the card that is to be destroyed, minus a small piece. The pencil is withdrawn and the card is wrapped in a bit of white paper. At the ends the paper is tucked into the card and closed by pasting on some cigarette tobacco, so that it will resemble the genuine article. 3. Two small "pay" envelopes. In one of these is a pinch of tobacco and the piece torn from the card in the fake cigarette. 4. A package of genuine cigarettes. 5. A box of matches.

To exhibit the trick the package of cigarettes and the imitation article are in the left side pocket of the trousers. The two envelopes are in the right side pocket of the vest, and the box of matches is in the trousers' pocket on the right side.

The card to correspond with the one in the imitation cigarette is on the top of the pack. Going to one of the audience the performer makes the pass and forces the card. When the one who draws the card has looked at it and made a mental note of it, he is requested to tear the card in two, then in quarters, and again and again until it is in small pieces. In the meantime the performer takes the envelopes out of his vest pocket, and palming the prepared one offers the empty one to the person who holds the pieces of the card, with the request that he puts the pieces into it.

When it is returned to the performer, he turns to the audience and says: "I must ask the indulgence of the audience, but I have a craving for a cigarette. Will some gentleman oblige me with one?" As the attention of the audience is at that moment taken off the performer's hands, he takes advantage of it to exchange the envelopes. Addressing himself to the one who drew the card, he says, "Will you be good enough, Sir, to keep one piece of the card, so as to identify it later on?" While saying this he opens the envelope, takes out the piece of card, and then sealing the envelope hands both to the gentleman. Noticing that some one is offering him a cigarette, the performer remarks: "I have some of my own cigarettes, but prefer one of yours." While saying this he takes from his left-hand pocket the package of cigarettes, shows it, and puts it back. In doing this he gets rid of the envelope containing the pieces of the card and palms the prepared cigarette. Accepting the proffered cigarette with his right hand he pretends to put it in his left, but palms it and puts the prepared cigarette in his mouth, saying: "With my apologies to the audience I will take just a whiff of this." Taking the box of matches from his right-hand pocket he gets rid of the cigarette that is palmed. He strikes a match and attempts to get a light, but fails. Taking the cigarette from his mouth to see why it does not draw, he picks at it for a moment. Then opening it he discovers the card, and taking it out presents it to the gentleman who drew it. "Is that your card, Sir? It is? Thank you. Perfectly restored?—No? Ah, the piece is missing. You have it, Sir." The piece is produced and fits perfectly, proving conclusively that it is the identical card that was destroyed. "But where are the pieces that we put in the envelope?" asks the performer. The envelope is opened only to find that the pieces are gone and in their place is the tobacco of the cigarette.

The Clock:
This trick, which dates back many, many years, has been revived within the last two or three years in a

greatly improved form. When first exhibited, the motive power was electricity and the clock was a piece of fine but delicate mechanism, easily put out of order. After a while some clever fellow took hold of it and changed it so that it might be worked by a string, but the way in which the arrow, that serves the purpose of a hand, was connected with the string was decidedly awkward. In time, however, some other clever fellow remedied that by stretching the string *across the frame* from which the clock was suspended. In this way when hanging the clock in place, the string was caught over the little grooved wheel at the back of the dial, that keeps the arrow in place.

Even then the trick was restricted to the use of the conjurer who had his own stage to work on, for it needed an assistant back of the scenes to pull the string, and that was almost an insuperable objection on the vaudeville stage.

It remained for a third clever fellow an experienced performer, with a genius for mechanics, Mr. Frank Ducrot, to devise an entirely new way of working the trick, so as to dispense with an assistant.

The clock is simply a dial of clear glass or what is better of transparent celluloid. When made of the latter the numbers and the inner and outer ring are cast in one solid piece of brass, thus almost precluding the danger of breakage. In the center of the dial is fitted a brass piece with a hole to admit of a spindle. This spindle which is of steel, passes through the exact center, from the back to the face of the dial, and through a corresponding hole in the arrow which is thus attached.

On the other end of this spindle is a small, deeply grooved wheel. Over this wheel is a strong, black thread. Before exhibiting the trick, the dial is prepared by being set in a frame, and one end of the thread is attached to a light spiral spring concealed in the upright of the frame. The other end of the thread after passing over the groove of the wheel is carried down through the upright, coming out at the foot. From there it is led to a table, at a little distance from the frame, and laid on it. A sharp, black hook is tied to this end of the thread. In its normal position the arrow points to twelve, but at a pull on the free end of the thread it will move to any desired hour, and will be brought back to twelve by the action of the spring which is nicely adjusted. But how can the thread be pulled without attracting the attention of the audience? The performer quietly picks up the little hook and sticks it into the leg of his trousers. He is now free to move away until the thread becomes taut. When that occurs a very slight movement of the leg or the least pressure of the body against the thread, will cause the arrow to revolve. It is absolutely under his control, and he can set it twirling round the dial if he wishes.

Sometimes a light weight is substituted for the spring. If desired, the clock may be hung from a cord that is attached to two chairs, or in other ways, according to the fancy of the performer. We are indebted to the courtesy of the inventor of this method of working the trick, Mr. Frank Ducrot, for this explanation, which has never been published till now.

Some performers use a loaded hand that may be set

by means of a ratchet to point to any desired hour.   This
may be combined, with advantage, with the method first
explained.

Wine or Water:

"Things are not always what they seem," but though
the wine of this capital trick is only an imitation of the
real article, it is always well received by an audience,
and that, from a performer's point of view, is the first
thing to be considered.   Besides, it requires very little
practice or skill, which is a still further recommenda-
tion.

In presenting it a China, quart pitcher, filled with
water, and about twelve or sixteen tumblers are used.
To prove that the water is not doctored in any way, a
glass of it is offered to the audience and the performer
takes a few swallows of it.   He then proceeds to fill
the tumblers, pouring into them, alternately, wine and
water from the pitcher.

"It may seem strange to the average man and woman,"
says the performer, "that at my own sweet will I can
pour from a pitcher that is absolutely not prepared in
any way, wine or water.   But one thing must be remembered, that when the surrounding atmosphere has
become thoroughly impregnated with the fumes of the
wine, especially a wine produced by a weird magical
process, it becomes exceedingly difficult for most people
to distinguish whether wine or water fills the glasses.
Many of you may imagine that these glasses are filled
with water; others are positive that they are filled with
wine; while still others, looking with a somewhat dis-
torted vision, see both wine and water.   There is noth-

ing in the pitcher, as you all may see. Let us fill it again.'' Here he empties the contents of the glasses into the pitcher, and almost immediately refills the glasses. ''And now see what we have—wine, the pure juice of the grape. Once more, let us fill the pitcher.'' As he says this he empties the glasses into the pitcher, and then refilling them there appears to be nothing but water. He calls attention to this, and then, correcting himself, adds: ''Excuse me, I have made a mistake. There is one glass of wine.''

For a third time he empties the glasses into the pitcher, and pours out all wine, and finally turning it back into the pitcher, ends the trick by filling all the glasses with water, with which he started.

As our readers probably surmise this is a chemical trick, and the solutions for it are made as follows:—

Six of the glasses are perfectly clean; in each of six others there is one drop of strong tincture of iron, put in about half an hour before attempting to exhibit the trick. Two other glasses are about half filled with a saturated solution of oxalic acid (a deadly poison) in water, and in another is some strong ammonia. To prevent the fumes of the latter from passing into the room, the glass is covered with a heavy napkin folded several times. Last of all, a glass is quarter filled with a saturated solution of tannin in water.

In a row on the performer's table are the six clean glasses and the six containing the iron solution, arranged alternately. Behind these, in the following order, are the glass containing tannin, one glass with acid, the one with the ammonia, and the second one with acid.

To begin, the performer fills a clean glass and the

glass with tannin with water from the pitcher. The clean glass he offers to the audience, but seldom finds any one to take it; then he takes a swallow of it himself. Then he empties both glasses into the pitcher, thus adding the tannin to what was pure water. Next he fills the clean glasses and those containing the iron with water from the pitcher and they will seem to be filled alternately with water and with wine. Turning the contents of the glasses into the pitcher, and refilling the tumblers at once, they are all filled with wine. Before filling the last glass the performer takes hold of one of the acid glasses in such a way as to conceal its contents, and, as he fills it, says: "All wine—no! here we have water and here" filling the twelfth glass, "is wine." When the pitcher is again filled from the glasses, the acid that goes in with the others bleaches the solution perfectly and on filling the glasses again nothing but water is seen. Picking up the glass that holds the ammonia and filling it, it appears to hold wine, but of a lighter color than any of the other glasses. Turning the contents of the glasses into the pitcher, wine is again produced, the ammonia nullifying the action of the acid. Once more the glasses are filled with wine with the exception of the second acid glass, which the performer has filled. Finally, the pitcher is again filled and when the contents are poured out for the last time, it is found there is nothing but water, "Which is only right," says the performer, "for as we begin so shall we end."

Let us advise our readers who would attempt the trick to experiment first for the proper proportions of acid, tannin, and ammonia, as they vary in strength, always bearing in mind that the smaller the quantity used, the better it will be. Let us also caution experimenters to empty the pitcher and glasses into a sink as soon as the trick is finished as the solutions are deadly poisons.

Some performers affect to sneer at this trick because neither the water nor the wine may be drank after the first glass has been emptied. Yet Mr. Kellar, who was supposed to stand high in his profession, frequently included it in his program, and in our experience of many years we do not remember that we ever heard any objection to it from the audience. To silence the captious critics, however, we present here formulas for liquids that produce nearly the same effects as those already described, and yet may be drank at any stage of the trick. Who originated them we do not know or we should be glad to give credit for them.

In presenting the trick a glass pitcher holding about a pint of water, and five whisky glasses, that hold about four ounces each, are brought forward on a tray. In the pitcher, besides the water, is about half a teaspoonful of liquor potassæ; glass No. 1 contains three to four drops of a solution made by dissolving in an ounce of alcohol as much phenol-phthaleine powder as will cover a dime; glass No. 2 is clean; glass No. 3 contains another three or four drops of the phenol-phthaleine solution; glass No. 4 contains a pinch of powdered tartaric acid dissolved in a little water; and glass No. 5 is prepared the same as Nos. 1 and 3.

In beginning the trick the performer picks up the pitcher and pours into the glasses alternately, starting with No. 1, wine, water, wine, water, wine.

He then mixes the contents of Nos. 1 and 2, when both will become wine. To show that he really uses water the performer takes a swallow of No. 4; then picking up No. 3 (wine) he is about to drink it, but just as it reaches his mouth it turns to water, which he drinks. Following this, he mixes Nos. 4 and 5, when lo! both glasses contain water.

The contents of Nos. 1 and 2 are poured into the pitcher when all is seen to change to wine. Nos. 3, 4, and 5 are now poured into the pitcher when the entire contents become water.

The effect of changing wine into water just as the performer is about to drink it is brought about in this way: Just before he picks up glass No. 3, the performer takes a mouthful of the acid solution in No. 4, but instead of swallowing it, he keeps it in his mouth. As he lifts No. 3 to his mouth, he ejects into it the acid solution from his mouth, causing the "wine" to change to "water," which he then drinks.

The liquor potassæ must be kept in a green glass bottle and be tightly corked.

There is nothing harmful in any of these solutions and the performer may drink them—wine or water or both—without experiencing any bad effects, though, personally, we do not believe that such concoctions were ever meant for the human stomach.

The Blackboard Test:

The performer seats his assistant, generally a young girl, on the stage, and between her and the footlights he stands a small blackboard. Then he invites one of the audience to come on the stage to act as a com-

mittee. Supposing that the girl is on the left of the
stage (which is the right of the audience) the performer
seats the committeeman on the extreme right. The
blackboard is between them, and while the man can see
its face from where he sits the girl is too far back to
get even a glimpse of it. The performer asks the man
to write three lines of five numbers each, one line under
another. Before the man begins, the performer blind-
folds the girl. To "make assurance doubly sure" he
folds two small kid gloves into a wad and places one
in each eye of the girl and over these he binds a handkerchief. "All light being now shut out," he says,
"please write down your numbers." When this is done,
the girl adds up the lines. The secret of the trick is
that the performer adds up the columns mentally and
then by cues conveys to the girl the particular numbers
that she needs to know. These cues are used in sen-
tences addressed to the committee-man in a low voice
that does not reach the audience. The performer never
speaks to the girl, unless she makes a mistake. In that
case he gives her the proper cues. These cues consist of
the first consonant of the first word in the sentence. To
make this clear let us suppose that

1 is represented by	T or D, as in This, That, There, Do, Does, Don't
2 "	"	"	N, as in Now, Name
3 "	"	"	I, " " I, In
4 "	"	"	R, " " Right, Write
5 "	"	"	L, " " Let, Look, Well, Will
6 "	"	"	J, " " Just
7 "	"	"	C hard, as in Can, Come, Quick, Go
8 "	"	"	H, as in Have, Here, How
9 "	"	"	P or B, as in Please, Be good
0 "	"	"	S, as in See, Sir

Let us illustrate this by supposing that the committee-man writes the following numbers:

$$9\ 7\ 5\ 3\ 1$$
$$2\ 4\ 6\ 8\ 0$$
$$1\ 3\ 5\ 7\ 9$$

These add up 135,790. The performer foots up the first column mentally, and turning to the committeeman, who is to add up the column and write the sum, he says, for instance: "That will do. See that your figures are plain." The girl mumbles to herself, as if adding up the figures and calls out, "Put down naught and carry one." For the second column the performer may say: "There, that's good. Please move so that the audience can see." Again the girl begins to mumble, and says: "Nineteen. Put down nine and carry one." For the third column, which adds up 17, he may say: "That's fine. Quick work, isn't it?" For the fourth column, "Down, all right. Well, go on;" for the fifth column: "That's all. I am obliged, Sir." The audience do not hear and the committeeman imagines that he is merely speaking in praise of the girl's work, and cleverness.

When the sum of the columns is written down, the performer hands the committeeman a light cane and requests him to point out or rather to touch some number. He does so and at the same moment the girl calls out the number. In this way three or four numbers are told. For this phase of the trick the performer uses other cues which he addresses to the committeeman. He is watched closely and just as his stick is about to touch a number the performer says (1) "Any one"—(2) "Any number;"—(3) "Any number you choose;"—(4) "Take any;"—(5) "Take any number;"—(6) "Take any number you wish;"—(7) "Choose any;"—(8) "Choose any number;"—(9) "Choose any number you wish"—(0) "All right."

When the committeeman is through the performer picks up the stick and rapidly points from one number to another, the girl, as rapidly, calling out the name. This is, simply a line of prearranged numbers, as, for example, the years in which the girl and the performer were born, but called out backward. Those familiar with the mnemonic cues, on page 310, will find it easy if they will take a line from some familiar song, as, for instance, "Don't you remember Sweet Alice, Ben Bolt," or "Hail Columbia Happy Land." Now and then, by previous arrangement, the performer points above or below a number, and the answer, "There's nothing there," is generally greeted with a laugh.

In describing the blindfolding of the girl we mentioned that the performer first placed a kid glove over each eye. This, instead of blinding her further, really helps her to see, for when the performer is putting the handkerchief around her eyes, she assists him by holding it, and at the same time moves the gloves so that they are on her eyebrows. This keeps the handkerchief away from her eyes, and she is enabled by looking down to see what is going on.

Another way of conveying the numbers is by the position on the back of the board of the fingers of the hand that holds the blackboard, as shown in the illustrations. Number 1 is represented by turning in the first finger; number 2 by turning in the first and second

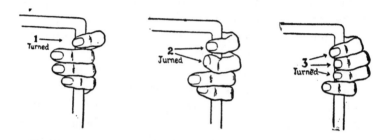

fingers; number 3 by the first, second, and third fingers turned in, and number 4 by turning in all four fingers. For number 5 three fingers lie flat and the second finger of the hand is turned in, the 3 and 2 equaling 5; numbers 6 and 7 are shown in the same way, that is, three

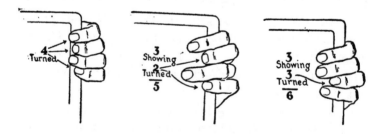

fingers are flat and the third finger of the hand is turned in, in the one case, and three are flat and the fourth finger of the hand is turned in the second. Number 8 has all four fingers lying flat, and number 9, all four

fingers flat, but spread apart. For 0 the index finger
and the little finger lie flat and the second and third
fingers are turned in. For 10 the four fingers lie flat,

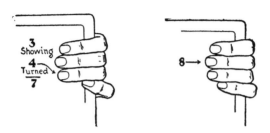

but the index is spread away from the others; for 20
the four fingers also lie flat, but the forefinger and
the second are kept together but spread apart from
the others; for 30 the four fingers are again laid flat
with the little finger spread apart from the others.

There is still another way of communicating numbers,
and that is by dividing the face and the body into
squares by imaginary perpendicular and horizontal lines.
Each of these imaginary squares is numbered, say, as
shown in Fig. 191: The right side of the forehead,= No.
1; the right ear,= No. 4; the right jaw,= No. 7; the
middle of the forehead,= No. 2; the nose,=. No. 5; the
chin,= No. 8; the left side of the forehead,= No. 3; the
left ear,= No. 6; the left jaw,= No. 9; any part of the
neck or throat,= 0. In the same way, the body is divided: The upper right side on a line with the shoulder,= 1; the right side, lower down,= 4; near the right
lower pocket of the vest,= 7; the upper part of the
body, just below the chin,= 2; about the pit of the
stomach,= 5; about the center of the waist,= 8; the

upper left side, on a line with the shoulder,= 3; about the center of the left side,= 6; the region of the left lower pocket of the vest,= 9; and at the bottom of the vest in the center,= 0. In addition to this, the stage curtain or the space it occupies is also divided into

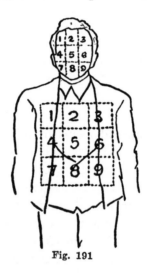

Fig. 191

imaginary lines, numbered in the same way, and by looking up or down or straight ahead; by turning the head to either side, and directing his glance toward the spot occupied by these imaginary numbers, the performer can give his assistant any number in the imaginary squares. At other times numbers, especially the decades ten, twenty, and thirty are signaled by taking a step forward, backward or to one side, as agreed upon between the performer and his assistant. By combining these various methods any number under a thousand may be conveyed rapidly and imperceptibly. Of course a great deal of tact is needed in order to give the cues in a natural way, so as not to excite suspicion. That it is done successfully is unquestionable, but not to any great extent for two reasons; first, it is not generally understood, and secondly, it requires considerable rehearsing.

Much thought has been spent on the different silent methods of communicating numbers. One of these is synchronous counting, that is, two people count together in the same time, studying this by means of a metronome. This requires a very correct ear, and at best is liable to errors. Another and better method is that in which the performer counts the breathing of his assistant by watching the rise and fall of her breast. The most simple and in our opinion the best is by means of our reliable old friend, a length of fine black silk thread. One end of this is tied to the assistant's thumb, the rest of it she holds in her hand. When the performer bandages her eyes, she passes the thread to him. He takes his position alongside the blackboard, and by a prearranged system of long and short jerks conveys to her the required numbers.

A well known performer gives a very striking example of what he calls his control of his wife's mind by allowing some person to select any page in a book and to choose a line in that book. He holds the book and his wife soon after opens a second copy of it at the page selected and begins to read at the very line chosen. Our readers will at once see how easy it is to convey to her the number of the page and the line by means of his fingers at the back of the book, combined with one or more of the methods we have described.

A Water Trick:

This is considered one of the best of the tricks produced in recent years. When the curtain goes up seven large metal jars are seen standing in a row on a board. This rests with one end on the back of a chair and the other on a small table that also supports a tub. In order that our explanation may be clear let us suppose that the jars are numbered 1 to 7, beginning with the one on the left of the stage. Picking up Number One, the performer holds it with its mouth toward the audience, to show that it is empty, and to prove that Number Two also is empty, he drops Number One into it. A moment later he removes Number One and places it on the board in its original position. He continues in this way, first showing a jar empty and then dropping it momentarily into another until all the jars are shown to be empty. When Number Six is taken out of Number Seven the performer shakes a duck out of the latter, and then proceeds to pour from the jars, beginning with Number Six, enough water to fill the tub.

Should you ask us whence the water and the bird, we, in the language of Hiawatha,

> " . . . should answer your inquiries
> Straightway in such words as follow: "

While only seven jars are seen by the audience at any one time, thirteen are used in the trick. Six of these are perfect, while each of the seven others has a longitudinal oval hole near the bottom. As they appear on the board at the start Number One, which has a hole in it, stands first. Number Two is made up of two jars, the outer jar with a hole in it, the inner jar perfect (really a lining) and nearly filled with water. Five other jars are arranged in the same way. Care is taken always to cover the hole in a jar, so that it may not be seen by the audience.

To begin the trick the performer picks up the first jar, which, the reader will remember, has a hole in it and is not double, and holding it with the mouth toward the audience, remarks, "This jar, as you may see, is absolutely empty, and so also is this next one." As he says this he drops Number One into Number Two and immediately brings it out again, and with it the perfect lining of Number Two. Number One is now filled with water, and the performer stands it in its place on the board. Then he picks up Number Two, which is now without its lining and has a hole in it, drops it into Number Three and at once takes it out with the lining of Number Three. In this way he goes on to the end.

Fig. 192
The dotted lines show the hidden jar with the hole.

All the jars are now full, except Number Seven, which has a hole in it and is without lining. This he picks up and shows it is empty. He rests it for a moment on the end of the little table with the mouth toward him, ostensibly to move the tub a little. As he leans forward, his left hand seizes a duck that lies, tied up, at the back of the table, and brings it up into the mouth of the jar. This is not done rapidly as that would attract attention, but by drawing back the left side, which is away from the audience, and leaning forward with the right and stretching out the right arm, as if to move the tub, he introduces the duck into the jar. Then the right hand grasps the lower end of the jar, and shakes the duck out on to the stage. Immediately following this he catches up Number Six, empties it into the tub and follows it with the other jars until the tub is filled with water.

One performer substitutes lemonade for water and serves it to his audience.

APPENDIX

Flash Paper:

The following reliable formula for this most useful article in constant use by conjurers was furnished to the editors by one of the most eminent chemists in this country. If the instructions are faithfully followed, the paper will be white, burn without an ash, and will not rot.

1. The best white tissue paper must be used, and it ought to be cut into pieces of the required size.

2. Make a mixture of *strong* sulphuric acid, 4 volumes, and *fuming* nitric acid (sp. gr. 1.52), 5 volumes.

The first-named acid is to be poured into the second, stirring all the time with a glass rod. The mixture will be very hot, and must be left till cold before it is used (preferably, 24 hours). If the mixture is made in a jar the jar must be covered with a plate to keep out atmospheric moisture.

3. Pour some of the mixture into a glass or porcelain dish, as, for example, a dish used in photography, and put into it about ten sheets of paper, *one at a time,* pressing down each sheet with glass rods, one in each hand. When the sheets have soaked for ten minutes, take them out one at a time and turn them rapidly into a *large* volume of water.

4. If the sheets when taken from the acid are put into a small volume of water they will heat up, become jellified, and be of no use.

5. After the first washing, the sheets must be put into a convenient vessel through which a stream of water is kept running for at least two hours.

6. While this final wash is going on, a fresh batch of paper

may be put into *the same acid* in the dish, as that acid is good for about fifty sheets, or five batches.

7. Lastly, the thoroughly washed sheets must be placed, separately, between sheets of blotting paper and left to dry, which will take five or six days.

Conjurer's Wax:

This wax, which is repeatedly called for in descriptions of various tricks, may be made by dissolving by heat in a porcelain dish pure yellow beeswax, and gradually adding pure Venice turpentine, stirring it constantly with a glass rod. Care must be taken that it does not catch fire while it is being mixed. The usual proportion is one part of turpentine to two of wax, but as a great deal depends on the quality of the wax and the turpentine, experiment alone can determine the proportions.

The editors are using wax that was prepared ten or fifteen years ago from this identical formula.

Rope Tying:

The best rope for these tricks is Silver Lake sash cord, No. 8, the soft kind. It should first be well soaked in benzine and then be washed out with soap and water.

The Servante:

At the back of the conjurer's table is usually a padded shelf technically known as a *servante*, a French word that means *dumb waiter*. The name, however, is not appropriate in this case, for so far from being *dumb* it *answers* the performer's purposes very effectually. This shelf extends nearly the whole length of the table. On it the conjurer lays such articles as he may need to pick up without being seen by the audience. He also drops on it articles he may want to get rid of. The *servante* is made in different shapes according to the needs and

fancy of the performer. Sometimes it is only a strong paper
bag reinforced by muslin strips and hung at the back of a
chair. At other times it is a canvas bag fitted to a wire frame
and suspended by small hooks to the back of a chair or a
table. One performer, Ducrot, when entertaining in a private
house uses an ingenious *servante,* made to resemble a handkerchief, and this he throws carelessly on top of his table. It is
arranged on a small metal frame so that part of it forms a
bag that will hold a large orange. Two small pieces of spring
steel serve as clamps to hold it on the table. Extending about
it on all sides is a dark silk handkerchief. When the performer is done with it he deliberately folds it up and sticks it
in his pocket without arousing the slightest suspicion.

A Pull:

A simple *pull* is made of black elastic cord. It should be
of such length that when stretched one end may be attached
to a button of the trousers on either the right or the left side,
and from there passed inside the vest, across the performer's back and down the opposite sleeve, ending in a loop of
strong black thread that goes over one of the cuff buttons.
When it is needed to vanish, say, a handkerchief, the performer draws the loop into his hand, runs the handkerchief
through the loop, and then releasing it, away goes the handkerchief up the sleeve.

The only trouble with this *pull* is, that the elastic loses its
elasticity and for that reason is not altogether reliable. A
better *pull* is made by substituting a strong black cord for the
elastic. At one end of the cord is a loop to go over the
trousers' button; to the other end is fastened a piece of fine
catgut ending in a large loop. The right arm is bent at the
elbow and held at the side. The catgut loop goes over the
right thumb. To vanish the handkerchief it is passed through
the catgut loop; then the arms are extended to full length and
the handkerchief disappears in a flash. In using this *pull*

the performer has to call it to his aid as soon after he comes on the stage as possible, on account of the constrained position of his arm.

There are other *pulls,* mainly mechanical, that rely on a cord attached to a spring barrel. When noiseless, some of them are good, but the second method that we have described is the best and most reliable, when it can be used at the beginning of the trick. Instead of fastening the cord to the trousers' buttons some performers have it hanging just outside the armhole of the vest. A ring is on the end of it, and when it is to be used the performer gets hold of this and gives it a sharp pull. A little practice will soon satisfy a performer as to which method he prefers.

A Slip Knot:

In the description on page 183 of "A Handkerchief with Seven Corners," a slip knot is mentioned. This is made by first tying a square knot, as shown here. One corner of

Fig. 193
A square knot.

Fig. 194
How to tie a square knot.

the handkerchief, which is here printed in black, to make the description clearer, is taken in one hand and the body of the handkerchief corresponding to that corner in the other hand, just below the knot. Then it is pulled. The result will be that one corner will be tied ROUND the other, as shown here. While it has all the appearance of a fair knot, one corner may be pulled entirely out without destroying the folds in any way. A silk handkerchief must be used, as one of linen or muslin is apt to jam.